WORKERS' COMP FOR EMPLOYERS

HOW TO CUT CLAIMS, REDUCE PREMIUMS, AND STAY OUT OF TROUBLE

JAMES WALSH

MERRITT PUBLISHING, A DIVISION OF THE MERRITT COMPANY

SANTA MONICA, CALIFORNIA

Workers' Comp for Employers: Taking Control

Second edition, 1994

Merritt Publishing
1661 Ninth Street
P.O. Box 955
Santa Monica, California 90406

For a list of other publications or for more information, please call (800) 638-7597. In Alaska and Hawaii, please call (310) 450-7234.

Library of Congress Catalog Card Number: 93-078268

Walsh, James
Worker's Comp for Employers — Taking Control
How to cut claims, reduce premiums, and stay out of trouble.
Includes index.
Pages: 334

ISBN 1-56343-066-5
Printed in the United States of America.

Acknowledgements

This is one of the first in-depth treatments of the workers' compensation crisis written for employers across the country. It takes a broader view of insurance markets, legal precedents, regulators, and financial schemes than most similar works. It advocates reform in a way that should have more direct meaning for readers than most previous suggestions.

Of course, assembling this package required assistance from various sources. The author and editors have many thanks to make.

To start, the employee-owners of The Merritt Company — from the president to the sales support staff — have made this project possible. The spirit of the book reflects the creativity and activism of the company that has published it.

On a more mechanical level, we'd like to thank: California Insurance Commissioner John Garamendi's office; Liberty Mutual Insurance Co. in Boston; California Indemnity Insurance; the National Council of Self-Insurers; the chambers of commerce in California, Florida, Minnesota, Nevada, New Hampshire, New Jersey and Wisconsin; the compensation insurance boards (or analogous agencies) of Arkansas, California, Florida, Louisiana, Massachusetts, Minnesota, Missouri, Ohio, Oregon, Texas, Washington, Wisconsin; the National Council of Compensation Insurance in Boca Raton, Florida; the National Federation of Small Business; Annette B. Haag & Associates and more individuals than space allows us to name.

Not everyone who helped will support — or maybe even tolerate — everything discussed or suggested in these pages. But they all played a role in the process. We needed to understand different and often opposing views before we could thoroughly analyze this thorny subject.

This book should be thought of as a work in progress. The workers' compensation problem will continue to evolve in coming years. We hope to continue tracking and analyzing its evolution.

Table of Contents

CHAPTER 1: THE PROBLEM

Workers' comp used to be so simple. A machinist, cut by an errant scrap of metal, saw a doctor at company expense and returned to work. A factory worker, maimed in a production line accident, got a small check every month. A police officer, injured in the line of duty, got enough to keep body and soul together.

How times have changed

Workers' comp still does these things for those who suffer workplace injury, but these days it does much more for countless others who don't come close to the workplace. Workers' comp has become a $70 billion industry whose real beneficiaries are people who stand at the elbow of the injured, offering "help" of one sort or another in exchange for some—a lot—of that money. These people suck the system dry — lawyers, doctors, chiropractors, physical and vocational therapists, and assorted healer quacks of countless persuasions. Meanwhile insurance bureaucrats, state regulators, politicians, and even the courts themselves stand by, hands folded.

All of these people have long since forgotten the original idea behind workers' comp — i.e., that the employee ought not to bear the cost of treating workplace injury. It was a good idea. But as the idea dims, the American economy labors under the weight of a system so inefficient, so astonishingly corrupt that it makes the mouth gape. Indeed, it is so out-of-whack that earnest and reasonable people despair of fixing it. Sometimes their eyes just glaze over. More often their feet shift nervously and itch to turn away. Occasionally their frustration boils over and becomes rage.

Rarely, however, does anyone attempt to do anything about this amazing problem. To employers, who stand witness to the destructive power of a good idea gone awry, the problem looks too big. It seems

The source of the problem: easy money

out of control. To all the others, the system ain't broke in the first place, so why fix it? There's too much money in it.

This book seeks to change all this, starting and ending with the only one who stands in position to act: you the employer. The book takes as its premise the notion that the workers' comp problem submits to one who determines to master it—period. It argues that the system is not out of control at all; it's just under the control of the wrong people. Indeed, the book argues that the problem gives birth to its own solution, and that it's your job to act as midwife in helping this birth to come about.

The Troubles You See

If you employ others, you know what troubles the system causes because you see them every day. The system corrupts the relationship between employer and employee. It assaults simple notions of justice and responsibility and turns them inside out. It breeds fraud and abuse, stripping away the virtue of labor and tempting good people to become scam artists. It threatens the bottom line and sometimes ruins businesses altogether.

It makes the blood boil.

Originally, the system struck a simple bargain between employer and employee. The employer assumed responsibility for the costs of on-the-job injury in exchange for immunity from tort liability. The employer bore the costs of injury, and the employee agreed not to take the employer to court.

Employers still assume liability for injuries. But lawyers and doctors do their best to corrupt the other party to the bargain: the employee. They find ways to turn the system into an alternative to work. They inflate claims, fake injuries, prolong and even abort recoveries, and otherwise make sure that getting the injured employee back to work becomes the last thing on the agenda. Unethical doctors run "workers' comp mills" in virtually every big city in the country, exaggerating and even fabricating injury claims. Bottom-fishing lawyers take these claims and manipulate insurers into forking over settlements without batting an eye.

The system can't reform itself

In all, they turn the system into an entitlement program whose real beneficiaries are themselves, not the injured worker. Some become so cynical that they don't care at all what happens to the injured employee so long as they — the lawyers and doctors — get their slice of the enormous workers' comp pie. These people know how the workers' comp system works, and they know how to exploit its weaknesses.

In this they connive with altogether too many employees who can't resist the temptations of a system awash with money. And they operate with the acquiescence, if not the connivance, of insurers who know that the money they fork over is really the employer's, not their own, and that there's more where it came from.

The Wages of Sin

This leaves the employer standing alone. Most of the time, the employer who faces a workers' comp claim assumes that justice will follow: an equitable settlement for the legitimate claim, nothing for the scammer.

When the system instead offers neither justice nor equity, the frustrated employer's first reaction is to expect someone else to fix things — politicians or insurers, as a rule.

It's a pretty dream.

Politicians don't even know what to do about the consequences of the problem, not to mention the problem itself. Among these are what insurers call risk flight — the disappearance of good risks from the insurance marketplace. The workers' comp system has become so complicated, so frustrating, and so expensive that low-risk employers simply opt out of it. They take themselves out of the market, either by removing their operations to states with less-troubled workers' comp systems or by dropping out of the system altogether — for example, by self-insuring their own risk or by leasing their employees. These employers leave the high-risk employers behind them, along with lots of trouble.

These higher risks — usually smaller employers who don't have the muscle to leave the system —

The time has come for employers to act

pull the marketplace into a spiral of increasing costs and diminishing returns. Insurers lose money and refuse to take new business; sometimes they refuse to keep existing business. They abandon whole industries, sometimes whole states. At some point (and usually sooner than later) the spiral sucks in the state, which imagines that it may resolve things by becoming the insurer of last resort.

But governments don't know how to run businesses. The state sets up a state-run pool, but as a rule this solves nothing at all. Sooner or later most state-run pools face bankruptcy and go begging to their legislatures for a bailout. The legislatures cough up some money and then take up the banner of reform — only to run into a buzz saw of special-interest lobbying from lawyers, doctors and the rest of those who feed at the trough of workers' comp. In state after state, reform attacks the wrong target — or else it attacks nothing at all.

Insurers have less power to change the system than the legislatures. And they probably have less incentive than they have power. They lose money on workers' comp, and they talk about changing the game, but they don't play the game with their own marbles, by and large. They play with the employer's marbles: *your* marbles.

This is not to paint insurers as the villains, however. It's just to argue that you ought not to expect much of them. Even if they had the power to change things, they don't have much reason to do so. Their interests lie in making money, not in restoring the old workers' comp bargain between employer and employee.

The Wellspring of Reform

Only one party can do that: you the employer. If reform is to happen, you must bring it about. Every other party with an interest in workers' comp has a position to protect, and none of those positions is yours. Employers have stood still for twenty years while doctors, lawyers, government regulators, and even some insurers twisted and tweaked the system to serve their own ends.

Now it's time to fix things. This is more than just rhetoric: As the employer, you fuel the workers' comp system with your premium dollars, and only you have power to say what happens to those dollars. So *you* must discipline the system. *You* must reclaim the original bargain between employer and employee.

How to begin the change

How?

Keep your end of the bargain.

Make sure your employees keep theirs.

Set up effective safety programs to prevent workplace injury.

Make sure that your employees get first-rate medical attention when an injury does occur.

Get the injured employee back on the job as fast as you can.

Monitor your health care professionals to make sure that they, too, want your employee back on the job.

Resist the spurious claim; make it hard for the bad apples among your employees to cheat.

Monitor your workers' comp insurance, to keep it as inexpensive and efficient as you can.

Avoid the traps of your state's workers' comp regulatory system.

Above all, remember that you *may* take control of this problem, and you *must.*

What's Ahead in This Book

This book tells you how to do all these things — and others. It helps you to cut costs and avoid exposures. It uses clear case studies to illuminate important points. It discusses the alternatives to commercial insurance — self-insurance, the big deductible, and risk pools — which give the employer the best chance to solve the problem once and for all.

In all, the book gives you the tools you need to take control, helping you to protect your business so that you may spend your time building it.

Only you can do this. Real reform *must* come from the grassroots. It wins only if employers — large and small — educate themselves about workers' comp

The difficult birth of real reform

and make good decisions. It happens one company at a time, as each employer reforms his or her own problem.

Don't fear doing so. And don't worry about those who would rather keep things as they are.

Instead, think of yourself as a midwife attending the birth of an heir in a big, rich, unhappy, and treacherous family. It's a difficult birth. By and large the members of this family — lawyers, doctors, insurers, regulators, politicians, and some ordinary working people — consider the newcomer an unwelcome heir. Some of the more murderous among them feel the threat so keenly that they would frankly prefer that the child not see the light of day at all. And they won't leave you alone. They stand at the door of the room where you work, all of them watchful, none of them hopeful that you will succeed, some of them downright dangerous. They don't like you.

Don't imagine for a minute that these people want to help; they're unreliable. But they don't control what you do when you're in charge. You control what you do. You must. And you've got to do this little job on your own.

So, before you start, shoo them away and shut and lock the door. Then wash up and get some water boiling.

Midwifing is messy business. Blood flows. Something wondrous happens. Afterwards, you clean up.

Chapter 2: The Social Context

The idea behind the system

Let's step back in this chapter and see how the workers' comp system developed. You will find this important because in grasping the elements of the history of workers' comp, you grasp the idea that underlies the system — and in grasping the idea, you take the first step in controlling the problem that workers' comp has become.

The first thing to keep in mind is that the system springs from a compromise between employers and employees. No abstract concept of law underlies it. No lasting political principles define it.

And nothing about it should intimidate you. Government has thrown up structures and legalisms around the workers' comp system, but time and again, when you think them through, you discover them to be the tools of interested parties, by and large — politicians who must please a constituency, insurers who confuse short-term results with long-term prosperity, lawyers who see big fees in your balance sheet, doctors who practice medicine out of caution, not care.

These structures and legalisms are not, in other words, insurmountable obstacles to your solving the problem. The system's costs grow at a dangerous clip, but you can bring them under control. Just don't buy what the politicians and the insurers and the lawyers and the doctors say about workers' comp — don't buy the workers' comp world as these people see it. And don't wait for them to reform it; they like things as they are, and even if they overcome their own inertia, they won't get the job done soon enough for anyone who runs a business.

And remember that, like the other difficulties you face in running your business, this one yields to one who determines to master it.

At its core, workers' comp is simply a deal struck by

A private system

employers and employees 1) to compensate workers for job-related injuries and illnesses and 2) to keep employers out of the Dickensian hell of the courts. It's a system of private settlement.

Both parties gain from the deal. Employers compensate workers for the actual costs of workplace injuries and illnesses — i.e., medical care and lost wages. In exchange, workers give up the right to sue their employers for negligence. The system assumes that each party wants to get on with things and avoid the time consuming, costly, and unpredictable hazards of civil tort proceedings.

A Strict Definition

The system revolves around a strict definition of employer liability in which negligence plays no part. Some people casually call workers' comp a "no fault" system, but it is more correctly a "no dispute" system. Employers do assume fault for workplace hazards, and they assume responsibility for the consequences of those hazards — i.e., financial loss to employees. But the workers' comp system is not a tort system. It works only if both parties keep negligence out of the picture.

To you the employer, the great benefit of the system is that it allows you to predict the financial risk of workplace hazards and to transfer this risk to your insurer. In doing so you control your own exposure to the costs of workplace injury or illness. You pay a premium to the insurer, a fixed dollar sum that represents the limit of your financial exposure. It becomes a cost of doing business.

So much for the ideal. You know very well how greatly the reality differs. But it's important to grasp the ideal because grasping it shows how to gain control of the problem. We can't put too much emphasis on this element of the workers' comp system; indeed, it's the wellspring of this book.

Early History

The need for a workers' comp system emerged with the late industrial revolution in Western Europe near the end of the last century. Old notions of work had centered around the individual: the farmer, the artisan, the merchant — manager and worker as one. As manufacturing became the primary effort of economic activity, manager and worker became different people, and their aims, interests, risks, rewards, rights and responsibilities diverged.

The interests of employer and employee

Common law seldom held the employer liable for injuries suffered by workers in his employ. Even if the employer were negligent with respect to a worker's injury, the employer avoided liability by establishing one of three mitigating circumstances:

1. Assumption of risk — i.e., the injury happened in the ordinary process of a dangerous job.
2. The fellow servant rule — i.e., the injury occurred as the direct result of another employee's actions.
3. Contributory negligence — i.e., the injured employee's own negligence contributed in a significant way to the injury.

A Stacked Deck

Employers may resort to these legal principles even today to contest workers' comp claims. Used correctly, they can be very effective defenses.

As you can imagine, workers found the deck stacked against them as the Twentieth Century began. Manufacturers made things by the use of machines, and machines are dangerous. So factory jobs were dangerous, and employers commonly turned their backs on injured employees by arguing that workers knew the dangers of the job going in. If that didn't work, employers found some way to blame an injury on the action of another worker, or on the negligence of the injured worker himself. It was almost impossible for an employee to win compensation for a workplace injury.

The First Attempts

The tables turned, however. Employers realized that popular sympathies, sooner or later reflected in the court system, made negligence claims a potent threat. The workers' compensation system began to evolve.

The states respond to the need

Germany, with its sophisticated network of unions and guilds, produced the first systematic workers' comp processes. The guildsmen knew from experience that holding employers hard to tort liability might satisfy a sense of justice, but it didn't always provide the most timely results for an injured worker.

Many countries relied on state-run welfare programs to support injured workers. The Germans (and, soon after, the British) applied these mechanisms to the new needs of the industrial economy.

In the United States, the model took longer to emerge. As in Europe, it developed here as the number of factory workers grew. But it was the states, not the federal government, that responded to the needs of injured workers. Their efforts focused on providing an equitable alternative to litigation, with its attendant uncertainties for both worker and employer.

The early workers' comp programs were similar in several key ways. They depended on:

1. Strict definitions of employee and employer;
2. The employer's assumption of fault;
3. The employee's surrender of the right to sue;
4. Medical benefits for workplace accidents;
5. Wage-loss benefits for disability and death benefits for fatalities; and
6. Local administration.

Initially, employers supported workers' comp even more enthusiastically than their employees, since the system shielded them from the onerous negligence exposure.

The first state-run programs appeared as early as 1910; by 1950, all the states had instituted some form of workers' comp. But this didn't assure blanket coverage. In half the country, employer participation remained optional well into the 1960s.

Changing the Terms

As time passed, employers and employees sought to change the terms of the compromise to fit their needs. It was a series of subtle moves — shading the definition of liability in one case, expanding the definition of workplace in another.

No rigid standards of proof

For the most part, employees came out the winners in this exchange. They took advantage of the leverage that their sheer numbers gave them with politicians, and of the increasingly litigious business climate. Inexorably they expanded the injuries covered by workers' comp, and the benefits paid.

In this they discovered the fundamental weakness of the system, and they exploited it. The system sought to keep everybody out of the clutches of the courts, so the claims process did not hold to the courts' rigid standards of evidence and proof. The process allowed for a more liberal use of causality, and workers found it relatively easy to expand their claims, especially once they got help from lawyers.

Rules That Encourage Compromise

As an employer you have doubtless felt your jaw drop on more than one occasion as you contemplated the claims that employees make in workers' comp cases — and in this book you will find ample evidence to support the idea that the whole thing just spins out into never-never land. The bodies which serve as judge and jury in workers' comp cases — the mediation boards, the review commissions — follow rules that encourage compromise, and as often as not, this means a continuous erosion of the employer's position. Says one New York state workers' comp judge:

> *The [workers' comp] system isn't a court of law. The assumption in these cases is that an injury has occurred. The main question isn't whether or not to find for the injured party; it's how much that injured party deserves in settlement.*

In fact, most claims never reach a mediator or review board at all. Workers' comp insurers settle all but the most egregious claims with few questions, whether you like it or not. Indeed, they don't leave it up to you to decide whether to contest or to settle; their policies leave that question to the discretion of the insurer. And they settle even when you know a

Lawyers know the weakness

claim to be outrageously false. And the regulatory system backs the insurer. State regulators encourage the quick settlement of modest claims.

Claimants and their attorneys know these things. As a rule they take care to keep their claims modest, and they don't care that when you add all their modest claims together, you're talking about a lot of money.

It follows that most of the contested claims that come before review boards involve self-insured employers, who generally have more specific knowledge of and direct financial interest in — and, therefore, more reason to fight — outrageous claims.

People spend more time on the job than they spend doing anything else except maybe sleeping — unless, of course, they sleep on the job. This goes for the plant worker putting in a few hours of overtime as well as for the salesperson on the road two hundred days a year.

This fact alone suggests that workers face a greater risk of injury on the job than off. Add to this the dangers presented by heavy machinery, complex chores, or even simple stress, and a significant financial risk emerges.

Factor in the sometimes testy relations between employers and employees and workers' comp moves from a significant risk to a critical one.

The Key Issue

But the key issue in workers' comp has never been the innocence or guilt of the employer — barring gross negligence, of course. That's why calling it a "no-fault" system misses the mark.

From the employer's perspective, it's all fault.

Except under a few specific circumstances, workplace injuries are assumed to be the employer's responsibility. That's the central assumption of workers' comp.

But, as we have already pointed out, employers don't mind supporting the system. It eliminates the erratic exposure to negligence litigation — and makes it possible to insure against the financial exposure of the lost wages and medical costs attending upon worker injury. And it gives employer and employee an incentive to make the workplace safe. In a 1970 survey, one big workers' comp insurer found that almost 90 percent of its customers considered the workers' comp system a net positive. At the time, Richard Nixon was proposing to establish the Occupational Safety and Health Agency, and employers pointed to the workers' comp incentive to make the workplace safe as an argument — unsuccessful, of course — against federal regulation.

The feds weigh in

Still, until the 1980s, the pros generally outweighed the cons of the workers' comp system, among employers. Since then, the cons have tipped the scale. Employers have seen too many big settlements.

The spirit of the historic workers' comp compromise between employers and employees is long gone. Lawyers actively seek workers' comp cases, and they have no interest in gaining their claimants a timely settlement. They want big settlements, and they'll wait for them.

Recent History

You can probably trace the change in the climate to 1970. The federal government entered the field in a big way with the passage of the OSH Act. And exposures escalated.

The act did not address workers' comp issues directly, but it created a body of federal law to which employees could point to support their claims. For our purposes, the act serves as a good example of how governmental structure has grown up around workers' comp issues.

The bureaucrats who drafted the OSH Act saw that workplace safety standards varied from state to state, and they thought it their duty to make things regular. It's in the nature of the federal bureaucrat to do these things.

The act implicitly rejects one of the basic tenets of workers' comp — i.e., that the historic compromise between employer and employee would bring about workplace safety.

A new party to the deal

Instead, the drafters of the OSH Act designed it as a governmental arbiter of what employers considered a market factor. OSHA could impose steep fines, and even shut down plants, long before the first employee injury ever occurred. OSHA could set standards for workplace safety and enforce compliance.

Noncompliance became tantamount to negligence in workers' comp cases — where negligence wasn't supposed to apply.

Thus, as far as employers were concerned, OSHA eliminated the two big positives of the workers' comp system: indemnity from negligence suits and the incentive to promote workplace safety.

About the same time, Congress passed the Federal Employees Compensation Act, which did address the workers' comp issue directly by extending protection to federal employees. And it passed other laws, among them the Federal Employer's Liability Act, the Longshoremen's and Harbor Workers' Compensation Act and the Federal Coal Mine Health and Safety Act, ensconcing the federal government as a party to the workers' comp compromise.

In addition, beginning in 1972, the National Commission on Workmen's Compensation Laws elaborated on the various federal edicts and suggested extensive standards and terms for state workers' comp enforcement. This has become a regular yearly process.

Loading the Gun

Again, this federal activity didn't seek to supplant the state-run workers' comp system. It did, however, load the gun in support of the employee and justify a consistent and aggressive regulatory overview of the question of workplace safety.

The federal laws also spurred an explosion in workers' comp claims. Lawyers had largely stayed away from the field prior to the 1970s; the system deterred manipulation and creative interpretation. But the passage of FECA, OSHA and the rest brought thousands of gray pages of bureaucratic rambling into the picture. And lawyers found all sorts of room to expand the field of play, not to mention the fruits of winning the game.

What had begun as a simple, lawyer-free attempt to ensure that injured workers got their just due became a nightmare more complex, more costly, and more hazardous than anyone could imagine. It became a legal hell. It ceased to be a market-driven mechanism for workplace safety. It became the civilian arm of government enforcement. Settlements went from modest to outrageous. The system, which had been cooperative, became contentious.

Politics muddies the waters

The big domestic workers' comp insurers didn't do much to resist these changes, though they should have.

They just raised premiums.

Since 1984, workers' comp insurance premiums have increased faster than the Consumer Price Index every year. In 1970, the total cost to employers of workers' comp claims was $4.9 billion. By 1976, that number had jumped to more than $11 billion; by 1980, to $22.3 billion; and by 1988, to $43.3 billion.

By 1991 the number had leapt to $62 billion.

The Politics

Through the first fifty years of its existence, the workers' comp system operated largely outside the realm of politics. Employees injured on the job received medical treatment for what could heal and compensation for what could not.

This changed in the late 1970s and early 1980s. Workers' comp became political and the politics muddied all efforts to limit costs.

When the federal government interjected itself into the system, it opened a floodgate of claims. Together, federal and state regulations now form a rigid and very legalistic framework for the system.

The states' codes remain different in many ways, but the similarities outweigh the differences. And what differences remain cause more trouble than good.

Few people think of Maine—rural, rugged, scenic—as a hotbed of labor and industry trouble. But the

The state as insurer of last resort

state has suffered much at the hands of workers' comp reformers, and its history stands out as a cautionary tale of good intentions gone very wrong.

The trouble began with an attempt to increase workers' comp benefits in 1986. Those who backed the effort sold it under the popular banner of reform, arguing that it was only sensible and just to give injured workers a little more money while they recuperated.

Ominously, the reformers took their lead from federal workplace safety standards. And they were generous. The reform put Maine's benefits among the nation's highest.

But the state foolishly failed to allow insurers to increase premiums to reflect the new benefits. And it did nothing to bolster the state-run assigned risk workers' comp fund.

Trouble didn't follow as quickly as some insurance types thought. A few voices complained through the late 1980s that the state's number would eventually come up, but Maine kept true to its vision of fairness.

Insurers Abandon the Market

By 1989, the trouble began in earnest. A handful of smaller workers' comp insurers abandoned the market, saying they couldn't keep paying high benefits from low premiums. Their clients had to take insurance from the state pool, a sort of assigned-risk plan, which was itself operating in the red.

A year later, Maine's legislators started talking about workers' comp reform anew. This time, they meant cutting benefits and raising premiums. But they ran into fierce opposition from labor, and the efforts proved fruitless.

Besides, it was too late. In 1991 and 1992, one commercial workers' comp insurer after another pulled out of Maine.

The state's employers had no choice but to seek coverage from the overburdened state pool. In late 1992, with 90 percent of its employers in the pool and no private sector insurance writers actively writing business in the state, Maine began limiting benefits at last. The legislature ditched the old system, installed a business-labor board with power to recommend specific reforms, and created an employer-funded mutual insurer to supplant the state pool.

When the system falls out of balance

Crucial Elements

The reform package took other, almost unheard-of steps: It required workers' comp claimants to pay their own attorney's fees. And it cut benefits and mandated mediation.

All of this aimed at restoring the state's system to its origins: a lawyer-free, simple, speedy process by which workers might gain compensation for medical costs and lost wages. It almost came too late, however. Maine's workers' comp system was the basket case among basket case systems.

Oregon found itself in similar straits in the 1980s, and it found a viable solution.

Oregon's problems, like Maine's, began when the legislature decided to do something about benefits, previously among the stingiest in the country. Business leaders loved the system, but they discovered that, as developments in Maine showed, legislators can't resist pressure from great numbers of people, especially when they present legitimate complaints. The state's benefit schedule hurt too many people.

Unhappy Parties

As we have argued, workers' comp is a common law contrivance between employer and employee. It falls apart if either party becomes unhappy enough.

Exactly that happened in Oregon. The state thought it did business a favor by keeping benefits low. But the imbalance hurt workers, and it engendered a snowstorm of litigation as workers and their lawyers sought to obtain just compensation. Costs skyrocketed. Lawyers from Washington and California spent a lot of time flying into Oregon.

Businesses, especially small ones, spent a lot of time moving out.

What reform really means to insurers

Finally, in 1988, Oregon began a serious overhaul of its system. The result was a reform act that 1) doubled disability benefits for most claims, but 2) compelled employers of more than 10 workers to form safety committees, 3) applied tighter definitions to compensable injuries, 4) required injured workers to seek care from HMOs and similar systems, and 5) enforced mediation as the sole solution to disputed claims. Like magic, Oregon's employers saw premiums fall two years in a row.

Why can't more states streamline their programs as Oregon has? For one thing, lawyers remain enmeshed in the system in state after state. For another, the political will to change doesn't reach a critical mass until the crisis itself becomes unbearable. The art of politics is the art of accomplishing the possible — and putting it off until you can get away with it.

For yet another, smart politicians see the position of state insurance commissioner as a springboard to higher office, and they sometimes find a greater opportunity in creating tension than in resolving it. Thus they play employee against employer, and both against insurers, and they regulate loudly. They show little interest in any reform that promises peace to a troubled market unless it also promises promotion.

In the face of all this, insurers continue to speak of workers' comp reform in grand terms. What they really dream of is a reform of the federally-fostered "reforms" of the 1970s. That just isn't in the cards. And their plans would do little for most small and medium-sized employers. To workers' comp insurers, in short, reform means higher premiums.

Where Change Comes From

Given this interest, not to mention the political nature of workers' comp, it goes without saying that insurers don't initiate change; they only reflect it.

You as an employer must look to yourself to solve your own workers' comp problem. You can't wait for the country to become less litigious, or for insurers to stop confusing short-term results with long-term prosperity, or for politicians to identify their own interests with those of society as a whole. You must analyze your own problem, master the issues of workers' comp, and manipulate the terms in your favor — and, in the process, take back control of the whole system.

The impact on the bottom line

Notwithstanding the troubles of workers' comp, you decide whether it will be a management priority or an unavoidable bother, a constructive tool or an expensive headache, a point of contention or a source of cooperation. This isn't just high-flying language. These choices have a direct impact on your bottom line. If you make the right choices, you encourage workplace safety by systematizing and informing workers of potential dangers. You enlist their support in promoting their own welfare. You stem the flow of money to those others who profit from the real mess that workers' comp has become — insurers, lawyers, and doctors. And both you and your workers benefit.

CHAPTER 3: THE MECHANICS

The who, what and when of workers' comp

In this chapter we take you through the mechanics of a workers' comp claim. The process presents many opportunities for expensive missteps, and you may already know some of them. But read on. You can turn these opportunities for missteps into opportunities to cut claims and benefit yourself and your employees.

In the best of all possible worlds you get no claims in the first place. In the worst of all possible worlds you face many claims and mess every one of them up. In the real world you get claims and you seize the opportunity to manage them effectively: Your employee gets treatment, receives prompt compensation for medical costs and lost wages, and returns to work, all with the least possible interruption to your business operations — and with minimal consequences to your insurance premium.

You have two choices when you get a claim. You can let someone else handle it, for example your insurer, and hope for the best, or you can handle it yourself. Let your insurer handle it and you guarantee that when push comes to shove, the insurer follows its own interests, not yours. Handle it yourself and you guarantee 1) that your employee receives his or her just due and gets back to work as rapidly as possible, and 2) that the claim doesn't balloon into a costly, lengthy nightmare.

The Mechanics

If all goes well, the typical workers' comp claim follows these steps:

1. The injury occurs.
2. The employee receives prompt care and goes home to recuperate.
3. The employee files a claim.

4. The insurer makes prompt payment of medical costs and lost wages.
5. The employee recovers and returns to work.
6. Your workers' comp premium doesn't go through the roof come renewal time.

What happens when a claim goes badly

If all goes badly, the claim follows these steps:

1. The injury occurs.
2. The employee receives prompt care and goes home to recuperate.
3. You make no effort to follow the employee's recuperation or assure the employee of your concern.
4. Feeling neglected, the employee becomes a couch potato, sees a daytime TV commercial in which a lawyer promises the moon, and succumbs to the lawyer's blandishments.
5. The lawyer files a big claim and does everything possible to delay settlement, not to mention the employee's return to work.
6. The employee begins a round of visits to a lengthening list of workers' comp doctors, chiropractors, physical therapists, emotional therapists, family therapists — you name it — each of whom suggests a regimen of very costly treatment absolutely necessary to the employee's recovery.
7. The insurer offers a settlement which the employee and the lawyer turn down.
8. The employee and the lawyer contest the claim formally, alleging soft-tissue injury, stress, emotional trauma, etc.
9. The employee finds it amusing to spend eight hours a day visiting doctors, chiropractors, etc. and consulting with the lawyer, and does not return to work.
10. Your operation limps along in the absence of the worker, forcing you to hire and train a replacement.
11. The hearing date nears, and you spend countless hours with your insurer and, maybe, your

lawyer preparing for it — and countless hours wondering what your insurer will do to your premium come renewal time.

12. Just before the hearing begins, your insurer and the lawyer reach a settlement that makes your teeth hurt.
13. The worker and the lawyer go their merry way, and you hope never to see either of them again.
14. You see your insurer at renewal time, and your increase in premium does indeed go through the roof.

You see how each of the steps in the claim that goes well can mushroom into the nightmare of the claim that goes badly. Let's take things one at a time, so that you can prevent the disaster of the claim that goes badly. Remember that for the sake of simplicity, we use the word injury to mean either injury or illness, as we do throughout this book.

The serious injury makes the system spin

The Injury Occurs

A machine operator at XYZ Manufacturing Corp. catches his hand in a gear, lacerating it and breaking bones.

Workers' comp cases begin with some form of injury to an employee. Usually, but not always, the injury occurs at the workplace or in the course of work. The vast majority of workplace injuries (some surveys suggest as many as 80 percent) require only minor attention and have no noticeable impact on the employee's status.

The remaining few injuries are serious, and they make the whole workers' comp system spin.

The National Council on Compensation Insurance[1] puts a serious injury into one of four categories: specific physical, cumulative physical, specific mental, or cumulative mental.

Specific physical injuries demand immediate treatment; their causal link to the job should be very

[1]The NCCI, an association of workers' comp insurers, collects statistics and develops policy forms and insurance rates.

The causal link to the job

clear—a cut or burn from a shop machine, a broken bone from a fall. Cumulative injuries result from the gradual or long-term impacts of the workplace; their causal links are often more difficult to establish — respiratory diseases from polluted workplace air, repetitive motion injuries.

Physical injuries, obviously, affect the body. They are usually easy to detect and diagnose with the exception, of course, of soft-tissue injuries to the muscles and tendons. These can defy even sophisticated medical detection.

Mental injuries are also tough. Sometimes they're obvious — e.g., the stupor that some chemicals cause when inhaled. Sometimes they're very difficult to substantiate — e.g., the stress caused by acute job pressures or mood swings caused by psychological abuse.

The Lawyers' Frenzy

Workers' comp lawyers love cumulative and mental injuries, with their inexact definitions and fuzzy causality. Give them a case presenting a combination of cumulative and mental injuries and the frenzy begins.

Workers' comp lawyers, backed by some expert testimony, add another category to the NCCI's four: mental/physical injuries. According to the legal theory, these occur when a pre-existing mental claim leads either to a physical injury or to the conditions which allow a physical injury to follow. As you can imagine, these are difficult to establish, since the pre-existing mental condition will itself often be difficult to prove. For the same reason, mental/mental injuries—when a pre-existing mental injury leads to another — are also hard to prove.

But lawyers love to litigate the physical/mental double whammy. They contend that an established physical injury leads to stress or depression which becomes an additional workers' comp claim.

The Worker Receives Medical Care

The XYZ Corp. employee rushes to the hospital, where doctors examine the hand, set bones, and stitch cuts.

Since most workers' comp injuries surface during

working hours, you the employer control the circumstances during the critical moments after an injury occurs. How you respond makes a big difference in how the claim plays out thereafter.

Medical costs take less than 40 percent of the settlement money insurers pay out each year. The real problems come from lost wages and other long-term results. Even so, it makes sense to provide the quickest and best medical care in the wake of an injury. Doing so demonstrates your concern and allows you to assert control right away.

Asserting control early on

Knowing What to Do

Someone will be nearby when your employee suffers the injury. This individual — and everyone else who works for you — should know what to do: go to the aid of the injured worker, summon emergency assistance, and alert management.

Instruct workers to do these things via a formal, ongoing program. Keep them informed about the location of first aid supplies and facilities. Keep ample supplies on hand. Consider employing a health care professional. If you can't, train your workers in first aid and keep them up to speed.This investment produces two important returns. It assures that a bad injury doesn't get worse from neglect or from slow response, and it makes all of your employees confident that you value their wellbeing.

Let's stress the second point, and think about it from the standpoint of the injured employee. Shyster workers' comp lawyers send runners to prowl the halls of hospitals, looking for depressed and lonely workers who want to blame somebody for their suffering and, with a little help, might target an uncaring boss. It's scary enough to suffer an injury, and doubly so when the injury may threaten one's livelihood. You make things worse when you give your employee reason to think that you don't care.

Too much is at stake for you *not* to care. Make sure that your employees know you do.

The Claim

The employee leaves the hospital several hours after

Make sure to keep in touch

the injury. In the days that follow, while the worker recovers at home and sees a doctor, the employee files a claim for medical costs incurred and for wages lost while recuperating.

How a claim starts almost always indicates how it plays out. The smart employer makes sure that someone — perhaps even the employer personally — keeps in touch regularly, maybe daily, with the injured worker and helps out with filing the claim and with taking care of the many other personal, family and work-related details that crop up in the wake of an injury (See Appendix Twenty-One). Never forget the tassel-loafered prowlers in the hallway.

In some cases, the injured employee spends an extended period in a hospital under care. More often, hospital care is short-term. In either case, workers' comp insurers usually pay for the medical costs without complaint.

Contention Arises

The point of contention comes after the worker has received medical treatment and seeks compensation for lost wages.

Every state uses its own formulas for calculating how to compensate workers for lost wages. The most common formula holds that an employee unable to work receives two-thirds of normal salary — to a limit of around $400 a week — until the worker can return to the original job or train for another.

No worker needs an attorney to make a compensation claim; the original idea was to keep lawyers out of the picture altogether. But workers' comp lawyers aggressively pursue injured employees. They run television ads ("Have you been injured on the job? Your boss's workers' comp insurance can pay you thousands of dollars right now!"), radio spots and print ads encouraging workers to seek legal representation. These lawyers work on a contingency basis and make their money from lost-wages settlements. They have no interest in — and often actively resist — your plans to get an injured worker back on the job quickly. They want long recovery periods, or no recovery at all.

onto the shoulders of others — competitors first, and then taxpayers. Eventually everybody loses.

A 1990 report written by Gov. George Deukmejian of California concluded that intentionally misclassified workers cost the nation more than $40 billion. The report estimated that California itself annually lost $2.3 billion in tax revenues from illegal misclassification. In a Congressional study released the same year, Rep. Tom Lantos (D-California) called Internal Revenue Service enforcement of federal misclassification laws "non-systematic . . . subjective . . . and inconsistent."

Across the country, employers save millions of dollars a year by bending a murky law that government doesn't enforce very strictly.

The pool shrinks, the problem worsens

The States Clamp Down

But the employer who considers joining these ranks goes forewarned: The states have started striking down on evasive classification. Gov. Deukmejian's report caused some tremors of change in California. The state Assembly considered legislation to give contractors legal recourse against competitors who flagrantly misclassify workers. This legislation, like bills written in no fewer than two dozen other states across the country, follows legislation approved in Connecticut in 1990.

State regulators, contractors' groups and building trade unions all support this approach to workers' comp enforcement. So do most lawyers' lobbies, needless to say.

There are other dangers to misclassifying employees. It encourages workers to file fraudulent tax returns. Shifting workers to contractor status doesn't eliminate exposure — only the workers' comp mechanism. The employer entertains grave risk if a "contractor" suffers an injury on the job and, lacking workers' comp protection, sues the employer for negligence.

Even so, some employers must use independent contractors. Those who do must prepare for state-run labor audits based on the IRS guidelines — and, in some cases, based on IRS tactics.

Who controls the method

Why does the regulatory establishment allow the lines to blur between employment and contract work, if it objects so strongly to industry's response? The answer is a common one: bad planning.

In general, the nature of the relationship between suppliers and users of services is one of the most troublesome issues facing businesses. Whether a given worker is an employee or an independent contractor highlights some of the fundamental changes facing the post-industrial economy.

Business relies on independent contractors to avoid the restrictions and obligations imposed by onerous labor legislation. Regulators and legal theorists recognize this, and seek to elaborate the rules of employment status to recover lost ground. They presume that the shift to contractors constitutes some kind of not-so-ill-defined fraud.

But the law holds the distinction between an employee and a contractor to turn on whether the worker controls the method of his or her work. This simple concept has led to several controversial decisions by the National Labor Relations Board, the main bureaucracy in charge. The federal courts, reviewing the NLRB's decisions, tend to go along.

The Right to Control

The NLRB emphasizes that it is the *right* to control which is of paramount importance, not the *exercise* of that right.

In one well-documented case, the applicability of common-law distinctions between employees and independent contractors surfaced some decades ago in a dispute involving newspaper boys in Los Angeles. The question: Were the newsies entitled to union representation for purposes of collective bargaining?

The NLRB applied common law in a manner that classified the newsboys as employees, since newspaper distributors controlled the manner of their sales. But the Ninth Circuit Court of Appeals found that the board had ventured too far from common-law standards.

The courts go along

In *NLRB v. Hearst Publications*, the U.S. Supreme Court reversed the appeals court and broadly expanded the labor board's position. The court found the right-to-control test of common law unsuitable for defining the meaning of employee under the National Labor Relations Act. It ruled that common-law classification could be replaced by a set of broad interpretations suggested in the National Labor Relations Act. As a group, these interpretations broadened the criteria for defining employee status to include economic and even social factors.

In short, the court felt compelled to call the newsboys employees because of their relative lack of bargaining power and the high degree of their dependence on distributors.

This opened workers' comp to a flood of litigation. Smart lawyers suddenly found it easy to manipulate the definitions of employee and employer.

Congress got its two-cents worth in through the Taft Hartley Amendment. This law expressly overrules broader tests and unequivocally reinforces the control test. But if you think that should have settled it, think again.

'A Maze of Precedents'

Confusion reigns, leading a former chief judge on the federal appeals circuit to complain:

> *On consideration of that issue [whether parties are employees or independent], I find myself in a maze of precedents with few standards for decision discernible.*

He admitted that Congress had clearly ruled the common-law definition of independent contractor to be the basic guide. But he had to acknowledge the broader definitions of the NLRB and the Supreme Court.

On the same topic, labor courts in Canada have done a lot of innovative work. They permit some classifications of independent contractors to engage in collective bargaining and otherwise behave like employees.

Some Canadian courts endorse so-called "organization tests," which determine whether services performed are "integrated" with the activities of the principal. These tests sound self-referential, but they do seem to stand up to legal scrutiny.

In the face of all this, at least one American commentator has advocated that the U.S. labor system abandon common-law concepts when determining employment status, but the traditional analysis remains intact.

First Things First

For the employer, the best time to settle the nature of the relationship is before it commences.

The employer (or the worker) may request a determination letter from the Internal Revenue Service by submitting Form SS-8. The instructions require an employer to complete the form for one worker representative of the class of workers whose status is in question.

The beginning is also the time to decide who controls the work. If the employer goes beyond explaining the result to be obtained, the worker is probably an employee.

Thus it helps to establish contractor status if you only explain the result you want and predicate compensation on reaching it.

You strengthen your position if you draw up a written agreement detailing the worker's duties and the terms and conditions of the service arrangement. The document should incorporate the common-law factors and, most important, recite the parties' intent to create contractual independence.

If the provider of services stands on equal footing with the putative employer, the latter must remain wary of tricks like late-hour attempts to change the terms of the contract between the two. This is known as restatement of the rules of agency. If the worker succeeds here, he or she can lead a court to infer employer control and employee status, even if other factors point the other way.

Independent contractors and employees may perform identical services for employers, but they can be identified differently depending upon the decision of the employer, the application of certain statutes, or — most erratically, it seems — by judicial interpretation.

Ultimately, the issue carries important implications for both worker and employer. And the risk of retroactive reclassification poses a significant financial exposure to anyone who engages another to mow a lawn or clean a carpet.

The ultimate determination in any one case involves a finding of law and is subject to endless consideration by appellate courts.

A Horror Story

A costly good deed

Some employers and labor specialists argue that the distinction between employees and contractors is so subjective that employers can't rely on it to protect themselves from workers' comp exposures. And horror stories exist to support their skepticism.

Thomas Hoppmann was a homeless man who did odd jobs at the First Southern Baptist Church of Cupertino, California. The church paid decent money — $5 or $10 an hour — to needy men and women who could help with maintenance and repairs.

One weekend in 1986, as Hoppmann helped to repair the roof of the church, he fell and fractured his heel and elbow.

Church officials took him to a hospital for treatment, but trouble ensued. Hoppmann was on welfare, and he didn't want the church to pay his medical bills because he feared losing eligibility.

But the church did contribute to the hospital bill, and in consequence the state did investigate and suspend some of Hoppmann's benefits.

He, in turn, filed a workers' comp claim against the church.

First Southern regularly paid Hoppmann for his work as part of its relief ministry to help the poor and unemployed. Church ministers believed that many needy people didn't want handouts but would work for assistance.

When coverage begins

But the California workers' comp appeals board had little interest in the church's charitable works. It ruled Hoppmann a church employee because he kept coming back for work, and at a negotiated hourly rate.

In the spring of 1989, the board ordered the church to pay two years' back wages and $80,000 in disability to Hoppmann.

Treacherous Waters

The church's experience shows how treacherous these waters are. The IRS makes them even more dangerous. It aggressively seeks employment taxes from employers who use the services of independent contractors.

Given this, and all the new legislation restricting the employment relationship, it becomes a crucial decision how you classify workers, with serious consequences.

It's impossible to make generalizations about all workers in this regard. As usual, the employer should look to the essence of each work relationship and determine what level of control and dependence is necessary to achieve the desired result.

Physical Circumstance

When and where is an employee covered by workers' comp?

Workers' compensation protection extends to any employee engaged in his or her job. Thus from the first minute of the first day of employment, the worker becomes a potential exposure to the employer.

And the workplace only begins the exposure.

Most workers' comp boards extend employee protection to any activity undertaken "in the course of employment," commonly abbreviated COE.

COE means that any activity directly linked to a job qualifies the employee for workers' comp coverage. For example, a sales rep on the road making presentations is covered by workers' comp in most states. So is an executive attending a work-related seminar.

But neither would be covered going to a nonbusiness dinner later in the evening. A service technician is covered while making a repair in a customer's offices but not while driving to and from work.

The 'going and coming' rule

Legal Theory

In workers' comp it matters whether the injury is job-related, not whether the employer or employee is at fault. As one state court has ruled:

> *[T]he test is not the relation of an individual's personal quality to an event, but the relationship of an event to an employment. The essence of applying the test is not a matter of assessing blame, but of marking out boundaries.*

One of the central difficulties in workers' comp lies in defining those boundaries.

In August 1983, the Ohio Supreme Court embarked on a new and potentially troublesome course in identifying work-connected injuries. *Littlefield v. Pillsbury* marked a substantial turning point in workers' comp law.

A Pillsbury employee suffered an injury while returning to work from lunch. The worker won workers' compensation because his injury stemmed from a special risk emanating from his employment. This case went against the "going and coming" rule, which denies compensation for injuries arising from accidents that occur on the way to or from work.

The court ruled that the employer created an atmosphere in which the employee had no choice but to drive to and from the worksite during breaks.

Littlefield is significant not only because of the context in which the accident occurred but also because of the policy ramifications underlying the decision. The ruling relieves individual workers of the risk of certain travel-related injuries.

Workers' comp experts argue that *Littlefield* distorts the "going and coming" rule and alters the grounds on which courts determine whether an injury is work-related.

Like most states, Ohio had required that an injury occur "in the course of" the injured worker's employ-

The courts rule in differing ways

ment to be compensable. But like the courts in other states, Ohio's found these terms deceptive, and they applied them to real facts and circumstances in widely differing ways.

Employers can try to finesse solutions to the exposure—and plan for the worst. Expect the courts to interpret the phrase "in the course of employment" to extend to virtually any harm which befalls an employee during the ordinary workday.

And if only it stopped there.

Many states cover injuries "arising out of employment" (commonly abbreviated AOE), and if you think the courts have trouble figuring out what "in the course of employment" means, they have just as much with AOE.

Workers' comp experts describe AOE as any job-related circumstance which plays an active role in the development of an injury. It can include problems that occur miles from the workplace and months after a job.

Clearly, AOE covers a multitude of sins, all of which threaten the employer. Injuries which can be said to have arisen from employment include many of a cumulative nature, including psychiatric problems. (Chapter 7 shows that psychiatric troubles such as stress have quickly become the most damaging workers' comp claims.)

Disqualification

What disqualifies an injury?

It might seem hard to imagine *any* injury which could not be construed as arising out of employment. But most states agree in pointing out those circumstances that eliminate an employer's exposure.

They include injuries, even occurring COE or AOE, which result from:

1. Intoxication with alcohol or illegally-used drugs;
2. Self-inflicted harm or suicide;
3. An altercation or physical conflict in which the injured employee is the aggressor;

4. A felonious act committed by the employee;
5. Horseplay or other reckless behavior during work hours; and
6. Travel to and from the worksite unless the employer controls the method and means of transportation (with the exception of the loophole opened by the Ohio courts in *Littlefield*).

Alcohol plays a big role

Some employers believe that intoxication plays a greater part in the incidence of workplace injuries than suggested by the limited data available. The data suggests that intoxication plays a role in 8 to 12 percent of workplace injuries.

Of course, employers can exercise great control over reckless horseplay in the workplace by banning it and disciplining workers who engage in it. They can exercise similar control over intoxication — if they tread lightly.

No Compulsion

Employers commonly attack the problem by implementing alcohol abuse and drug testing and counseling programs. Many report unquestioned success, but they achieve this success by avoiding anything that smells of compulsion. The law prohibits employers from requiring that problem workers enroll in such programs, so successful programs must emphasize the personal and social benefits of overcoming substance abuse. They sell problem workers on the benefits of sobriety, in other words.

But these employers keep a strict eye on their own benefits, too — not to mention their liabilities. The employer who keeps a tight rein on intoxication in the workplace demonstrates a commitment to workplace safety. Workers' comp lawyers hate to see this. Defense lawyers like to see it. So do insurers. It lowers the risk and, hence, the workers' comp insurance premium.

It also allows employers to establish so-called "patterns of behavior" at troubled plants or among troublesome employee groups. This sort of evidence doesn't always divert a workers' comp claim, but it can limit the damage.

The level of control

The small employer may find it prohibitively expensive to maintain a substance abuse program. But the fact is that an aggressive effort limits exposure, and a single incident involving an intoxicated worker can bear devastating fruit. Consider your own situation carefully. Analyze the costs and benefits, and if you see no clear path either way, give the greater weight to safety. An ounce of prevention is worth more than a pound of cure.

The Vital Question

More than anything else, the Who, What, and When of workers' comp comes down to the issue of control. The tools and guidelines discussed in this chapter help to determine the level of control exercised by employer over worker — a vital issue in workers' comp claims. Once you establish the level of control, the rest follows.

But the best way to avoid a devastating workers' comp claim is to prevent injury in the first place. It also helps, as we see here, to understand the legal grounds on which claims play out, and to cover all your bases. You don't prevent claims by relying on legalities, of course. But you must know them if you are to mount a solid defense against a questionable claim, and institute a program offering long-term solutions to the big problem of workers' comp.

The legalities don't make for creative solutions, and they fail in the face of a judge or panel determined to find lavishly for the worker. But, when a claim looms ahead, they are the place to start.

CHAPTER 4: CLASSIFICATIONS

How the system works

Now we home in on one of the most important, least understood, and easily abused aspects of workers' comp: employer classifications. It's a rich lode — and a treacherous one. Learn the intricacies of employer classifications and you arm yourself with a powerful weapon to cut your costs aggressively. Gain control here and you influence the regulatory climate that governs your workers' comp bill far more effectively than you can in most other respects. But proceed cautiously. Go too far and you get yourself into trouble.

The Mechanics of Employer Classification

Employer classification lies at the center of workers' comp.

Each state classifies employers according to the businesses in which they engage. The NCCI list, used by most states, ranges over hundreds of classifications from accounting to yarn dyeing.

The theory here is that, by and large, employers engaged in the same business show the same claims experience, and ought therefore to pay the same premium for workers' comp insurance. It's not a bad idea — in theory. After all, it stands to reason that employers who build skyscrapers expose their workers to greater hazards than, say, employers of clerical workers.

In practice, however, if you don't pay attention, you can end up in a classification that 1) doesn't fit your business and 2) costs you a bundle. Later on we show you some examples of how the system goes awry, and how you can fight it, but for now, let's start with a description of how the system works.

In setting workers' comp rates, the state first pools the claims experience of the employers in each clas-

'The business of the employer'

sification. This is the central data for pricing workers' comp insurance policies.

In doing so each state relies on Rule IV(A) of the NCCI's Basic Manual. This rule makes a crucial distinction:

> *The object of the classification system is to group employers into classifications so that the rate for each classification reflects the exposures common to those employers. Subject to certain exceptions . . . it is the business of the employer . . . that is classified, not the separate employments, occupations or operations within the business.*

Note the emphasis on "the business of the employer." The idea is that the rate you pay for workers' comp insurance should reflect the average accident record of employers like yourself, plus a bit to cover the overhead expenses of your insurer. Thus, the worse the accident record among employers like yourself, the higher your premium.

Each state publishes rates for the classifications at least once a year. You pay a "base rate" expressed in terms of each $100 of your payroll:

$$\text{Base rate} = \frac{(\text{payroll} \times \text{manual rate of classification})}{\$100}$$

For example, the 1990 NCCI standard form set the base rate for high explosives manufacturers at a whopping $14.18 per each $100 of payroll — a number that ought to make you thankful if your own fascination with things that go bang faded with your childhood.

'Experience Rating'

Insurers use classifications to report workers' comp claims and to evaluate applications for insurance from employers like yourself. But it's not cut and dried. If a premium exceeds a certain amount (about $6,000 a year in 1989) it becomes subject to "experience rating." This helps or hurts you according to how many claims your business shows. You pay through the nose if you show lots of claims — that is, if your "experience" is worse than the average for employers in your classification.

You save money if your experience looks better than the average.

This alone should give you a powerful incentive to do something about claims, about which we go into greater detail later on. Experience rating can cut your costs substantially, but the classification into which the state puts you makes an even bigger difference.

Some employers push too hard

Aggressive employers know this, and some of them push hard, sometimes too hard, in seeking to get themselves into a cheaper classification. The following case study brings this issue into clear focus.

The Paper Trail

In 1991, Imagineering, Inc., a Maine-based producer of outdoor furniture, got into a nasty fight with its workers' comp regulators over classifications. The fight went to the state supreme court and sent aggressive employers around the country ducking for legal cover.

Imagineering made and marketed its furniture (under the trade name Weatherend Estate Furniture) from three separate facilities, all located in preppy Rockland, Maine. The company's workers sawed and milled raw lumber into furniture parts at 3 Gordon Drive. Other workers assembled the parts and finished the furniture at 6 Gordon Drive. Still others displayed and sold the furniture at 374 Main Street.

Like all employers in Maine, Imagineering paid workers' comp insurance premiums based on a percentage of its payroll.

To establish Imagineering's classifications, the state consulted NCCI's Basic Manual of Workers' Compensation Insurance Classifications (the "Basic Manual") and a reference book known as the Scopes of Basic Manual Classifications (the "Scopes Manual").

Prior to 1988, Imagineering's entire manufacturing operation fell under classification Code 2883 (furniture manufacturing) and its retail operations under classification Code 8044 (store: furniture and

Separate payrolls, separate entities

driver). Its outside salespeople and design and clerical workers received standard exception classifications (of which more anon) as allowed by the Basic Manual.

Imagineering paid tons of money for workers' comp insurance for those employees classified under furniture manufacturing — one of the highest-risk classifications in the Scopes Manual.

Code 2883, on the other hand, is where furniture-manufacturing workers go who are "not otherwise classified." This classification covers a multitude of high-risk workers, including those who process rough or surfaced lumber, plywood or fiberboard into finished products.

In an attempt to lower its workers' comp rates, Imagineering painstakingly split up its furniture manufacturing operations by moving all of its milling equipment and personnel to 3 Gordon Drive and all of its less dangerous assembly equipment and personnel to 6 Gordon Drive.

Its strategy was to limit the number of employees who fell into the expensive Code 2883.

A Single Corporate Entity

The company went even farther. Although it continued to operate as a single corporation, Imagineering began to maintain separate payrolls for each operation and took care not to cross train any of its employees.

But Maine's regulators refused to go along. They would not allow Imagineering to break its operations into separate classifications, and the Maine courts agreed. They ruled that the company's efforts to separate operations didn't go far enough, that it was still essentially one manufacturing operation even though it used adjacent buildings.

In rejecting Imagineering's appeal, the Maine Supreme Court made an important observation:

> *Although developed and administered by NCCI, the rules contained in the Basic Manual and the Scopes Manual are equivalent to administrative regulations because they are subject to the ap-*

proval and periodic review of the Superintendent of Insurance and have been incorporated by reference into Bureau of Insurance Regulations.

This is important because it validates the NCCI's authoritative power. (If you think about it a minute, it also reflects the ad-hoc nature of workers' comp regulation.) Rarely does a private sector industry group wield the kind of regulatory influence over a multi-billion dollar business held by the NCCI.

Good but not good enough

The Maine Supreme Court thought Imagineering's efforts good but not good enough to merit separate classification.

It noted that the Scopes Manual explicitly states that Code 2883 "contemplates the manufacture of furniture and frame parts which are assembled into chairs, buffets, dining room sets, dressers, chests, beds, tables, couches, china closets and other furniture. [It] further contemplates the finishing of such furniture by sanding or buffing, followed by the application of the stains, varnishing, lacquer or paint. Basic Manual Rule IV(C)(3)(f) states that '[a] classification designated ["not otherwise classified"] shall apply only if no other classification more specifically describes the insured's business.' "

A More General Theory

The court set out a more general theory from rules in the NCCI's classifications manual:

. . . each employer is "assigned the one basic classification which best describes the business of the employer within [the] state."

The rules specifically state that "it is the business of the employer within a state that is classified, not the separate employments, occupations or operations within the business."

The object of the classification procedure is to assign the one basic classification which best describes the business of the employer within a state. Subject to certain exceptions described in this rule, each classification includes all the various types of labor found in a business. It is the

Hung up on a fine point

business which is classified, not the individual employments, occupations or operations within a business.

According to the Basic Manual, an employer should be assigned more than one classification only if "a classification requires operations or employees to be separately rated" or "an employer operates a secondary business within a state."

So Imagineering lost. Every employer who sees classification as a loophole should remember this ruling. Classification is not a loophole. You have to master it if you want to control your workers' comp problem, but you can't abuse it. The courts broadly interpret the rules limiting the use of classifications. As we show you in this chapter, the courts go along with those employers who do their homework, but not with those who get sloppy.

This makes your job difficult but not impossible. Imagineering failed to exploit the "secondary business" allowance to get some of its workers into less costly classifications. Its failure doesn't mean that you will fail, too, if you take this tack. Indeed, being aggressive with your classification remains your best strategy in many circumstances. But don't expect an easy job of it.

'Secondary Business'

The NCCI Manual doesn't actually define the term "secondary business" but does say that all of the following conditions must exist before a single employer qualifies for more than one classification:

1. You must conduct the secondary business as a "separate undertaking or enterprise."
2. You must keep separate payroll records for each business.
3. You must separate each business physically by structural partitions and carry them on without interchange of labor.
4. State law must not prohibit the assignment of separate classifications under the language defining the applicable classifications.

Imagineering got hung up on that last point. Its

2883 classification did "anticipate" all kinds of furniture manufacturing. Most classifications don't.

The Standard Exceptions

Before we go on, let's spend a minute on the standard exception. Aggressive employers seize on the standard exception as a tool to cut their costs—and they sometimes rue the day they ever thought of doing so.

Small risk, low cost

In workers' comp insurance, certain low-risk classes of employment go into classifications separate from other ratings. The Basic Manual states:

> *Some occupations are common to so many businesses that special classifications have been established for them. They are called standard exception classifications. Employees within the definition of a standard exception classification are not included in a basic classification unless the basic classification specifically includes those employees. The standard exception classifications are clerical office employees, drafting employees, drivers, chauffeurs and their helpers and outside salespersons, collectors or messengers.*

The idea is that these jobs pose such a small risk of worker injury that they belong in one low-cost classification. Many employers try to jam their workers into the standard exception even if the work the employees perform doesn't qualify. You may find this tempting, too, but it can cause trouble. When state regulators and insurers smell fraud, they look first to the standard exception. So don't try to get away with any fancy stuff here. As one East Coast risk manager says, "The standard exception is the cheapest premium on the books. But there are better places to hide."

The key to saving insurance and self-insurance costs is to change rate classifications from high-risk groups into low-risk groups. But in order to cut what you pay for employees slotted in each classification, you have to change job descriptions, work habits and sometimes even company structures, too.

The change can be difficult because — as we have stressed — the state applies classifications to em-

Doing your homework

ployers, not employees. Regulators don't allow you to use different classifications for workers doing the same work in a single worksite, just to save on insurance premiums. You have to justify the different classifications, and that means doing your homework.

Obviously, an explosives maker with a dozen manufacturing employees and a dozen clerical employees should classify the groups separately. The manufacturing workers cost more than $14 per $100 to insure, the clerks around 25 cents. Separating them saves the employer more than $20,000 a year.

But the separation can be difficult.

Costly Ignorance

Most workers' comp forms allow you to choose your own classifications for workers. Ignorance can be very costly here, as the following case proves.

In 1978, New York-based Harry Wolsky Stair Builder, Inc. filed an "Application for Classification of Industry and Premium" with Ohio's Bureau of Workers' Compensation, seeking coverage for employees of an operation it wanted to set up in Ohio. The company described its operations as a "manufacturer of stairs (wood)." This should have put Wolsky's workers into classification 4883.

But the Ohio bureau mistakenly put Wolsky's workers into a more costly classification, 2731 — wooden pallet manufacturing — and set premiums accordingly.

Wolsky didn't catch the error for six costly years. In early 1984, the company received the bureau's payroll report describing its activities as wooden pallet manufacturing—classification 2731. Wolsky immediately informed the bureau of the error and requested a refund of the overcharged premiums, calculated at more than $38,200.

The bureau, following an audit, refunded only $13,268, reflecting overcharges paid after December 31, 1981. On technical grounds it refused to refund the overcharges paid in earlier years. Ohio regulations limited refunds to overpayments made within 24 months of the current payroll reporting period — a sort of statute of limitations.

Wolsky filed suit seeking full reimbursement. But it didn't have much more luck with the courts.

Wolsky alleged that Ohio violated the company's constitutional right to equal protection under the law. The company argued that the Ohio bureau observed no statute of limitations when it came to dunning employers for underpaid premiums more than two years old, so it should have no grounds for refusing to fork over what Wolsky had overpaid.

Making the best case

Too Late in the Game

The Ohio Court of Appeals and Supreme Court disagreed. They rejected the constitutional noises on the grounds that Wolsky made them too late in the game. Wolsky had appealed the classification assessment on two occasions — first to the state industrial commission's adjudicating committee in 1986 and then to the commission itself in 1987. On both occasions, the courts noted, Wolsky focused on the premiums, ignoring the more important fact that the classification was wrong in the first place.

In any event, the courts found no evidence that either the industrial commission or the workers' comp bureau ever denied a request for hearing. Wolsky simply didn't make the best case.

On top of this, the courts supported the two-year limit. Ohio law allows for refunds when the bureau makes "adjustments as to classifications, allocation of wage expenditures to classifications, amount of wage expenditures, premium rates and/or amount of premium." In the Wolsky case, the bureau overcharged the company between February of 1978 and December of 1981. But the company's status as a wooden staircase manufacturer never changed — a crucial distinction, the courts said.

The overpayment resulted from a mistake by the Bureau of Workers' Compensation, not a mistake by the employer, the courts said, but this did not entitle Wolsky to a refund of more than two years' worth of overpayments.

Wolsky, the Ohio Supreme Court said, "was informed by the bureau, during the period at issue, that its premiums conformed to its classification. The [company] had no reason to object to the premiums, while assuming that the state properly charged it for insurance coverage."

In other words: caveat emptor. It was the company's responsibility to know the classification structure well enough to know that it was being overcharged.

One Employer Wins

In a similar case, the Oregon Court of Appeals ruled in 1992 that an employer who had incorrectly classified some workers was not liable for additional workers' comp insurance premiums.

Oregon insurance regulators had tried to hold the employer liable for the additional premiums when they discovered the misclassification, years after SAIF Corp., the state-run workers' comp insurer, had written the policy.

The courts countered that the carrier wasn't entitled to bill the employer retroactively because it didn't demonstrate 1) that the employer knew or should have known that employees were misclassified, 2) that it had provided inaccurate information, or 3) that it had changed work activities of employees after risk classifications had been approved.

The Oregon Court of Appeals wrote that:

> *[The e]ffect of changing employer's payroll from one risk classification to another was to change classification of work activities of employees on basis of [a new and] different assessment of risk of injury. . . .*
>
> *[R]eclassification may occur [only] by assigning work activities to a new classification or by changing classification from one class to another.*
>
> *An administrative agency is not at liberty to limit or restrict the terms of a statute. Clear, unambiguous statutes are to be construed according to their plain meaning.*

At bottom, this impenetrable language means that, since the state agency had no grounds in statute to reclassify the employer, it couldn't demand the higher premiums.

The highest class

An Important Dissent

This case produced an important dissenting opinion that stands as a touchstone for any employer who gets aggressive with classifications. As noted, the majority concluded that Oregon law precluded the state from reclassifying the employer's payroll. The dissenter — the chief judge — argued otherwise. He quoted Oregon workers' comp law:

> *At the time a workers' compensation guaranty contract is issued, the insurer shall give written notice to the insured of the rating classifications to which the insured's employees are assigned and shall provide an adequate description of work activities in each classification. The insurer shall not bill an insured for reclassifying employees during the policy year unless:*
>
> *(a) The insured knew or should have known that the employees were misclassified;*
>
> *(b) The insured provided improper or inaccurate information concerning its operations; or*
>
> *(c) The insured's operations changed after the date information on the employees is obtained from the insured. . . .*
>
> *When there is an interchange of labor without verifiable records, the entire payroll of employees who interchange shall be assigned to the classification representing any part of their work which carries the highest authorized premium rate.*

An "interchange of labor" occurs when an employee at different times performs work described by two or more classifications.

The State's Ability to React

The dissenting judge voiced his own opinion about the state's ability to react to aggressive use of classification:

Who may divide payroll

> *[Workers' comp law] permits an employer who has been assigned more than one rating classification to allocate payroll to the different classifications, provided that it maintains verifiable records to substantiate its allocation.*
>
> *If the employer fails to maintain verifiable records for an employee, the insurer can reallocate the payroll for that employee to the highest authorized classification. The only time that a "reallocation" can possibly occur is after the employer has submitted its total payroll and verifiable records to its workers' compensation carrier. Therefore, an insurer's authority retroactively to adjust an employer's payroll is a necessary adjunct of the statutory and administrative scheme.*
>
> *. . . the legislature intended that employers that are assigned more than one rating classification may divide their payrolls. [Oregon law] effectuates that intent but precludes manipulation by enabling insurers to adjust an employer's payroll on the basis of the employer's records. Were the law otherwise, employers could allocate all payroll to the lowest assigned rating classification and then preclude the carrier from challenging that allocation by asserting a bar on reclassification.*

Don't take this dissent to mean that the law precludes your doing all that you can about your own classifications. Instead, take it as a measure of what regulators will argue if you do. Expect them to give close scrutiny to your effort, so keep your paper trail in good order, don't act foolishly, and argue your case forcefully. Splitting a given job or group of jobs into two class codes is difficult. It isn't illegal — but will almost assuredly come under fire, either from your state regulators or from your insurer. If you lose the fight, your insurer may deny a claim and leave you holding a very heavy bag.

Dealing with Regulators

State agencies have ultimate control over classifications, but they take their lead from the forms you submit. (See Appendices One & Five.)

If you choose more than one class for different operations, the workers' comp bureau will want to see distinctions among the operations in payroll, worksite and training.

Close scrutiny from the state

Anticipate the scrutiny even if you think your regulators too overworked to pay attention to your operations. They can't audit every classification, but they do look for aggressive cost-control efforts involving classifications. In this the workers' comp bureaucracy resembles the IRS, and classifying employees resembles doing your taxes. Smart work saves money. Too much aggressiveness draws attention you don't want.

But the fact remains: The best and fastest way for you to save money is to classify your workers so as to gain the lowest rates. Here are the best ways to start:

1. Order an updated copy of the state's classification list and read it carefully, looking for classes that apply to operations and even to specific job titles. Often, more than one classification applies to a given job.
2. Discuss the classifications with an agent or underwriter—in detail. Don't accept what they tell you uncritically; too many employers do. And don't wait for your agent or underwriter to suggest the appropriate classifications for your operations. Instead, take the initiative and make your own suggestions. After all, who knows your business better than you do?
3. Support your arguments with specific data on what your workers do — and prepare to set up separate payrolls or payroll categories.
4. Keep different training programs for different classifications. Don't cross train. And keep a paper trail showing how your training programs differ from one another.
5. Separate the physical plants in which employees in different classifications work. If you can't, set up separate entrances and exits.
6. Control access to dangerous operations — fanatically. Many manufacturing firms go so far as to segregate the workshop floor, putting more dangerous machines in separate rooms and re-

Support your own position

stricting access with keys or coded ID badges.

7. Get to know your state's classification and appeals processes. Most states try to make these processes user-friendly, notwithstanding the cumbersome nature of bureaucracy. Some refund premiums if the workers' comp agency forces higher-risk classifications on an employer who can make the case for lower ratings. If you lose at this level, you may want to take your case to the state courts.

A particular caveat: Employers studying the classification lists should always beware of NOC ("no other class") ratings. Avoid these if at all possible. They almost always cost more than existing classes, sometimes double or triple as much.

Long-Term Impacts

As you manage classifications to minimize premiums and risk levels, don't lose sight of the fact that these ratings have long-term implications for your business and your workers.

For starters, the courts often use work classifications to determine complicated workers' comp settlements, with consequences that may not please you.

Let's look at two examples of how this can come into play.

In 1969, a state circuit court ordered the Kentucky Workmen's Compensation Board to pay construction worker Herman Stacy permanent total disability even though Stacy had suffered an injury that caused only partial disability. The board appealed but lost — and in the process set a precedent for the importance of work classification.

Stacy suffered his injury in a fall from a scaffold. Uncontradicted testimony showed that he worked heavy construction projects requiring lifting, stooping, and bending.

A physician testified on behalf of the workers' comp board that Stacy suffered from only a 15 percent permanent partial functional impairment.

But Stacy testified that he could no longer do the extensive manual labor required of a heavy construction worker. And he had plenty of support. Fellow workers corroborated what Stacy said. A doctor testified that Stacy couldn't return to doing heavy work "at least for a prolonged period of time, and very likely . . . permanent(ly)." Another doctor said Stacy would always have to wear a back brace and do no heavy lifting, stooping or bending.

Yet a third doctor testified bluntly that, when it came to doing heavy manual labor, Stacy was "totally disabled."

So there was no doubt about Stacy's injuries; they were real and lasting.

The workers' comp board didn't deny this. Instead it argued that, since Stacy remained fully mobile and otherwise healthy, his disability counted for only 15 percent of his previous wages.

How 'partial' becomes 'total'

A Different Classification

The court of appeals held that because the injuries to his back and knee rendered Stacy unable to do hard manual labor, the board's award for only 15 percent permanent partial occupational disability was in error — this, even though Stacy had suffered only partial functional impairment.

The court went on to distinguish between impairment of bodily function from the purely physical standpoint and "occupational disability" — the impairment of bodily function as it relates to an occupation.

Stacy's injuries left him unable to do hard manual labor. His occupational classification had been "heavy laborer — skilled," and he could no longer fulfill the requirements of that job. This, the court said, entitled him to an award for total permanent disability, even though he might do other kinds of work.

The court added that, had Stacy's occupational classification been different — say, skilled construction without heavy labor — the board might justifiably have given him an award for less than total disability. The court directed the board to review Stacy's ocupational classification, but it loaded the process by ruling that it had been improper, given the facts of the case, to translate a 15 percent permanent partial functional impairment into an award of 15 percent permanent partial occupational disability.

The point? The Kentucky court read a risk/reward relationship into its decision to award full disability benefits to Herman Stacy. He did dangerous work. Therefore he earned more and fell into a higher classification. Hence a higher award.

An Incentive to Be Strict

When push comes to shove, this risk/reward relationship lies at the center of all classifications. As you think through Stacy's case you see a great incentive to classify employees as strictly as possible. (Your insurer ought to see the same incentive but may need your help in doing so.) Classifying your employees aggressively doesn't just save front-end premium dollars. It also limits your exposures. In Stacy's case, the court ruled that he deserved full disability because his classification had explicitly identified his duties as heavy manual labor. Had Stacy's employer pushed for a less specific classification, Stacy might not have won full benefits.

You fall into a trap if you attack the classification system on constitutional grounds, as we see in the case of Ohio-based nursing home operator Quality Health Service, Inc. In 1980 Quality Health filed a class-action suit attacking the Ohio Industrial Commission on the grounds that it set basic rates unfairly.

Quality Health noted that the commission charged lower rates for operators of for-profit nursing homes than for operators of nonprofit homes. It went on to argue that, since most nonprofit nursing homes were church-affiliated, the difference in classification amounted to religious persecution.

The company tried to make another constitutional argument: that the different classifications for for-profit and nonprofit nursing homes violated the equal protection and due process clauses of the U.S. and Ohio constitutions.

Other employers succumb to the allure of this argument. They seldom succeed, and Quality Health didn't, either.

The equal protection trap

No Violation

The Ohio trial court found no violation of the company's constitutional rights and no evidence that the Industrial Commission had acted in violation of its statutory duties. The commission had no grounds for treating for-profit and nonprofit nursing homes differently, the court said. Indeed, in 1979, the workers' comp board had considered merging the two classifications.

In addition, no data existed justifying higher premiums for for-profit nursing homes. If anything, the reverse was true. The evidence showed that the Ohio Industrial Commission had requested an actuarial survey to determine whether there was a significant statistical risk difference. The study showed that for-profit nursing homes posed a statistically smaller threat to workers than did nonprofit homes.

At the trial, the state bureau had one of its actuaries, a fellow of the Casualty Actuarial Society and a member of the American Academy of Actuaries, testify that malpractice insurers commonly discriminated between for-profit and nonprofit hospitals and nursing homes.

A former director of the underwriting section of the Ohio Bureau further fanned the fires by testifying that, had it fallen to her, she would determine classification on the basis of whether or not a particular nursing home associated with a church. (She did not, as it happened, have authority to determine classification.)

Unambiguous Ruling

Quality Health hung tough. It appealed — only to lose again. The Ohio Appeals Court unambiguously ruled that regulators hadn't violated equal protection laws because the classification rested on a difference that bore a reasonable relationship to the facts.

The facts govern the outcome

The Quality Health case tells a cautionary tale. Too many employers resort to the constitutional argument because they don't want to do the homework that really solves their problem. Instead they sue, arguing that the classification system is so fundamentally unfair that it violates the ambiguously-worded Fourteenth Amendment.

And they lose. Unhappy employers do much better to steer clear of constitutional arguments. What works on "L.A. Law" doesn't work in real life. Time and again, the courts hold the employer responsible for his or her own workers' comp fate. Employers who seek solace in constitutional hand wringing don't stand much of a chance.

The solution to managing classifications lies in working with — or on — your state's regulations, as the following cases show. All involve employers who creatively managed classifications to their advantage. In each case, state regulators audited or otherwise confronted the employer — not a process you want to endure — and all ended up in court. The results stand as a good guide for how much aggressiveness is too much.

The Mr. Lustre Car Care Center Case

In late 1989, Mr. Lustre Car Care Center came before the Oregon Court of Appeals to make its case for splitting jobs into different classifications.

Mr. Lustre's facility consisted of an enclosed tunnel for car washing and an office area, separated from the tunnel by a concrete block wall and windows. A customer waiting area, which displayed auto accessories, adjoined the office area.

Customers came to a window in the wall of the office area with "menus" describing the car wash services they wanted. Office workers tallied the charges and sold the accessories, accepting payment and making change. They did bookkeeping, record keeping, correspondence and general office work. They did not work in any other area of the facility.

Management tried to classify the office employees under the standard exception for clerical office employees. But the standard exception defines clerical office employees as:

All employees engaged exclusively in bookkeeping, in record keeping, in correspondence, or in other office work where books or other records are kept or correspondence is conducted.

This classification applies only to employees who work in areas physically separated from other operations by structural partitions and in which work of clerical employees as defined in this rule is performed exclusively.

If such an employee has any other duty, the total payroll of that employee shall be assigned to the highest rated classification of operations to which the employee is exposed.

An integral part of work

Regulators had ruled that, beyond their clerical functions, the employees of Mr. Lustre carried out diverse cashiering functions as an integral part of their work. These cashiering functions made the bookkeeper/cashiers something other than clerical office employees, the regulators ruled. They pointed out that the NCCI's Basic Manual allowed such employees to receive the standard exception only if they worked exclusively as clerical office employees.

Mr. Lustre countered that the Scopes Manual said that "other clerical employees or operations assigned by analogy to [the standard exception] are bank tellers . . . horse and dog race track parimutuel clerks and cashiers; bus terminal ticket sellers; airline or helicopter ticket sellers . . . away from airport or heliport locations."

Since these responsibilities included cashiering, Mr. Lustre argued, the cashiering duties of its employees should not exclude them from the standard exception.

'By Analogy'

The court of appeals sided with the regulators. The court ruled that the "by-analogy" language of the Scopes Manual covered employees for whom no other class applied. In contrast, it ruled, Mr. Lustre's employees did fall within a governing class — namely, Automobile Service Station and Drivers, the relatively expensive NCCI Code 8837.

When no other class applies

Furthermore, the standard exception applies only if the employee performs the described duties exclusively, the court said. If the employee has "any other duty," the rule classifies the worker with the employer's governing class.

Mr. Lustre also tried the old equal protection argument. The court, as have so many others, rejected it out of hand. It said, tersely: "A finding in petitioner's favor on that claim would not be supported by substantial evidence."

When to Investigate the Options

Two lessons stand out here. First, Mr. Lustre relied too much on the plainly defined standard exception. Too often, employers don't investigate their classification options when they start out — that is, when they first file their workers' comp papers. Then, when the state or the insurer lands their workers in an expensive classification, the employers run to the only option they know — the standard exception.

Second, had Mr. Lustre created a paper trail separating the clerical employees from car wash employees early on, it might have made the case for a different classification for the office workers.

The paper trail is essential. You must set up a company structure that treats different operations as discrete units if you want separate classifications to stand up to legal scrutiny. Overwhelmingly, regulators and the courts presume that employers should be treated as single entities. You pay dearly if you defy this presumption without preparing the way.

Just ask Ohio-based Viox Builders. This company put together a much more substantive case than Mr. Lustre, but still fumbled it away.

Viox Builders, a general construction firm, sued the Ohio Industrial Commission on the grounds that the commission improperly denied the company's request for manual classifications. The company chose an aggressive legal strategy — an action for declaratory judgment, which demands quick decision from an appeals court.

The trial record showed that Viox's divisions competed with outsiders for work on projects undertaken by Viox. For example, the company's plumbing division might bid against outside plumbers to obtain the plumbing work on a project for which Viox served as general contractor.

At the same time, the company's skilled employees worked on other projects as well. For example, an electrician from the electrical division might work on an outside project unrelated to any of the company's ongoing contracts.

Given its unusual operations, Viox sought ten separate manual classifications for its workers: cabinet shop, testing facilities, landscaping, and plumbing, electrical and general contracting, among others.

Fumbling your case away

A Near Miss

Viox almost made its case. The company had the corporate structure to support its contention that its units operated separately. The NCCI manual includes discrete entries for the classifications Viox wanted. The company even had some paper trails.

But it failed to prove conclusively that its divisions operated independently. It allowed the Ohio Industrial Commission to establish the presumption that one employer meant one classification.

The Ohio Appeals Court ruled:

> *The Industrial Commission did not abuse its discretion by denying [Viox] additional manual classifications and granting only single manual classification under general construction . . . each division under general contractor classification was exposed to similar hazard and segregation of bookkeeping between divisions was incomplete . . . separate classification is inappropriate where a labor segregation is incomplete, thus allowing employees of one division to work for other divisions, as [Viox] admitted occurs. . .*
>
> *In essence, to warrant additional manual classifications, each division would have to maintain its own separate employees. Alternatively, in*

One class for each employer

the absence of complete segregation, plaintiff at a minimum would be required to maintain bookkeeping that reflects which labor expended within a division was applicable to the manual classification assigned. As [a senior state workers' comp regulator] explained, a single manual classification is assigned "because of the problem of segregating labor in a manner which is acceptable to the bureau, and also the problem of segregating claims into these different manual numbers in order to arrive at a rating—merit rating or penalty rating for the employer."

. . . [Viox]'s bookkeeping, to the minimal extent evidenced in the record, does not indicate a verifiable segregation of labor expended within the various divisions. . . .

The words in this ruling tell the story: "incomplete," "at a minimum" and "to the minimal extent evidenced." Viox had the right idea. It did the right things. It just didn't do them completely enough to satisfy the court.

The main hurdle to making first-dollar premium savings remains that regulators classify by industry, not by the work done by individual workers. And the law does not require that they give you a break if your workers do different things presenting different hazards. You have to prove your case.

Of course, many employers assume that they can make aggressive claims as to the nature of their business and get away with it. Sometimes they do; the workers' comp bureaucracies in most states seem so inaccessible and ponderous as to appear ineffectual. But don't count on it.

In a pointed 1992 management column, the *Minneapolis Star Tribune* told the story of a Minnesota furniture retailer classified by the state's workers' comp bureau as a furniture manufacturer. This translated into a premium of more than $8 per $100 of payroll instead of the more appropriate $4.36.

The reason for the disparity, the retailer was told, was that he fell into a classification that included both retailing and delivery of furniture.

He argued that his store functioned solely as a showroom. His workers took orders there, but the furniture came from a North Carolina manufacturer and the delivery went directly to the customer. Outside agents — not store employees — moved furniture in and out of the Minneapolis store.

Different Job, Different Rate

The retailer pursued the issue, arguing that a company that didn't deliver furniture should not have to pay the same rate as one that did.

He wound up on the phone with a representative of the Minnesota Workers' Compensation Insurers Association, the industry data-collection agency that establishes workers' comp classifications and advises insurance companies on rates. According to the newspaper, the conversation went something like this:

> *Bureaucrat: I'm sorry, sir, but the category for furniture is listed under the rate of furniture/delivery.*
>
> *Retailer: But I don't deliver furniture!*
>
> *Bureaucrat: I'm sorry, but that is the category that the underwriters have assigned to you, and we can't change just because you don't have the incidental delivery category.*
>
> *Retailer: But it's not incidental. That's what's driving up the rate.*
>
> *Bureaucrat: Our underwriters work hard to come up with these categories, and we can't change them.*

The bureaucrat didn't tell the retailer that there might be as many as eighteen or twenty other retail sales classifications into which he might fall. The bureaucrat also failed to mention that the retailer could request a survey to determine whether he had been properly assigned and that, if all else failed, Minnesota — like most states — has an appeal process that the retailer could pursue if his questions persisted.

As this employer discovered, it's tough to face the glacial whims of the workers' comp bureaucracy.

Glacial whims

And bureaucrats forget that the system should serve employers. And, yes, it helps to have the blood pressure of an 18-year-old when you pick one of these fights.

But sometimes you win — if you make a strong case and fight hard. In the last case study of this chapter, the bureaucracy of the Ohio Industrial Commission takes it on the chin.

A Strong Case

Minutemen, Inc., was an Ohio-based temporary help agency (THA) that supplied workers to various companies for specific assignments. As we know, the basic rate applies to all employers within a given classification so as to spread losses among all in the group. But under Ohio law, the basic rates for THAs reflected the actual labor of the worker — that is, the manual number of the occupation practiced by the employee while on assignment. Thus, for a machinist assigned to XYZ Corp., a THA would pay $2.90 per $100 of payroll, as determined by the corresponding manual classification. XYZ Corp., of course, paid the same rate for permanent employees doing the same job.

In 1985 the Ohio Industrial Commission changed the rules for THAs. It refused to let them use the same manual classification numbers — 226 in all — as the employers to which the THAs assigned temporary workers. Instead, the commission came up with nine classifications applicable only to THAs. These super-classifications purported to reflect the character of the business to which a THA assigned a given worker: manufacturing, construction, transportation, etc. But it was pretty loose.

Employers of permanent employees, meanwhile, continued to pay premiums reflecting the 226 classifications.

If you smell a plot here, you're not alone. Ohio's THAs did, too. They figured out that the new rules crammed 117 occupational classifications into just one of the new super-classifications, "manufacturing," with a basic premium rate of $7.62 per $100. This meant significantly higher premiums in 102 of the 117 categories. Under the old system, for example, a THA paid $2.90 per $100 for a machinist. Under the new, it paid $7.62 for the same employee.

Adding insult to injury, the $2.90 rate still applied to XYZ Corp.'s permanent employees — so that vastly different rates applied to people doing identical labor on the same shop floor.

Differing rates for the same labor

The new rules sought to discourage companies such as XYZ Corp. from using significant numbers of temporary employees — that is, from using THAs to provide permanent staffs. The rules' real effect was to make it highly unlikely that XYZ Corp. would do business with a THA at all.

Minuteman Inc. argued that the new classifications 1) didn't reflect the hazard and 2) violated equal protection laws. It sought to compel the Ohio Industrial Commission to reclassify occupations or industries by degree of hazard and to reimburse all overpaid premiums.

The Ohio Supreme Court considered two questions pertinent to the appeal:

1. Did the super-classifications reflect the real hazard?
2. Did they violate equal protection law?

Ohio law requires that the Industrial Commission "classify all occupations according to their degree of hazard," the court said; hence the 226 classifications.

The Actual Hazards

But as Minuteman Inc. argued, the nine new super-classifications didn't reflect the hazards actually faced by the workers, the court said. It pointedly noted that the commission continued to apply 226 classifications to other employers.

The Industrial Commission didn't put up much of a fight. It argued weakly that the "new classifications . . . are easier for THAs to understand and the Bureau of Workers' Compensation to administer." Even more weakly, the commission suggested that temporary help was "historically less skilled and/or trained than . . . permanent employ[ees]."

The court wasted no time jumping down the commission's throat.

It forcefully ruled that the commission could not break the law for its own convenience and fob the misdeed off as a benefit to THAs.

The law mandated that the commission classify occupations according to hazard, the court said. So get to it.

As for the skills of temporary vs. permanent workers, the court answered that "besides being unsupported by any evidence of record, the point, even if true, is irrelevant."

Minuteman Inc. returned to the cheaper classifications. Employee leasing remained a viable alternative for small and unestablished employers.

And Minuteman Inc. made a case that employers like Viox should note: Somebody put the matter of Ohio's super-classifications on the desk of someone who didn't think the matter all the way through.

Lesser Beings

This happens all too often. And it's a big mistake. Don't give your workers' comp problem to some lesser being — a bureaucrat, an insurance broker, an attorney, a manager — to solve. No one understands it as well as you do. Aggressive classification can save you potfuls of dollars in insurance premiums each year. But you must do your homework, and you must defend your aggressiveness aggressively.

Chapter 5: Cost Containment

Taking action after an injury occurs

In this chapter we take up something that bewilders all too many employers — cost containment. It ought not to. It's not as confusing as it appears, and like everything else in workers' comp, it yields to one who determines to master it. And in yielding it gives up great benefits in the form of dollars on the bottom line.

Cost containment seeks to control the *medical* costs attendant upon an injury — the flow of dollars to physicians, chiropractors, physical therapists, and the array of health professionals and quacks who stand so ready to help the injured employee, whether the employee really needs it or not. More generally, cost containment is the art of limiting your exposure to workers' comp losses *after* an injury occurs, often by means resorted to *before* the injury occurs.

We'll show you what we mean here throughout this chapter. First let's establish one very important fact. In the world of workers' comp, medical care costs too much. But it lies wholly within your power to control these costs. You just have to know where to look for them and what to do when you find them.

Strong Evidence

The health professionals who wax fat on workers' comp protest loudly when you accuse them of milking the system, but the evidence against them is pretty strong. In 1990 the state of Minnesota looked into the matter and concluded that, on average, doctors and hospitals charged almost *twice as much for workers' comp cases* as they did for injuries covered by Blue Cross.

Now, you can explain away this discrepancy, in part, on the grounds that state law in Minnesota, like state law elsewhere, mandates a lot of treatment in workers' comp cases. Hence higher fees.

Twice as much is too much

And you can argue that the ever-present threat of litigation makes health care professionals prone to caution in workers' comp cases. They gather more information and form their judgments more slowly for fear of second-guessing themselves under the stern gaze of some lawyer holding forth before a jury in court. The Minnesota study found a great deal of fear of this kind among health care professionals treating workers' comp injuries.

But twice as much is too much no matter how you look at it. The study found that health professionals charged the same fees where treatment was standardized (as with a broken bone) but greatly differing fees where it was not. They charged more, in other words, where they had discretion as to treatment.

And given some discretion, they probably did more work for workers' comp patients because they knew that more money was available to pay for their services, whatever their worries about the tassle-loafered ones with the stern gazes.

The study reviewed more than 75,000 medical workers' comp claims and some 8,000 claims from the files of Blue Cross. It found that for back injuries, health professionals charged 2.3 times as much for workers' comp cases as for regular Blue Cross customers. For strains and sprains, they charged 1.95 times as much. For cuts, they charged 1.55 times as much.

No serious student of workers' comp doubts that health care professionals do the same in other states. A separate study established that Minnesota's medical costs for workers' comp cases roughly compare to those in nineteen other states. Reason urges the conclusion that the disparities between workers' comp and other cases in Minnesota exist in these other states, too, and probably in every state in the Union.

The Broader Context

Now let's put all this in a broader context. The relation between health care professional and patient is really that of seller and buyer in any marketplace. The health care professional sells a service, treatment, in exchange for the buyer's money. Only in this case the buyer's money has come to appear to be someone else's: the employer's or maybe the insurer's, the buyer isn't sure just which. In a normal marketplace the seller expects to meet with resistance on the part of the buyer — a reluctance to part with money — as the seller's price becomes dear. But in the workers' comp marketplace the buyer doesn't part with his or her own money, so the seller never encounters this resistance. *The money belongs to someone else.*

The seller makes the price ever dearer and, meeting with no resistance, gives a loud hurrah. This brings more sellers to this particular corner of the marketplace, all finding that money flows in their direction unchecked.

What distorts the market

What distorts this marketplace? Government, of course. Government and the insurer. Government distorts *any* marketplace in which it appears. It distorts this one by making treatment mandatory and leaving nothing to the discretion of the putative buyer, the injured worker. The insurer distorts it because *it isn't a buyer* and has no inherent interest in resisting the blandishments of the seller. Insurers don't part with their own money. It's the employer's money. And insurers know that there's more where it came from.

The Intervener

Where do you come in? You intervene in the marketplace as the buyer. You step in on behalf of the injured employee and supply the missing element, resistance. You keep an eye on the seller's price, weigh it against the seller's service, and stiffen your back when the price gets out of whack. You say no.

And you do it right away.

More specifically, you:

1. Choose the health care professional first consulted by your injured worker;
2. Negotiate fees;
3. Monitor treatment; and
4. Get your injured employee back on the job as soon as possible.

Saying no at each step

Note how you say no at each step. In choosing the physician you look for someone who knows how to treat workers' comp cases and agrees up front that the object of the game is to get the worker back on the job, not to get rich. You make it clear that you want expertise and a commitment to this goal. You say no to anybody who doesn't sign on to your agenda.[1]

In negotiating fees you weigh service against cost and say no when they don't balance out. You give notice to the health professional that you intend to ride in front on this particular horse, reins firmly in hand — your hand.

In monitoring treatment you ensure that your injured employee gets good treatment and that you put a stop to things when the regimen becomes unnecessary or promises no significant improvement in the employee's condition. You put yourself in position, in other words, to say no when your health care professional wants to provide treatment out of caution, not care. (See Appendix Four.)

In getting your employee back to work you ensure that the injured worker understands the target. You say no to the worker who would abuse the system. You teach all of your workers that you do not countenance cheating.

Rational Market Discipline

By doing these things you accomplish what neither of the other parties — the health care professional and the injured employee — can. You position yourself to say no every time one of the parties seizes the opportunity to go too far. You supply rational market discipline in a transaction which otherwise proceeds without it.

All of this presupposes that you leave none of these matters to someone who has no stake in the outcome. You do the footwork and undertake the negotiations yourself.

Start out as you do when seeking a relationship with any professional provider of services. Poll your

---

[1]In Colorado, workers' comp officials found that medical costs and lost-wage costs dropped 29 percent when the injured employee saw a physician chosen by the employer.

peers for referrals; ditto any professional or trade organizations to which you belong. Check with medical authorities to find the specialists in your area. Interview the promising candidates. Get the details as to background and experience. Inquire into your candidates' cost-saving techniques of treatment and management with respect to workers' comp cases.

Avoid the workers' comp mills

Most important, check out the track record. Talk with other employers who use the services of your promising candidates and find out whether they have in fact saved money on treatment costs and, later, on insurance premiums. Check with workers' comp authorities and your insurer as to the record and reputation of the provider.

Above all, stay away from the "specialists" who work hand-in-hand with your local trial attorneys. You can identify them by checking the ads in any trade or professional publication, state or local, directed at trial lawyers. These "specialists" run workers' comp mills in every big city in the country, and they don't walk on your side of the street.

Look especially at HMO and PPO organizations. Aggressive health insurers find these groups a good alternative to the traditional private-practice health professional. Some HMOs and PPOs set up specialty operations concentrating on workers' comp cases, and these show great promise for providing high quality, cost-effective medical care.

Big Dividends

Don't stint on your time here. It will pay big dividends. The Minnesota study mentioned earlier reported that, although employers sought to cut their insurance premiums, they made little attempt to contain medical costs because they found the whole matter so confusing. Instead they focused on cutting wage-replacement benefits for injured workers.

Don't fall into this trap. You have to get too many unreliable people to go along—your legislature plus your governor — if you want to cut wage-replacement benefits. State law regulates these benefits,

Don't count on the pols

and, unaided, you exercise virtually no control over the forces that impinge here. In any case, as Chapter 13 of this book shows, it isn't easy to get politicians to do anything at all about workers' comp, not to mention getting them to do the right thing at the right time.

So don't count on them. It lies within your power to do a great deal about workers' comp, starting with the costs of medical treatment for injured workers, and you reap big benefits by seizing control.

Indeed, in recent years medical care costs have mushroomed more rapidly than any other element in the workers' comp stew. In one year — 1987 — these costs rose more than 11 percent. Medical costs made up 30 percent of workers' comp costs in 1980. Now they exceed 40 percent nationwide and approach 50 percent in some states. In general, workers' comp medical costs more than doubled between 1980 and 1988. The average lost-time claim, meanwhile, cost $6,000 in 1980 and more than $10,000 in 1990.

Similar Numbers

You would find similar numbers if you tracked down the records for your own business over the same period. You can bet, in addition, that costs will increase over the next decade. So if you make no more than a 10 percent dent in medical costs now and keep it up over a decade, you will see a big difference. The Minnesota study proposed that the state undertake some mild reforms — freezing the fees for standard treatments for one year, containing them in later years, and establishing a review system to ride herd on insurers — from which the study expected to squeeze savings of about $30,000 per year, or 10 percent of the $300 million spent annually on medical costs. Surely bigger savings would come from an aggressive cost-containment program of the sort argued for here.

In 1992, the consulting firm Lynch Ryan and Associates probed the importance of establishing a good relationship with a group of health care professionals. By an overwhelming majority — 77 percent — employers felt that good relations with the health care professionals helped in reducing workers' comp costs. None considered such relationships unhelpful or neutral.

Two more points before we move on: First, if you contract with an outside administrator to handle workers' comp claims, take a close look at the arrangement. Do you pay the administrator the same whether a claim settles rapidly or not?

A stake in keeping a lid on costs

If so, you need a new arrangement — and maybe a new administrator. Too many outside administrators think like insurance company employees; too many of them actually are. They add up your claims, tack on overhead and profit, and send you a bill. They have no stake in keeping costs under control.

If you do business with an outside administrator, make sure that the administrator signs on to your agenda. Give the administrator an incentive to keep uppermost in mind the importance of settling a claim rapidly and at the lowest possible cost relative to benefit — and of getting your worker back on the job soon. Hammer the administrator if you find cases dragging on toward 90 days. The longer an injured employee stays home, the less likely he or she will return. The employee who stays home a year rarely returns at all. Keep track of average claim times for your business, your industry, and your administrator. Start jumping up and down when the numbers get out of whack.

Discretion Over Fees

Second, find out whether your state mandates fees for health care professionals in workers' comp cases, or whether your insurer has discretion.

If the former, make sure that your insurer monitors the process closely. The state rating bureaus track claims using a special identifying number which shields the name of the employee. You can match numbers to your own records, however, to make sure that claims from other employers don't end up in your lap. Not uncommonly, employers find that the numbers don't match — with the result that the rating bureau tags them with claims actually filed by other employers.

Enlist your employees in the fight

If your insurer has discretion in setting fees, check the policy. Make sure that the fee schedule applies where you operate. You don't want to pay Los Angeles rates for medical services provided in Dubuque. Run a random check occasionally to make sure that your insurer pays the right amounts for the right treatment. It's one thing for an insurer to pay the correct fee for setting a broken leg. It's another to pay the fee for a broken leg when the employee suffered only cuts and bruises.

Equally important, let your employees know what these fees are. Do this as part of an ongoing program to educate your employees about workers' comp in the modern economy, and about the specific threat that it poses to your operations and their jobs. Don't be chary with your information, either. The more you share these matters with your employees, the easier it is to sign them up for the fight against abuse.

The Fruits of Victory

You gain enormous leverage over your workers' comp bill when you enlist your employees in the fight. The nation's safest utility controls workers' comp costs by emphasizing safety and bringing employees back to work as soon as possible. Consumers Power of Jackson, Michigan, practices management techniques that cut down on the number of accidents and reduce the costs of claims that do occur.

Consumers Power, which self-insures its workers' comp exposure, won National Safety Council awards five times in eight years for posting the fewest lost workdays among large U.S. gas and electric utilities.

Unlike many companies, Consumers Power gives responsibility for managing a claim to those who hold responsibility for preventing claims in the first place; it assigns management of workers' comp claims to the safety and health department, not the legal department.

It's a great idea. The arrangement brings a broad perspective to the work of the safety and workers' comp specialists, and fosters communication between the specialists and the injured worker on the mend.

Meanwhile joint employer-employee safety committees, introduced in 1983, reduce injuries by monitoring safety practices regularly.

An incentive for all managers

Senior managers review all workers' comp claims involving lost work time. This gives lower level managers a real incentive to avoid such claims in the first place. If they screw up, they must answer to their supervisors.

When injuries do occur, the company uses health care professionals familiar with its worksites and operations. Consumers Power encourages these providers to emphasize an injured employee's abilities, not his or her disabilities. All this seeks to bring an employee back to work as soon as possible. Michigan law helps by requiring employees to use employer-chosen health care professionals for the first ten days after an injury.

The company treats recuperating employees with respect and allows them to participate in decisions about their return to work. The company allows them to come back for as little as two hours a day. This bolsters their enthusiasm and makes it difficult for would-be malingerers to stay away.

The Key

The key to all of this: open communications among providers, employees and supervisors.

The regulatory environment supports programs like Consumers Power's. New state rules allow employers and insurers to implement cost containment measures such as utilization review.

Not all states give the employer such leeway in controlling medical costs. California and Florida notoriously give the injured employee complete freedom to choose a physician. Not surprisingly, the workers' comp problems in these two states rank among the worst in the nation. New York, on the other hand, requires that the employee choose an authorized physician in a timely manner. The employer may require that the worker get a second opinion to determine whether treatment should terminate or the employee should transfer to another doctor. The state sets health care professional fees by schedule, and it resolves disputes through a strictly structured arbitration system.

You can, in short, do much to control costs by controlling your employee's choice of physician. Bear in mind, however, that your first responsibility is to ensure that the employee gets quality health care. Containing costs comes second. Whatever you do to contain costs, make it an outgrowth of your search for quality care and not a mechanism for saving money at your employees' expense. One lawsuit over misdiagnosis or mistreatment can wipe out the short-term savings generated by manipulative and faulty health care.

Job Safety and Injury Prevention

The employer who prevents an injury from happening in the first place saves all of the hassles and headaches associated with the claim, not to mention spiralling premiums.

Two things come into play here, and they affect job safety more than anything else: employee safety committees and safety training.

All too often employers go through the motions in setting up safety committees and safety training programs. They start off by hanging some splashy slogans here and there, and they orchestrate some phony fanfare and do some speechifying. But that's it. They show no continuing commitment and instead turn matters over to second-line managers. Worse, they give these managers no stake in the success of the effort, no incentive to see to it that it bears fruit. The managers attend the meetings of the safety committees but soon make no effort to hide the fact that they would rather be elsewhere. The meetings drag on, and pretty soon everyone knows that what management really wants is that everyone pay lip service to safety, not that everyone contribute to it.

As for safety training, the programs lose touch with

the dangers workers really face as they go about their tasks. The training becomes rigid, focusing on things that have nothing to do with what happens on the shop floor.

Workers take up their rights

Employees see through this in a minute. And when an accident occurs, they take up their rights under workers' comp law as a weapon of revenge.

It you take safety seriously, on the other hand, you make it a pervasive part of the workplace environment, not something to think about only once in a while.

You start with the presumption that the workplace presents certain dangers, that you can identify them, and that your employees want to eliminate these dangers as much as you do.

You set up committees consisting of people who actually face the dangers, and their supervisors. You keep the committees small, so that the members of each can focus on what they do themselves, not on what other people do in unrelated jobs far away in the manufacturing process.

You put these committees under the guidance of supervisors and workers who show a genuine commitment to safety.

Setting Goals, Measuring Progress

You insist that the members of the committees pay attention to the realities of the day-to-day workplace. You make sure that they analyze what they do step by step — a difficult task, and easily slighted. You set them to thinking up solutions, to setting goals and measuring progress.

You check with your insurer for safety experts who understand the problems of businesses like yours. You pick the brains of these experts for safety measures that apply to your operations. You pick the brains of your peers who run similar operations.

Most of all, you see to it that everyone has a stake in the outcome. You give employee and supervisor an incentive for success. You listen carefully to the ideas that come out of the safety committee meetings. You implement the good ones right away. In

No job is static

short, you turn a problem, job safety, into an opportunity.

And you do the same with safety training. No job is static. Every job changes with time, just as every business changes with time. Your training program must change as the work changes. It must speak to the actual needs of your employees, and it benefits them to the extent that it changes as their needs change. It succeeds if it becomes an ongoing part of what everybody does, if everyone commits to it, and if they see and taste the fruit it bears.

The 1992 Lynch Ryan survey on workers' comp found that more than 90 percent of employers agreed on the importance of providing a safety orientation to new employees. When asked about training new employees specifically on what to do if injured, 58 percent thought it very important. A slightly smaller number, 52 percent, considered it helpful to provide regular, ongoing training for existing employees on what to do if injured.

And the overwhelming majority supported management tools like safety committees to disseminate information and encourage participation.

The Payoff

To the employee, the real benefit of an effective, ongoing, focused safety program is the sense of empowerment that it gives. The employee exercises influence; things change, things *get better* because of what the employee does.

It's impossible to overstate the good things that flow from this. Employees stop demanding their rights. They take on responsibilities. They look out for one another. They look out for the enterprise.

Will-Burt Co., a contract machine firm in Orrville, Ohio, has achieved spectacular results by involving employees in all aspects of what the company does.

In 1985, Will-Burt started a remedial education program that has given each of its 300 employees the equivalent of a 12th grade education. Through a companion program, the company offers instruction equivalent to two years of college. The programs allowed the company, in 1989, to replace traditional floor supervisors with elected team leaders.

The combination of education and empowerment creates a tremendous level of peer responsibility. People watch out for each other. They make sure that no one gets hurt.

The result: It rarely happens.

Keeping tabs on the injured employee

The company doesn't let anyone fall through the cracks of the workers' comp system if an injury does occur. It engages in aggressive contact and follow-up from the minute an employee suffers an injury. It checks in every day the worker remains in the hospital and every day he or she rests at home. It gives the injured employee no chance to assume that no one cares, no incentive to call the lawyers who fill daytime television with commercials boasting of their prowess in wringing the workers' comp system of rich settlements.

The Workplace Atmosphere

Central to this effort is the company's "work hardening" program to get injured or ill employees back to work as soon as possible. Working with its insurer, Will-Burt offers rehabilitating employees jobs to get their bodies attuned again to the workplace atmosphere. It really doesn't matter what the interim job is; sometimes the employee works as little as an hour a day in an area completely unrelated to his or her regular job. The important thing is to give the employee something gainful to do, something important to the success of the company — and something that gives the employee tangible evidence of his or her own recuperation.

Says CEO Harry Featherstone: "We don't ask the doctor what the employee can't do, but what he *can* do."

In addition, Will-Burt conducts a mental health program which brings in local psychologists to see employees on company property at reduced rates.

All this paid off handsomely. Injury claims plummeted after the company instituted these programs. Will-Burt slashed its workers' comp tab from $178,000 in 1985 to $7,200 in 1992. It shot for $3,000 in 1993.

Wage loss claims

You have less room for maneuvering as regards wage loss claims than you do with medical costs. As a rule the states dictate wage loss claims, and insofar as they involve only your employee and your insurer — and no third party, such as a physician, with whom you can negotiate fees — you can't do much about them.

Still, you do well to keep an eye on wage loss claims, specifically on medical costs associated with wage loss claims. These yield to the same cost containment techniques discussed earlier.

The employer who self-insures the workers' comp exposure gains an advantage here. The self-insured employer takes the faceless, nameless, deep-pocket insurance carrier out of the picture altogether, so that the employee bent on abuse must face up to the fact that he or she abuses the employer and everyone else at work: real people, in other words.

This deters a good many employees otherwise tempted to taste the fruits of the workers' comp system. As we discuss in Chapter 10, self-insurance yields a great many other benefits as well. But even if you can't self-insure, you gain some of the advantages by choosing a high deductible on your workers' comp policy instead. In effect a high deductible makes you self-insured to the limit of the deductible and opens up the possibilities for cost containment managerial techniques discussed in this chapter.

Four Triggers

Four disabilities trigger wage loss benefits: temporary partial disability, temporary total, permanent partial, and permanent total. As a rule state law dictates that the employee who suffers a temporary partial or temporary total disability receives a fixed sum, up to two-thirds of former wage, for the duration of the disability. The employee who suffers a permanent partial or permanent total disability receives either a lump sum or periodic payments.

Health care physicians play a part here insofar as they define the extent of the disability and predict its duration. Treatment continues at least until the employee reaches what insurers call the point of maximum medical improvement — the point at which doctors determine that the worker's condition probably won't change substantially. At this point, the parties usually agree on what, if any, long-term compensation the worker will receive.

A key element in cost control

Return-to-Work Programs

A good return-to-work program gives you plenty of room for maneuvering; indeed, few cost containment programs of any kind pay such big dividends.

For starters, you control your return-to-work program from beginning to end.

You also ensure good relations with the injured worker — a key element in any cost containment effort. Indeed, return-to-work programs presuppose good relations between employer and the injured employee. They also keep the injured employee focused on the real tasks at hand: getting better and getting back to work.

A good return-to-work program probes the abilities of the injured worker to determine whether the worker can return to his or her original job or needs to train for a new one. It also keeps the employee in psychological condition to work. This in turn keeps the worker's skills sharp and so prevents further injury.

Employers of all sizes make use of back-to-work programs offered by workers' comp insurers. Large enterprises employ trained rehabilitation experts who set out a regimen of rehabilitation, usually undertaken in facilities at the worksite, and measure the worker's progress toward recovery, or the lack thereof. This gives the employer control over both program and costs. It also gets the injured employee back to the worksite on a regular basis.

Some programs give injured workers the use of exercise equipment which subtly exposes the malingerer — a gym with basketball hoop and a discreet video camera, for example. You know you've spotted trouble if the worker complains of shooting leg pains and then, seeing no one around, picks up the ball, shoots a few baskets, and chases up and down the court. A worker can drop guard with exercise machines as well.

The proper care at the right time

Not that you must consider such efforts sneaky. Exercise and rehabilitation facilities exist partly for therapy and partly for purposes of measuring the injured worker's progress. Exercise helps the injured worker to recover strength and confidence, and under the supervision of a qualified rehabilitation specialist, the worker gains many benefits from a regimen tailored to the worker's injury and condition. It is important, of course, that you make sure that injured workers use exercise equipment only with supervision; you don't want a worker to push too hard too fast and suffer a relapse or, worse, yet another injury.

Qualified rehabilitation specialists formulate a regimen for recovery, assess the worker's progress, oversee retraining, and even accompany the worker on doctor's visits, making sure that the worker receives the proper care at the proper time. The specialist can also help the employer figure out what jobs the injured worker might fill upon returning to work.

Work-Hardening Programs

Many employers use work-hardening programs to expose the injured worker to the tasks he or she will encounter during a normal workday upon returning to the job. Once again, the benefits range from the confidence the worker gains in his or her own ability to the concrete knowledge the employer gains as to what the worker can do.

Few employers doubt the benefits they gain from a good return-to-work program. The 1992 Lynch Ryan survey found that 81 percent of employers saw the value of maintaining an active return-to-work strategy. Ninety five percent of the group maintained programs involving modified duty — a temporary work assignment performed by an injured worker.

Eighty one percent considered the strategy very helpful. Eighty percent viewed modified duty very helpful in reducing workers' comp claims, and the rest found it somewhat helpful. Thus, the group was unanimous in agreeing on the value of such programs.

Similar numbers lined up behind the importance of weekly contact. Seventy five percent considered it very helpful and the rest somewhat helpful.

A helpful strategy

Return-to-work programs show that the employer cares about the injured worker. They pay for themselves by helping the injured employee mend rapidly and maintain confidence in his or her ability to work. They keep communications open and build good will in times that can breed adversity. They keep work skills sharp and prevent further injury once the employee gets back on the job. And they save money by making it less likely that the employee will fall into the embrace of a workers' comp lawyer.

A Success Story

Indeed, a good return-to-work program saves *lots* of money. In the mid-1980s, Chesebrough-Pond's, Inc., the New York-based conglomerate, initiated a cost containment safety strategy that reduced workers' comp costs more than 90 percent in just three years.

In the three years immediately preceding the effort, the company's workers comp costs had risen from less than $3 million to more than $10 million — and threatened to hit $18.5 million the next year.

Chesebrough-Pond's had no choice but to bring these costs under control. Management saw that it might add substantially to annual profits if it kept its workers' comp bill within a reasonable limit. At the time profits ranged around $100 million annually, and management knew that in order to generate $10 million in profits, Chesebrough-Pond's would have to increase sales or, in the alternative, buy an ongoing company with annual sales of almost $200 million.

Management wisely decided to spend a few million dollars reducing workers' comp costs.

The plan attacked the problem from four angles: better personal protective equipment, new workplace rules and employee safety committees, better accident investigations, and a smattering of safety incentive programs.

A 10-point plan of attack

In less than three years, the company cut workers' comp costs to less than $5 million per year. To get to this point, Chesebrough-Pond's followed a 10-point strategic blueprint.

First, it hired a claims manager. Only a handful of corporations employ in-house claims managers. Too many hire an outside claims manager who pays claims and adds overhead. Chesebrough-Pond's claims manager saved the company his own salary almost ten times in his first year.

Status Reports

Second, it developed an in-house claims status report. Insurers use claims status reports all the time, but they mainly help the insurer's own underwriters judge the risk at renewal time. They don't help the employer manage specific claims.

Chesebrough-Pond's wrote its own software to translate the claims status reports issued by its insurers into a single report useful to management. The reports allowed the company to look at the entire history of a claim. The software made the reports user-friendly by avoiding insurance and medical jargon.

Third, it improved site conditions. Chesebrough-Pond's concentrated on quick-fix solutions to simple problems, rather than obsessing on the jargon and minutia of ergonomics. It installed simple footrests, tilted work stations, adjustable work platforms and minor tool adaptations. And it listened to its employees in deciding what to do.

Indeed, Chesebrough-Pond's took care to bring its employees along at every step, carefully explaining the improvements, detailing the role of the employee, and showing the benefits to both employee and company.

A Good Lawyer

Fourth, it hired a watchdog lawyer. Protests came from the company's insurers, broker, and even its own risk manager, but Chesebrough-Pond's hired the most aggressive and successful workers' comp attorney it could find to handle difficult cases. This attorney visited plants, studied the company's cost reduction program and interviewed line managers. The lawyer became an expert on the realities of the workplace at Chesebrough-Pond's — as much an expert as the company's workers themselves.

The value of in-house expertise

Fifth, the company improved diagnosis and treatment. It hired a corporate medical director even though most of its losses came from soft-tissue injuries resulting from repetitive task stress.

The company brought in a medical consultant to investigate the common histories of three types of repetitive stress injury. The investigation found that in every case, workers suffered permanent and total disability because of mistreatment *after* the injury occurred. Given proper treatment, these cases could have been resolved in a matter of weeks, the investigation found.

Together with the in-house medical director, the company used a certified occupational therapist, a chiropractic consultant and physical therapists to develop exercise and physical therapy programs for injured workers.

Sixth, the company provided alternative work. Recognizing that it is better for a rehabilitating employee to work a little than not at all, the company developed a return-to-work program. The program tailored responsibilities to the worker's physical restrictions so as to readjust disabled workers to the demands of their regular jobs gradually.

Employee Involvement

Seventh, the company made sure to involve employees at every step. It allowed workers to undergo treatment or therapy on company time. It developed an educational program called "It's Your Body." The program illustrated how stress plays a role in disabling injuries. The program compared workers' bodies to those of professional athletes and encouraged workers to do warm-up and warm-down exercises. It tailored exercises to specific jobs.

Eighth, the company made sure that management reacted immediately to employee complaints of work-related injuries or stress. This required that supervisors assist employees immediately, adjust the work environment and, if necessary, marshal medical assistance.

Ninth, the company improved its job placement procedures. Management realized that federal law limits what an employer does in hiring workers. Like other employers, Chesebrough-Pond's tried to make up for this handicap by concentrating on job placement, with scant improvement. Employees with histories of carpal tunnel syndrome found themselves in jobs demanding upper extremity force and repetitive movement — making a bad situation worse. Chesebrough-Pond's adapted NIOSH standards for testing employees for appropriate job placement.

Tenth, the company instituted better management controls. It set up monthly case reviews and key indicator reviews. It supplemented its ordinary accident investigation forms with a "Strain Supplement" for musculo-skeletal injuries. It kept track of workplace modifications at various plants and offered successful efforts to other divisions.

Not least, it tracked physicians with high failure rates and attorneys associated with failed settlements in the past, and it developed a safety manual under a committee made up of manufacturing division heads.

Benefits to the Bottom Line

In all, it was an extraordinarily successful program. It cut Chesebrough-Pond's workers' comp costs by 90 percent in barely three years, with benefits that flowed straight to the bottom line. And it ensured that the company would continue to profit from the effort simply because it involved nearly everyone from the worker on the production line to the supervisor to the manager to the senior executive in charge of the division. To be sure, the company spent money on this effort, but it saved far more.

You may not have the resources to set up an elaborate return-to-work program like that at Chesebrough-Pond's. But you can play a decisive role in the rehabilitation of every injured worker — with benefits to your own bottom line. The responsibility for what happens on your own production line falls on your shoulders, and whatever your resources, you have it in your power to solve your workers' comp problem. You create the atmosphere in the workplace. You have more to do with employee morale and workers' comp than anyone else.

Power to solve the problem

Involve your employees in your efforts to improve safety. Listen to what they say, treat them well and fairly when injury strikes them, and you go a long way to avoiding the devastation of workers' comp claims.

Another Success Story

In the mid 1980s, Minnesota-based 3M Corp. decided to give responsibility for workers' comp claims to its employee benefits department, rather than the risk management department. In fighting hard to save every dime, the company's risk managers had alienated workers and squandered millions of dollars. They processed claims inefficiently. They pressed for early settlement only to end up with disputed claims anyway. Even simple cases turned ugly and difficult.

In 1990, the company's workers' comp costs totalled $25 million.

The employee benefits department already handled group medical claims. Why not turn this expertise loose on workers' comp? Medical and workers' comp claims require similar services and documentation. And things go more smoothly with both types of claims when someone shows a reasonable concern for people's fears and pains.

Under the new setup, 3M's benefits department employs case managers with experience in workers' comp and rehabilitation. Each case manager holds responsibility for a specific geographic area, helping injured and ill employees find the most appropriate and cost-effective heath care in their area.

The company uses in-house attorneys with workers' comp experience to negotiate settlements with injured employees. The lawyers keep tabs on case law and new legislation, working with plant supervisors to make changes to plant or equipment to reflect these changes.

Concern for real pain and fear

3M fields case workers to keep in touch with each injured worker. These case workers stress returning to work; they work with injured employees to get them back on the job.

Another innovation: The employee benefits department has authority to decide when an employee should return to work, not the supervisor on the production line. This makes for some trouble among supervisors, but employees see the important distinction. They consider the employee benefits department an ally, and the people in the department work hard to maintain the relationship. It helps them to *manage* each claim.

The 3M team maintains regular contact with disabled employees, makes every effort to grasp the nature and the extent of each disability and the prognosis, and keeps tabs on the employee's capacities and limitations.

The company makes sure that the injured worker's health care provider understands the company's objective: to get the worker back to work early and safely. 3M encourages disabled workers to assume light duties in a return-to-work program.

The bottom line: 3M lowered its workers' comp costs by more than 20 percent by applying these measures.

The Payoff: Avoiding Claims

The techniques of cost control and cost containment seek to reduce your exposure to workers' comp claims.

Inherent in these techniques, as the case studies in this chapter show, is the idea that you can organize your operations so as to ensure that the workers' comp problem doesn't come up in the first place. You can run things so that workers' comp doesn't *become* a problem. You can ensure that your operations don't *invite* the problem.

In the best of all possible worlds your state government would establish guidelines for appropriate and reasonable levels of treatment, limit your employees' choice of doctors, limit fees and impose dispute resolution, and discipline greedy providers. But politicians aren't good at making the world better, much less at fashioning the best of all possible worlds. So don't wait for them to get on with it.

The solution within your grasp

The solution to your workers' comp problem lies within your grasp. You don't have to wait for someone else to do something. You can take control of this problem and devise a solution tailored to your own operations — a long-term solution with long-term benefits to your operations and to the people who work for you.

The ideas we present aren't quick fixes. They focus on the long range, and if they take more time and effort to set in place, they yield bigger long-term benefits. They may look incremental at first glance. But they can have a big impact on your workers' comp premium, sometimes bigger than the aggressive front end strategies we discussed in the preceding chapters.

Chapter 6: Fraud and Abuse

How the cards stack up

In the world of workers' comp, nothing angers the employer more than fraud and abuse. Together, they crystallize the system's ills. But of the two, abuse costs more — and causes far more trouble — than fraud.

The workers' comp system gives the employee the benefit of the doubt in matters of honesty and integrity. And when the employee violates the trust inherent in this formulation, the law stands by, hands tied — or folded. The insurance industry makes the appropriate noises about fraud and abuse, but when push comes to shove, it sticks the customer — you the employer — with the costs of fraud and abuse. You, in turn, stick your employees with these same costs, in the form of lower wages, or you pass them on to your customers, in the form of higher prices. Or you eat them.

So the cards stack up against you. As we argue throughout this book, however, you aren't without resources. You just have to marshal them yourself. You can't look to your insurer or your local prosecuting attorney, or for that matter your legislature, to help much.

The Distinction

We get to the specifics of what to do later in this chapter, but first let's distinguish between fraud and abuse.

People use the words interchangeably to describe workers' comp malfeasance. But they don't stand for the same thing. Fraud is a crime; abuse isn't. The individual who abuses the workers' comp system exploits its weaknesses and its bias in favor of the employee, whether truly injured or not. The individual who commits fraud subverts the system altogether.

The line between fraud and abuse

But the fuzziest of lines separates the two.

By and large the law says that fraud occurs when someone:

1) knowingly files a claim for an injury that didn't occur;
2) knowingly falsifies the details of a claim or exaggerates the scope of an injury; or
3) knowingly bills for services never rendered.

All those "knowinglys" make it instantly clear why it's so hard to enlist the help of the law in fighting workers' comp fraud. You can't sic a dog on a cat he can't see. Regulators pursue people who defraud the system — when they can make a case. Which is not often. They ignore abusers altogether. A growing number of states make workers' comp fraud a felony, and this deters some who would defraud the system. It means nothing to the many, many others who abuse the system.

Too Wide a Leeway

In workers' comp law, in other words, there's a vast difference between what a reasonable person considers thievery and what is — according to statute — punishable behavior. The law gives too wide a leeway to those who would abuse the system. Commonly they know their limits (they most certainly learn their limits when they fall into the embrace of a workers' comp lawyer) and they take care not to push beyond.

Given the hazy distinction between abuse and fraud, and given the bias of the law toward the employee, the real problem lies in proving that someone — an employee, physician or attorney — has knowingly pursued a false claim. More often than not, it costs more to pursue abusers, not to mention those who defraud the system, than it does to pay the claim. So insurers, as a rule, show no more inclination to pursue wrongdoers than do prosecuting attorneys.

Meanwhile, nationwide the costs of the workers' comp mess mount. In 1989, insurers lost money on workers' comp for the sixth year in a row. Specifically, for every $1 that they collected in premiums for workers' comp insurance, they spent $1.20 on benefits and expenses. In large part, medical costs fueled the losses. According to a 1992 report in the *New York Times*, the costs of caring for workers injured on the job rose 150 percent during the preceding decade. Worse, these costs inflated at a rate 50 percent faster than those for health care in general.

Costs outrun premiums

You can make the case that medical treatment soaks up so many dollars in workers' comp because state law mandates lots of it. Besides, the ordinary citizen may or may not seek treatment for a condition not related to the job — a back sprained pulling weeds in the garden, for example — depending on a number of factors: the individual's insurance deductible and his or her willingness to wait to see a physician who hasn't been on time for an appointment since long before medical school.

No Hesitation

But these factors don't apply in workers' comp, so the ordinary citizen, as ordinary worker, doesn't hesitate to seek treatment for a job-related injury. Besides, state law requires that the employer provide the employee with medical treatment for injuries suffered on the job, period.

This allows some health professionals to turn the system into a cash cow. It allows others to vindicate their propensity to practice medicine out of caution, not care, and subject people to treatments they don't need.

The aggressive few bilk insurers and employers so thoroughly that, in state after state, they hold the workers' comp system at their mercy.

Moreover, the bias of workers' comp tilts toward the worker anyway. Workers' comp pays first-dollar benefits — no deductible. This tempts the gardener to bring his or her strained back to work on Monday and report it, say, about mid morning. A 1992 study by the American Insurance Association estimated that cheating factors in 20 percent of workers' comp claims nationally — and many experts call this estimate conservative.

The middle class scammers

Such widespread deceit hurts more than the individual employer; it hurts the entire economy. Employers close up shop because they can't afford to buy workers' comp insurance. Or they stay open and do without it. Or they leave one state for another. Or they ship jobs overseas. In California, employers cited excessive workers' comp costs as their number one reason for leaving the state in 1991 and 1992.

The workers' comp crisis affects every employer's competitiveness in every marketplace. It affects the country's competitiveness in the global marketplace.

The Looter's Mentality

The evidence for estimating the extent of fraud and abuse is scant at best. In Oregon, the number of workers' comp claims dropped by about one-third after the state reformed its system, set up the state-run insurer SAIF Corp., and cracked down on fraud. Officials in other states estimate that fraud and abuse play a part in one out of every four workers' comp claims, overall.

Most workers' comp thieves come from the middle class. One study pegged the median income of scammers in the range of $40,000 a year.

This suggests that the thieves have decent jobs, enough to eat, a place to live.

What motivates them? Two factors, neither being poverty. First, they feel entitled. A decent job isn't good enough. Ditto honest pay for honest work. Second, they feel no sense of involvement. The scammer feels no connection to his or her faceless victims, making bad behavior easier to rationalize.

In any event, there's a lot of fraud and abuse. The real shame is that employers and regulators become numb to the outrage.

The system, which began as a protective structure for working people, gives haven to the conniving and the dishonest. People receive monthly checks from distant, monolithic insurers while they nurse injuries that never happened, didn't happen on the job, or healed long ago. Some collect more than one check. A direct marketer in Southern California tells the story of a job applicant who blithely admitted she was collecting permanent partial disability checks from the insurers of four former employers. The woman didn't get the job.

A little abuse wreaks havoc

Business columnist Peter Dexter calls this "a looter's mentality." Such people exploit a besieged system. But the tales of their misdeeds ought not to lose their shock value, and we present them in this book for their motive value: in the hope that they will drive you to take matters in hand and solve your own problem.

Worker Fraud

A little abuse can wreak a lot of havoc.

T.L. and Elizabeth Fahringer ran a small machine shop in Tampa, Florida, employing as many as several dozen workers, depending on the Fahringers' backlog of business.

Over four years leading up to 1990, however, the Fahringers almost lost their business to workers' comp. As Elizabeth Fahringer explains it, her company fell victim to three employees, encouraged by lawyers and doctors, who filed outrageous workers' comp claims.

None of the cases involved traumatic or even particularly well-defined injuries. Each focused on a hard-to-disprove cumulative injury of the sort that spells trouble to workers' comp insurers.

The shysters did their job well. In all three cases, the Fahringers' insurer elected not to fight. The Fahringers didn't like it, but they had no choice. They hired some unsavory types, some of whom made unsavory claims. It was a cost of doing business.

Then insult compounded injury. The last case involved an employee who claimed psychological damage and paralysis caused by an electrical shock. Elizabeth Fahringer thinks someone intentionally miswired a machine, but of course she can't prove it.

Forces beyond control

Once again her insurer rolled over and paid the claim. Then it raised the Fahringers' workers' comp premiums sharply, almost doubling them.

The Fahringers protested the hikes. The insurer temporized. A few months later, it dropped them altogether.

The Fahringers couldn't find another insurer in Florida's thin market for workers' comp coverage, so they had no choice but to join the state pool.

But the Fahringers' premiums still tripled. In a relatively narrow-margin business, this meant imminent insolvency.

Desperate, the Fahringers turned their workers over to an employee-leasing company as 1991 drew to an end. The change didn't come cheaply, but the leasing company managed to structure costs in a way that left the Fahringers something to live on.

Their business survived — but at the cost of abandoning the employer-employee relationship that had existed between the Fahringers and the people on their shop floor.

And now it exists at the mercy of forces wholly beyond its control — i.e., the state's willingness to tolerate employee leasing. Elizabeth Fahringer knows that sooner or later the state may crack down, maybe by making employee-leasing arrangements illegal altogether, maybe by making them just impractical.

The Case of Byron Gizoni

Lawyers saw their opportunity to loot the workers' comp system years ago, and as the economy went into recession in the late 1980s, the system became a trough at which altogether too many of them fed. Great piles of money — and more all the time — were at stake.

They have also twisted it to accomplish ends that only other lawyers can love, as the case of Byron Gizoni shows.

Byron Gizoni supervised workers in the loading and unloading of equipment on company barges for San Diego-based Southwest Marine Co. In April 1987, he fell through a hole in the deck of a barge and suffered disabling injuries to his back and leg.

Southwest Marine paid more than $15,000 for medical treatment and disability payments under the special federal workers' comp law covering longshoremen and harbor workers. Like many state laws, the Longshore and Harbor Workers' Compensation Act provides no-fault compensation and prohibits workers from suing for further damages.

Then San Diego lawyer Preston Easley hooked up with the injured longshoreman.

Suddenly, Gizoni was suing Southwest Marine in federal court for negligence under an arcane exemption.

Easley argued that Gizoni worked as a seaman aboard a vessel in navigable waters at the time of the injury and that he therefore stood covered by a different federal law. He cited the Jones Act, which allows seamen to sue employers for negligence — and recover damage awards in jury trials.

U.S. District Court Judge Gordon Thompson Jr. dismissed Gizoni's lawsuit, agreeing with Southwest Marine that Gizoni was not a seaman and that his job was not necessary to the navigation of the barge. Easley appealed to the activist U.S. Ninth Circuit Court of Appeals, which overturned Thompson's ruling and said it was up to a jury to decide whether Gizoni was a seaman or a longshoreman.

A trough at which many feed

'The Key to Status'

Southwest Marine appealed to the U.S. Supreme Court and lost. "The key to seaman status is employment-related connection to a vessel in navigation," the court said in a unanimous decision. "It is not necessary that a seaman aid in navigation or contribute to the transportation of the vessel, but a seaman must be doing the ship's work."

The case went back to U.S. District Court for a jury trial. Easley tried Gizoni's case on contingency, of course. Southwest Marine paid its lawyers by the hour. Gizoni won.

"This has opened a big door for shipyard workers, no question about it," Easley told a local newspaper.

A big door opens to abuse

Shippers warned that the case would doom an already ailing industry. They said insurance and litigation costs would double for U.S. shipyards, making it tough for them to compete with foreign builders. They were right.

Provider Fraud

Employers get emotional when they talk about fraud. They feel helpless in the face of a system that accommodates claimants no matter how outrageous their claims. But it's not just workers who defraud employers. The providers of health care can't resist the system's tendency to corrupt, either. Here malfeasance becomes a subtle thing, and difficult to prove.

SAIF Corp., the state-owned insurer that dominates the Oregon workers' comp marketplace, has sought to curtail fraudulent claims by prosecuting shifty doctors. But this hasn't improved things dramatically, as a high-profile case proved.

In June 1991, Oregon authorities indicted a McMinnville chiropractor and his wife on two counts of first-degree aggravated theft. The indictments alleged that the couple engaged in fraudulent billing practices with respect to their workers' comp patients. Oregon's workers' comp law made first-degree aggravated theft a Class B felony punishable by ten years' imprisonment.

The indictments named Edward Moore and his wife, Andrea. Edward Moore, a former president of the state's Chiropractic Physicians Association (OCPA), had operated a chiropractic clinic in McMinnville, in western Oregon, for more than twenty years.

The charges accused the Moores of overcharging SAIF Corp. by more than $40,000 during 1989 and 1990. The indictment alleged that the Moores charged higher rates for workers' comp cases, lower rates for others.

Moore's attorney saw a political motivation behind the case. Moore was a prominent man, and his attorney alleged that the prosecution constituted an effort to railroad Moore.

Papers filed with the court noted that authorities had seized Moore's patient records more than a year before, just after OCPA had concluded a high-profile but unsuccessful fight against a workers' comp bill that restricted the role of chiropractors.

Moore's attorney noted that the indictment came down just as the legislature began a new review of workers' comp. He argued that a serious criminal investigation would have proceeded to prosecution long before.

Prosecutors denied his allegations.

"Investigations involving billing take a long time to dissect," Jeff Maldonado, director of fraud investigators for SAIF, told a Portland newspaper. "We've been working on the investigation for more than twelve months."

Higher rates for workers' comp cases

The First Criminal Case

Moore wasn't the only chiropractor in SAIF's sights. In Oregon, as in the rest of the country, regulators hear more complaints about chiropractors than they do about any other kind of medical provider. Since February 1989, SAIF had targeted fourteen Oregon chiropractors with fourteen civil suits and five criminal charges related to dual billing. But the Moore case was the first to involve criminal charges under the state's 1989 workers' comp reform laws.

The trial began in mid-October, 1992, in Yamhill County. To the aggravated theft charges, the Moores responded that they had merely given their services at reduced rates to uninsured, largely needy patients.

Their attorney argued that, no matter what state workers' comp law said about rates, a doctor should always have the prerogative to give away services to poor people.

To their utter astonishment, state prosecutors saw this argument work. Seven days after the trial began, the jury returned two not guilty verdicts.

No one wants to find the bad guy

Said one: "Nobody ever wants to find a bad guy in these workers' comp cases. Everyone says they want reform. But the system is so big, it's tough to make the problems comprehensible (to the average citizen)."

The point: Don't stand around waiting for your local prosecutor to go after fraud. It's hard to make a case stick, and prosecutors want victories, not defeats.

Innovative Litigation

But the legal system isn't utterly impotent in the face of fraud and abuse. Reform-minded California insurer Zenith National sued Wellington Medical Corp., also based in California, in connection with a series of allegedly bogus stress claims. More specifically, the insurer made innovative use of the federal racketeering law, RICO, to press Wellington into a settlement that stands as a model for anyone else interested in 1) reform or, short of that, 2) taking matters into your own hands.

According to Zenith's suit, Wellington, a psychological treatment center, colluded with a ring of attorneys and claimants to foist exaggerated and sometimes wholly fabricated stress injury claims on Zenith and other insurers.

Wellington showed a decidedly checkered past.

Two years before Zenith made its charges, Wellington's CEO, Dr. Byron Crawford, had pleaded no contest to fraud charges and paid a $20,000 fine to the California workers' comp board. He'd hired unqualified staffers to write medical reports supporting workers' comp claims. A number of insurers, including Zenith, had relied on these reports to make settlements.

The next year, the workers' comp board sanctioned Crawford for doing the same thing.

In response to Zenith's racketeering charges, Wellington countersued, claiming that Zenith wanted to drive Wellington out of business because it served a patient base consisting primarily of minorities.

In late 1992, after heated negotiations, Zenith dropped the litigation in exchange for an undisclosed cash payment and Wellington's adoption of a number of administrative reforms designed to fight fraud.

Wellington agreed to:

1. Permit only licensed physicians and health care professionals to conduct medical evaluations;
2. Itemize the time spent by licensed professionals on each workers' comp claim;
3. Refrain from misleading advertising, especially regarding an employer's right to control medical care given to employees making workers' comp claims;
4. Inform patients of the penalties for workers' comp fraud;
5. Perform only one initial comprehensive medical exam per workers' comp claim;
6. Refrain from billing for treatment provided more than 30 days before an employer received notice of a particular workers' comp claim; and
7. Bill only the direct cost of a physician's services in regard to an initial medical exam.

A model victory

Zenith considered the settlement a victory, and it was. The settlement held Wellington to standards far stricter than those enforced by the state itself. In fact, the Wellington settlement stands as a blueprint for reformers everywhere. Such an agreement won't stop a claimant determined to defraud an insurer, but it does make cheating considerably more difficult.

Employer Fraud

Zenith wasn't the first insurer to make use of RICO in rooting out fraud.

In the summer of 1991, NCCI and the insurer Liberty Mutual made use of the federal racketeering act to launch an attack against a New England contractor. The lawsuit named a series of Rhode Island corporations, their officers and an insurance agency.

The suit alleged that the corporations were really a single construction company whose principals, faced with ballooning workers' comp premiums,

A series of shell entities

had formed one corporation after another to stay a step ahead of their insurers.

The case started with Atlantic PBS Inc., a construction firm specializing in port facilities and the first company in the alleged chain. Like many employers in high-risk occupations, Atlantic PBS had a poor claims record. The company couldn't get workers' comp coverage in the voluntary market and ended up in the Massachusetts pool.

Massachusetts had just begun administering its own pool in 1991. Like its counterparts in other states, the Massachusetts pool calculates the cost of a company's coverage on the basis of its claims history and its business classification.

New companies obviously show no claims history and so commonly pay less than established firms.

Back Premiums

Atlantic PBS, which operated in Southeastern Massachusetts and Rhode Island, not only had a poor claims record, according to the lawsuit. It had also failed to pay Liberty Mutual some $228,000 in workers' comp premiums over eighteen months.

But contractors bidding for business in Massachusetts must show proof of insurance. So, according to the lawsuit, two of the company's officials applied for workers' comp coverage under the name of a new company, INRI Construction Co.

The officials left only Atlantic PBS's clerical employees in the old company and transferred its construction workers to INRI. The result: a company with no claims record and, so, a better rate for workers' comp insurance. On various applications and pieces of paperwork, INRI listed its managers' home addresses as its business location.

Liberty Mutual had insured Atlantic and, unaware of the connection, wrote a new workers' comp policy for INRI. The insurance broker submitted a premium check to the insurer for $7,227 — initially noting Atlantic PBS's name in the memo space. At some point someone scratched this out and wrote in INRI instead.

Not that such minor sloppiness mattered. The check arrived late and the new company never arranged an audit for Liberty Mutual.

No claims meant low rates

The Insurer Catches Up

Eventually, Liberty Mutual's auditors determined that INRI had a higher payroll than it reported, that it had improperly classified workers, and that it employed construction workers who had worked for Atlantic.

The insurer cancelled the policy.

In mid-1990 the Massachusetts Department of Industrial Accidents issued a stop-work order against Atlantic and INRI. But according to the lawsuit, Atlantic/INRI officials just started a third company, Bee Gee Enterprises.

Bee Gee applied for insurance in Massachusetts, listing an Atlantic/INRI executive as principal. The company letterhead showed telephone numbers previously used by both INRI and Atlantic and the name of at least one other Atlantic/INRI executive.

This litigation — unusual in its use of the federal racketeering law — remained unresolved as this book went to press. RICO allows ordinary people to collect triple damages from wrongdoers who engage in racketeering — admittedly a loosely defined term in a loosely worded law. NCCI and Liberty Mutual intended to pursue the litigation to make an example of Atlantic/INRI/Bee Gee. If successful, the litigation may open an avenue for others.

Whatever the outcome of the suit, workers' comp officials in Massachusetts and elsewhere agree that corporate shell games contribute to the high workers' comp rates that dog honest employers. The NCCI sees fraud by employers as a widespread and growing problem throughout the country. "We're discovering it more and more," Terrence Delehanty, counsel to the NCCI, told a Boston newspaper. "It's a new field for us as far as fraud goes."

You prevent fraud and abuse by investing time and effort in two elements of your business over which you exercise control: hiring and safety.

Hiring and safety

When it comes to hiring practices, follow the adage that prevention is the best cure. This means hire the right people. Screen every applicant with the utmost care, even the worker who will push a broom— maybe especially the worker who will push a broom. Make sure that your applicant can do the work for which you hire him or her.

And be careful. You must comply with a roomful of state and federal laws, including the Americans with Disabilities Act and the EEOC's voluminous regulations thereon. You must comply with any labor contracts in force.

Vague Language

The ADA presents special difficulties because in this law Congress gave you language so vague that the courts may never clarify its murk. You can't screen for medical conditions or disabilities. You can't require pre-employment medical examinations or inquire into the existence or extent of any disability. You may ask such questions only after making an offer of employment. You may also undertake "task matching" — finding the most appropriate work for each employee. Take full advantage of this tactic. It's a good idea; it puts health-related inquiries into a nonthreatening context, and it involves the employee materially.

Before you take the plunge, however, get some good legal advice on this matter. Or explore it yourself if you feel up to plowing through the EEOC's voluminous regulations.

Above all, don't hesitate to spend time and money in finding and hiring the right people. In doing a good job here you engage in preventive management. You spend money now rather than throw it away later on when a cheater turns up on your payroll and hits you with a bogus claim or, even worse, litigation under ADA.

As you bring new people on board, make sure that they understand the importance of on-the-job safety. Set up ongoing safety programs and safety committees. Make sure the programs and committees pay attention to what your people really do in the course of the workday. Otherwise your workers will quickly see the irrelevance of the effort and turn away from it.

Stinting on Time

Make sure everyone participates, too. Don't stint on management's time and attention here; you want your people to know that you attach a great deal of importance to safety and that safe work practices involve everyone, from the broom pusher to the boss. Experience shows that an effective, management-backed safety program instills trust between employer and employee — and that the absence of this trust leads to nothing but trouble. As the chapter on cost containment establishes, trust and goodwill act as powerful weapons against egregious claims.

Show your workers that you consider on-the-job injuries a bother and you get lots of bother. Show them that you care for their safety, that your own well-being depends on theirs, and that you do more than pay lip service to the idea — and you get fewer injuries. Good employees commit to safety; they sign on. Bad-apple employees know they can't get away with funny stuff.

Make your employees sense the community of your interests. People want to involve themselves in all aspects of their work, not just the task itself. Capitalize on this. Seek input from your employees about how work progresses through your organization. Ask them how they would arrange things if they had their way. Reward them for good ideas — by instituting them.

The Environment You Create

This isn't just New-Age psychobabble. The environment that you create at work greatly affects what happens with respect to your workers' comp problem. Workers don't look for the opportunity to burn an employer who makes them feel they belong.

Make sure that your concern passes down to managers and supervisors. All must reflect the company's position — that legitimate claims get fair hand-

Spend money now, not later

Employees commit to safety

ling and illegitimate claims don't. Require that your workers report all injuries, major and minor, immediately. Insist that all details of an accident go straight to your insurer, including the names of any witnesses. And keep track of what happens at each step of every claim, from injury to settlement.

If you suspect fraud, start building your case early on. If necessary, hire an investigator who knows how to use a camera. You stand a good chance of fending off fraud if you can show an "injured" worker moonlighting for another employer — or even shooting baskets in the driveway.

Short of this, find out what services your insurer offers in reviewing claims for the signs of fraud; make use of them. Make use of your insurer's services in safety training, too. A good workers' comp insurer offers plenty of help in educating employers and employees alike on fraud, and in cracking down on the bad-apple worker who tries to cheat.

Above all, prepare yourself to fight the cheaters. The money in workers' comp attracts miscreants determined to defraud. The social agenda at the heart of workers' comp gives such people a number of tactical advantages. (See Appendix Seventeen.)

In everything you do, consider yourself the soulmate of the Korean business owners who armed themselves and stood guard on their shop roofs during the Los Angeles riots in 1992. They understood right away that the police couldn't protect them and probably wouldn't anyway. So they didn't wait; they did it on their own. Some actually fought off the looters with bullets — and we don't advise that you take workers' comp cheaters behind the barn and shoot them. The real deterrent was the shopowners' willingness to fight hard for what they had. Like these shopowners, you engage in a kind of civil war, and you win if you commit everything to it.

The Real Culprit

As passionately as you may feel about fraud and abuse, remember two important points:

Help from the insurer

First, in the scheme of workers' comp problems, fraud plays a smaller role than most people think. Abuse is the problem, not fraud — abuse and what you might call the institutional factor: the willingness of the system to countenance abuse, or its inability to do much about it.

Second, you limit your exposure to fraud and abuse by anticipating the problem.

Your best defense is a workplace that joins the interests of your employees with your own. And if you're the boss, the workplace is your creation. So don't blame the host of ills associated with workers' comp for problems that you can fix on your own. Above all, don't let your outrage at fraud and abuse stand as the be-all and end-all of your response; it's an illusory release. The real solutions demand steady effort and the often-mundane work of planning for the long haul. And they lie at hand.

Chapter 7: Stress and Soft-Tissue Claims

The fastest-growing complaints

If fraud and abuse don't spur you to do something about your workers' comp problem, the threat of facing a stress or soft-tissue claim surely must.

These claims ruin businesses, particularly stress claims. In the early 1980s, when stress-related claims first appeared, no one could have predicted the extent to which they would burden the workers' comp system. In fact, in some states they threaten to destroy the workers' comp system altogether.

In California alone, the number of stress claims rose from 1,282 in 1980 to an estimated 8,900 in 1991 — an increase of more than 700 percent in a little more than one decade. Meanwhile, on average each claim cost $13,200.

Among white collar workers, stress now plays a part in a majority of workers' comp cases nationwide. Among blue and white collar workers put together, stress figures in 11 percent of all workers' comp cases.

Increase in Claims

As for soft-tissue claims, repetitive trauma disorders figured in only 18 percent of the work-related injuries reported to the Occupational Safety and Health Administration in 1980. By 1990, they figured in 55 percent. Between 1986 and 1990 alone, the number of repetitive strain injuries rose from 45,000 to 185,000. Such injuries include carpal tunnel syndrome, tendon disorders, and lower back injuries.

Meanwhile musculoskeletal injuries eat up something between 33 and 40 cents of every workers' comp benefit dollar.

Not surprisingly, the increase in repetitive strain injuries corresponds with the spread of computers in

Work is stressful by nature

the American workplace. In 1981, the number of computer users stood at 6 million. In 1991, the number hit 50 million.

Things will probably worsen before they improve, and you don't have to look far for two good reasons: 1) the vague nature of stress and soft-tissue injuries, and 2) lawyers.

Work is stressful by its very nature — because work is creative. To be sure, some jobs are more stressful than others. But if your job doesn't subject you to stress, you aren't working.

It doesn't follow, however, that you can say just how much stress is normal for any given job. You can't set standards here and expect people to measure up to them. Stress is subjective, and some people handle it better than others, no matter what the job.

Soft-tissue injuries aren't subjective in exactly the same way, but like stress claims, they don't present the sort of hard evidence that doctors find with a disease such as cancer.

Little Proof Required

Enter lawyers. They have a field day with claims involving either stress or soft-tissue injuries because they don't have to prove much in such cases. To be sure, they *can't* prove much, but in state after state, the law makes it easy for them. At one point in California a disabled worker qualified for workers' comp benefits if he or she could demonstrate that stress contributed no more than 1 percent to the disability. The state later increased this threshold to 10 percent and then to 51 percent, but even that didn't make it hard to establish a case.

The burden of fighting such claims thus falls on employers, and they don't fare well. It's hard to prove a negative, and harder still to prove a negative in a case involving something so subjective as stress or a soft-tissue injury.

The better idea is to avoid such claims in the first place — specifically, by attacking the problem from four angles: employee hiring, work flow, supervision, and employee communications.

You save a lot of trouble by hiring the right people in the first place, and you get off on the right foot by paying careful attention to what happens in the job interview.

You hire people, not bodies

Whole libraries of books go into this subject, so we won't. For our purposes, let's proceed by keeping in mind the idea that in hiring you don't fill jobs and you don't find bodies. You hire people.

Remember that job interviews put the applicant under stress — and so give you a chance to observe unguarded, involuntary responses. It pays to sort through them in search of clues to the applicant's character.

The Interview

People send out all sorts of signals in a job interview, and if you pay attention and trust your own perceptions, you get a feel for character that will stand you in good stead. After all, it is character that distinguishes the fraud artist from someone whom you can turn into a committed employee, and the skillful interviewer of job applicants looks just as hard for the signs of character as for the individual's objective qualifications for the job in question.

For that matter, during the interview you send out signals of your own from which, nervous or not, your job applicant picks up an idea of your character.

You can use this, too, to your advantage, by keeping your job applicant ever so slightly off guard. See what happens, for example, when you ask your questions in somewhat testy fashion, perhaps demanding detailed answers to a number of tough questions in a brief time. In the alternative, appear wholly relaxed and let your applicant ramble on.

Either way, what you see in the interview may well be what you get on the job. Pay attention to body language, to tone of voice, to the hands and eyes. All of these tell stories you want to hear.

You must play by rules you don't set here, of course; the list of things you can't ask of a job applicant grows longer every day — too long to go into here. Keep your questions job-specific and away from

Be wary of the law's demands

matters that might violate the guidelines of the U.S. Equal Employment Opportunity Commission and any state bodies with similar regulations. Within these constraints, keep your eyes open.

Study the flow of work in your operations. Can you reduce stress by rearranging the flow, by reassigning duties or changing work rules? Look at the work itself. Can you refashion not just what your employees do, but how they do it, so as to relieve them of undue stress?

You can make a big difference by shifting tasks so as to render work less routine. You can make a bigger difference by doing for your employees exactly what you do for yourself in mastering your workers' comp problem.

How? People break down in routine jobs that make heavy demands wholly outside the worker's control. Businesses break down for the same reason — when they labor under demands wholly outside their control, and fail to cope.

You know all too well the demands the workers' comp system makes on your time and on the resources of your business. Nationwide, the system threatens to spin out of control, and makes countless employers feel vulnerable and at the mercy of the most whimsical of gods.

But it submits to one who determines to master it.

So does the problem of stress. And you solve the problem of stress just like you solve the workers' comp problem. You make up your mind to master it, you study it, and you find that what you *may* do, you *can* do — and that it makes all the difference. You gain control.

Supervision

Give your employees a say in how they get work done. Give *them* a sense of control.

But don't give them total control. Mankind is not perfectible. Employees need supervision, and they thrive under careful and consistent supervision. They get sick under inconsistent, unpredictable supervision — literally.

This goes for the supervision they get on the shop floor and the supervision they get during a performance evaluation. The coach who behaves in an illogical way does great damage. So does the disciplinarian.

Be aware that it's sometimes tough to see supervisory problems from the top. If you don't supervise your employees yourself, make sure to give them some means of expressing their feelings about management and about the workplace in general. In doing so you don't peddle psychobabble. You look for early warning signals from unhappy workers who might otherwise break down under stress and saddle you with big claims.

Communications

Above all, clue your employees in. People do a better job when they know what their employers expect of them, and why, and when they have specific standards for measuring their work.

On a broader scale, your employees need to know what's going on in the company — its prospects and plans for the future, which is in large measure their own. The fewer surprises you spring on them, the better they respond when you need them.

If you block communications, you don't just cut productivity. You buttress stress claims. Around the country, employers who fail to set clear work standards, who fail to respond to signals of trouble — who fail to communicate — guarantee that their employees do well in pressing stress claims. (See Appendices Three & Twenty.)

The Price of Failure

Stress claims can cost twice as much as any other kind of claim. But you can't blame the medical costs; they're no higher for stress claims than for others. The problem is that the employee with a stress claim commonly uses the services of a mental health professional, and you can count on the fingers of one hand the number of mental health professionals who work fast.

Thus the problem is lost time. Stress-related disabilities are hard to diagnose and tough to cure. And

Three types of stress claims

they lend themselves to anyone looking forward to a stretched-out recovery period.

Stress claims fall into three categories: physical-mental, mental-physical, and mental-mental. The differences among the three have to do with cause and effect.

A physical-mental claim refers to a mental disorder brought on by a physical accident. For example, an employee falls down a flight of stairs and breaks a leg, and then becomes violently afraid of going up or down stairs. The broken leg heals quickly and cheaply, but not so the employee's fear of stairs. Curing this disorder takes longer and costs much more.

As employer, you stand liable for the costs of healing both, according to most workers' comp laws.

In the Other Direction

Mental-physical claims reverse the process and complicate matters dramatically. These entail stress-generated illnesses or injuries, in other words, physical injuries caused by mental disorders. For example, a shop supervisor overwhelmed by constant, mounting job pressure develops physical symptoms. With no prior evidence of cardiac problems, she has a heart attack on your shop floor.

Your shop floor could be one of the safest on the planet, but you still stand liable for the costs of rehabilitating the employee.

And it takes lots of time and money to rehabilitate someone with a stress-induced heart attack.

Mental-mental claims plunge you into the dark depths of workplace psychology. These claims entail stress-related emotional ailments — emotional ailments caused by other emotional ailments. For example, the same previously-healthy shop supervisor suffers a nervous breakdown, not a heart attack.

You see in a minute that mental-mental claims mean trouble. Nearly all states allow them. Most define them liberally, if at all, in keeping with the vague nature of mental ailments in general.

And getting over a heart attack is a lark compared to getting over a nervous breakdown.

Mental claims attract lawyers

Worst of all, mental-mental claims attract workers' comp lawyers. They don't have to show physical symptoms in mental-mental claims, and almost any management error becomes admissible evidence favoring the injured employee. Workers' comp lawyers accuse employers of "illogical management" and have little trouble winning the argument. After all, the art of management is the art of choosing among alternatives. Given time, an artful workers' comp lawyer finds it easy to pick away at your choice and present some other choice as the smarter move.

What to Do

You can't eliminate workplace stress and probably ought not to. But you can turn stress into a creative, not a destructive force — so that it works for, not against your enterprise.

You can also act before a stress claim hits, whatever its origin or nature.

You can make the workplace safe. You can keep stress to a creative minimum. You can make sure that your supervisors understand stress problems and know how to deal with them. You can school your employees in the elements of safety-consciousness. You can keep uppermost in mind the idea that safety prevents mental as well as physical injury.

And if a stress claim does hit, you can contain the costs of treatment by using the techniques discussed in Chapter 5. All apply to stress claims.

In all of this your object is to make stress work for your business. These days people enter the work force with a knowledge of their rights under labor law and a willingness to use them to get what they want out of their jobs. Their values have changed, as well. Workers consider fairness and equity greatly important — sometimes far more important than pay. They want, and feel free to ask, employers to contribute to a workplace life of high quality. This presupposes an environment physically and psychologically safe.

The law stands behind employees

By and large the law stands behind these expectations, although no one argues that it speaks coherently on such matters. In piecemeal fashion the state legislatures modify workers' comp law to reflect the expectations of the modern worker. Not unexpectedly they leave behind a great deal of confusion for the courts to clear up. This gives the courts little choice but to interpret liberally, notwithstanding the bias of workers' comp law in favor of the worker in the first place.

The courts encounter their most difficult question in deciding whether an injury arises out of workplace stress. Employers wish the courts shared their own suspicion of employees who don't cope with stresses that other workers handle easily. If employers had their way, the courts would give greater attention to stress arising out of the employee's personal life — from family relations or personal finances, for example.

Notions of Cause and Effect

But the courts don't side with employers in these matters. They wrestle with notions of cause and effect made murky by the vague nature of stress-related nervous disorders. They generally back the worker who presents a physical disability caused by a mental stimulus, or the worker who presents a mental disorder caused by a physical stimulus. With far less consistency they back the worker who presents a mental disorder caused by another mental disorder.

The difference comes from the fact that the courts use symptom-specific definitions of cause and effect. Judges like to see separate and distinct responses to separate and distinct stimuli. More specifically, they want to see a "proximate cause" for a given injury; they want to identify connections between the injury and hazards in the workplace.

The courts have no trouble seeing cause and effect when they consider claims involving computer use and carpal tunnel syndrome, for example. They don't fret much with claims involving physical disabilities caused by mental stimuli, or with claims involving mental disorders caused by physical stimuli.

But they run into lots of trouble when they consider workplace hazards that precipitate mental conditions which, in turn, aggravate physical injury or, worse, aggravate some other mental condition. Or rather, they *would* have lots of trouble if they grounded their thinking in simple reason or in state law, which becomes inconsistent when it contemplates such hazards. But the bias of the workers' comp system goes to the worker, so by and large the courts ignore the ambiguities and side with the worker.

Tough to see cause and effect

It makes no sense at all for the employer to fight this bias. The better idea is to help your employees to identify the sources of stress and find ways of dealing with it to the benefit of all.

Help from the States

To a certain degree the legislatures recognize the difficulty of the employer's position in fighting stress claims. Alabama law speaks of injury as involving "the physical structure of the body," thus implying that mental injuries caused by nonphysical events don't qualify. Other states make things more explicit by specifically prohibiting benefits for conditions arising solely from stress. A few states limit recovery to certain situations; Arizona, for example, pays benefits for stress claims only if they meet rigorous diagnostic criteria.

Michigan pays benefits for mental disabilities "if contributed to . . . by the employment in a significant manner." The disability must arise "out of actual events of employment, not unfounded perceptions thereof." Alaska imposes the same limitation. Wisconsin law appears to prohibit mental-mental claims.

Colorado prohibits stress claims resulting from disciplinary action — a key limitation. The state requires that a worker support a stress claim with testimony from a licensed physician or psychologist. The claim must arise primarily from workplace conditions and not ground itself in circumstances common to all fields of employment.

Maine law outlaws stress claims arising from personnel actions; it allows "mental or emotional disabilities only where a significant contributing cause . . . is an event or series of events occurring within the employment."

Injuries to the 'Human Organism'

Other states don't impose this limitation; Kentucky, for example, compensates injuries to the "human organism," which appears to include injuries to mind and body alike. Arkansas law speaks only of injury arising out of and in the course of employment.

Vagueness of this sort leaves the courts to their own devices in deciding whether mental-mental claims qualify for benefits. Worse, such vagueness allows workers' comp lawyers to paint disciplinary action as a cause of stress, and the courts, lacking firm grounds in state law one way or the other, go along.

Originally, the courts saw no reason to treat stress-related mental breakdowns differently from stress-related medical conditions such as heart attacks. They did require that the employee point to specific conditions leading to the mental disorder.

But as time passed they came to base their decisions on highly subjective considerations — for example, that men and women react differently to the same stimuli, even that people of different ethnic and cultural backgrounds react differently.

In *Hansen v. Von Duprin*, the Indiana Supreme Court found nothing in state law to prohibit benefits for injuries arising out of the daily stress of working. In this case the worker, a woman, had sought benefits for mental-mental injury. She alleged she had left her job because of mental harassment from her immediate supervisor, a man.

Occasionally, the confusion benefits employers. In an Arkansas case, *Owens v. National Health Laboratories*, a courier who had suffered from mental illness for 25 years fell behind schedule on her deliveries one day and became so upset that she suffered a nervous breakdown. The court ruled against her on the grounds that she had not shown that more-than-ordinary stress had caused the breakdown.

A similar case, *Smith and Sanders v. Peery*, involved a man who lost his job in an economic downturn. The claimant, who had a history of mental illness, suffered a nervous breakdown when his employer told him he would be laid off.

Vague laws favor employees

The Mississippi Supreme Court reasoned that an injury must stem from an unusual event and that a layoff didn't qualify as unusual. It added the requirement that when a pre-existing condition contributes to an injury, a claimant qualifies for benefits only in proportion as the injury stems from conditions of employment, not the pre-existing condition. Thus the individual in this case could not claim benefits for any portion of the nervous breakdown attributable to his pre-existing condition.

Offending Justice

Despite these cases, vagueness in the law works to the benefit of the worker, and employers pay a big penalty in states with ambiguous law respecting stress claims.

In 1992, Florida gave rise to a workers' comp case which tortured justice in more than one way.

Ruth Jandrucko, a white woman, was attacked and robbed by a black man while delivering a package for her employer. Jandrucko suffered a broken vertebra during the attack. Worse, the attack made her unable to stand the presence of blacks any longer. She testified that they made her anxious and nervous.

She filed for workers' comp. The state workers' comp judge found a cause and effect relationship between the assault and Jandrucko's phobia, noting that she had had no problem working with blacks prior to the attack. Her employer, Colorcraft Corp., appealed the award but lost.

Jandrucko pocketed $200,000.

The legislature subsequently passed a bill barring workers' comp benefits in cases where a psychological disorder results in action amounting to discrimination against a class of people. The legislation did *not* affect benefits for physical injury leading to psychological disorder.

Simple notions of justice

If you think this confusing, you're right. Workers' comp law takes strange turns when it bumps up against ordinary notions of justice, and the courts have a hard time finding their way around, particularly when the legislatures don't help out.

In general the courts remain split as to whether to allow benefits for mental-mental claims and, if so, to what degree. For their part, the legislatures seem inclined to tighten the circumstances under which mental-mental claims qualify for benefits — when they seem inclined to do anything about workers' comp at all, that is. Commonly, they act only when they really don't have much choice.

The Case of Sedonia Sparks

Louisiana stands among these states. In 1989 the legislature began requiring that a claimant show clear and convincing evidence for mental-mental injury — a tough standard.

The legislature acted in response to a much-debated workers' comp case involving one Sedonia Sparks, who became manager of Tulane Medical Center's distribution center in New Orleans in 1984. Supervising 10 employees, she shortly realized that several of her people regularly smoked marijuana in the medical supply storeroom.

Sparks warned the employees. She also alerted her supervisor, upon which the employees started showing their resentment. Sparks became the target of petty theft and vandalism. Someone stole her personal property from a storeroom; someone urinated in her coffee pot.

In 1987, tensions flared between Sparks and one employee in particular, the supervisor of the supply room's weekend crew. Sparks complained that the weekend crew wasn't doing its job. Two employees — including one whom Sparks had warned about drug use — protested by not stocking the shelves of the storeroom. The hospital suspended the employees without pay for five days.

At this point a fellow worker told Sparks that "a lot of people around here want to kick your butt." This frightened Sparks, who left work the same day complaining of headaches. A physician diagnosed her as suffering from tension headaches, probably caused by depression from work-related stress.

Sparks began to suffer from insomnia, and she lost her appetite. A psychiatrist diagnosed her condition as an adjustment disorder — a form of depression that arises from difficulty in adjusting to stress.

Physical symptoms of stress

The Threat to Her Safety

Sparks sought workers' comp on the grounds that the threat to her safety caused her to suffer a disabling mental injury.

A Louisiana district court denied her claim, ruling that no accident had occurred to cause Sparks' disability and that, in any case, state law expressly forbade claims like hers.

Sparks appealed and won. The court refused to grant penalties and attorney's fees, but it did award Sparks $7,300 on the grounds that she had suffered temporary total disability lasting five months.

The kicker here is that, at the time, Louisiana law limited workers' comp benefits to "injuries by violence to the physical structure of the body and such disease or infections as naturally result therefrom." An ordinary person might read that language as excluding claims of mental injury, not to mention claims of mental-mental injury. But the law made things even more explicit, adding:

"These terms shall in no case be construed to include any other form of disease or derangement, however caused or contracted."

Case closed, right? Wrong. The appellate ruling argued that Sparks had become disabled due to job-related stress and had "suffered personal injury by accident arising out of and in the course of her employment. . . ."

The Louisiana legislature had no choice but to react to this decision by tightening the requirements for stress-related mental injury claims. It outlawed them unless the mental injury results from "a sudden, unexpected, and extraordinary stress-

The smart employer doesn't wait

related" occurrence demonstrated by clear and convincing evidence.

So in the end employers won the day in Louisiana. Eventually the weird twists and turns of workers' comp case law may provoke other legislatures to tighten up on claims involving nervous disorders; the trend goes this way, at least.

But the smart employer doesn't wait for the courts or the legislatures to act, because they just aren't reliable.

Soft-Tissue Injuries

Like stress claims, injuries to the body's soft tissues don't present much hard evidence. Physicians do poorly in substantiating damage to tendons, muscles and nerves just as they do poorly in understanding damage to the psyche. They deduce the injury from the symptom, not the other way around. They don't see the injury itself — as, for example, they see cancer cells. And they can't always posit a cause and effect relationship between the injury and conditions in the workplace.

All this makes for trouble for the employer.

In workers' comp, the definitive soft-tissue injury is carpal tunnel syndrome, which particularly afflicts people who use computers for hours on end. The disorder involves an inflammation of nerves located in the wrist, caused most often by repetitive motion.

Medicine can't do much about carpal tunnel syndrome. Some orthopedists do surgery to expand the room for nerves in the wrist, but this doesn't always solve the problem. For that matter, physicians often don't agree on the diagnosis in the first place, making it difficult for the cumbersome workers' comp system to sort things out — as the following case study shows.

No Unanimity

Rodney Marchione worked on the assembly line for the Delaware Seat Company in New Castle, Delaware. His job involved lifting 35-pound automobile seats every 55 seconds and wielding a 5-pound hand drill.

In 1985, Marchione began experiencing numbness and pain in his hands and wrists which he attributed to his employment. His family doctor, Harry Greenetz, an osteopath, diagnosed carpal tunnel syndrome.

Carpal tunnel syndrome

Marchione quickly filed a workers' comp claim seeking benefits for temporary-total disability. The Delaware Industrial Accident Board denied benefits, ruling that Marchione hadn't proven that he had carpal tunnel syndrome or that it stemmed from his work — or even that it had disabled him.

Marchione's mistake was that he saw too many doctors, and they couldn't agree on the nature or the cause of his trouble.

The key evidence came from the osteopath Greenetz and two physicians, Daniel Singer and Joseph Arminio.

Greenetz diagnosed carpal tunnel syndrome on the grounds that Marchione had a tingling sensation in both hands, showed a weakness in grasp, and complained of pain. Greenetz testified that Marchione's work caused his condition.

Auto Accident

But Singer, a specialist in hand and upper extremity problems, traced Marchione's trouble to a car accident one year prior to his employment with Delaware Seat. Marchione told Singer that he had braced himself against impact and experienced pain in his wrists after the accident. The pain reappeared after Marchione went to work for Delaware Seat.

Singer conducted a number of tests to determine whether Marchione had carpal tunnel syndrome, with mixed results. Marchione tested positive on some, negative on others. On a test to determine strength of grip, Singer felt that Marchione didn't give it all his effort.

Singer considered Marchione a good candidate for carpal tunnel syndrome, given the nature of his work. But he wasn't sure that Marchione actually had the condition.

Mixed results from tests

Marchione saw Joseph Arminio at the request of Delaware Seat. Like Singer, Arminio ran a number of tests on Marchione and came to the same conclusion. Arminio testified that Marchione appeared to have some irritation of the median nerve, which runs through the carpal tunnel, but he wasn't sure the irritation amounted to carpal tunnel syndrome itself.

"We are not absolutely sure why he has irritation, but there are two possible reasons," Arminio said. "One is the automobile accident and, of course, [the other is] his work record."

Three Doctors, Two Opinions

Thus the three doctors presented the Delaware Industrial Accident Board with two different opinions.

In his own testimony Marchione acknowledged the car crash but denied any injury to his wrists. He denied having told Singer that he had injured his wrists in the accident.

Given the conflict, the board had little choice but to rule that Marchione hadn't proven carpal tunnel syndrome. Delaware law allows benefits for an injury "possibly" related to an industrial accident only if other credible evidence establishes a causal relationship.

The board traced the pain and numbness in his hands and wrists to the car accident, not to his work. It accepted Singer as the reliable witness for this, not Marchione, whose varying testimony the board discounted as self-interested.

Marchione appealed but lost.

For his employer, the key to the case was the requirement of state law that Marchione establish a causal relationship between his injury and conditions in the workplace. Marchione failed to do so because three doctors looked at the same looked at the same symptoms and made two differing diagnoses — not uncommon in soft-tissue injuries.

In this case the conflict worked to the employer's advantage. More commonly, employers lose contested cases involving soft tissues for exactly the same reason. Doctors try to deduce the injury from the symptom. With soft-tissue cases, sometimes they start from symptoms so vague as to defy analysis of any kind — and they diagnose an injury anyway.

Most employers lose this fight

Workplace Solutions

The point? You do yourself a favor by finding workplace, not legal solutions to your ergonomics problems. If soft-tissue injuries puzzle physicians, soft-tissue *claims* usually trump anything you might try in court. Marchione's employer got lucky. Most of the time employers lose a fight over soft-tissue injuries once they become claims.

For starters, don't put too much faith in the notion that you can hire a consultant for a quick fix, or that you can find the perfect chair for your computer users or the perfect tool for the people on the shop floor. Few consultants really earn their keep; none knows as much about your workplace as you and your employees do. As for the perfect chair or tool, they don't exist — that is, no *one* chair or tool works for *all* your employees.

Involve your employees in your effort from day one. Take your time here, because you must use all the arts of smart management to enlist the support of your employees and keep them with the program. You get exactly nowhere with a program that doesn't benefit your employees, no matter how much fanfare you drum up in starting off.

Analyze the workplace. Look carefully for tasks that subject the employee to undue vibration, awkward extension, overexertion, and repetition. Ditto for what ergonomists call static loads — positions that concentrate weight in one part of the body, especially the limbs when extended.

Brainstorm with your employees about solutions. If their work requires lifting items from the floor onto a conveyor belt, how about delivering the items to them already elevated on a wheeled platform? If their work requires that they extend their arms to

Design stress out of the task

attach a component inside something else — for example, to a low corner inside a deep boxlike container — can you redesign the container to avoid the awkward extension? Can your workers devise different working positions to accomplish tasks that subject them to undue load? Can they realign things so that they don't carry awkward loads?

Solutions Must Address Problems

Check with your workers' comp carrier. Some insurers know a great deal about repetitive motion disabilities. You stand a good chance of getting valuable help if your carrier specializes in insuring employers like yourself. Remember, however, that your insurer's interest lies in preventing losses, not necessarily in solving your problems. Make sure that your carrier's "solutions" actually benefit your employees.

For that matter, make sure that your own solutions fit the individual and the job. Don't expect one solution to fit all; your employees will see through this in a minute, and if you end up damaging morale by subjecting everyone to a fix-all solution, you make things worse. Put another way, you need flexible solutions, not highly specific "bullet" problem solvers that ignore what people actually do in the course of their work.

Above all, make sure that your ergonomics program becomes an ongoing part of your workplace environment. Plan for the long haul. Make sure that everyone signs on and stays on. Give everyone a stake in the outcome. Set realistic goals — and measure progress.

Attracting Lawyers

Stress and soft-tissue injuries threaten the employer with a double whammy. Their ambiguities are bad enough on their own, and when you couple them with the broader ambiguities of the workers' comp system itself, you breed trouble. You also attract lawyers.

You work at a disadvantage in stress cases since, all things being equally ambiguous, the system favors your employee.

But you aren't helpless. You accomplish a lot by hiring the right people, supervising them fairly, and giving them well-defined jobs in a trusting environment with some degree of open communications.

A good solution won't break the bank

Things get easier with soft-tissue claims. A wealth of literature exists on the techniques of preventing soft-tissue injury, many of them simple and practical. And an industry has sprung up to supply workers with ergonomic devices and items of personal equipment that go a long way toward ensuring that soft-tissue injuries don't happen.

Even better, many of the preventive techniques don't require overhauling your operations, and the ergonomics devices and items of personal protective equipment don't strip your budget for capital improvements.

CHAPTER 8: VOCATIONAL REHABILITATION

Good programs work, bad ones don't

Vocational rehabilitation programs range from the truly useful to the truly outrageous. The best of them help injured employees to return to their old jobs or train for new. The worst constitute just one more ripoff of the workers' comp system, draining countless dollars away from insurers, employers, and ultimately employees themselves.

As the employer, you need to keep a watchful eye on any vocational rehab programs in which your injured employees engage to make sure that they profit from the effort. In doing so you learn much about the odd tendency of the workers' comp system to reward unproductive behavior, and about how to counter it. You also do a positive good in the world, on behalf of the seriously injured worker.

The Elemental Question

The discussion of vocational rehab starts with a question implicit in any discussion of workers' comp as a whole: What objectives, other than the paying of cash benefits, should the system have?

Those who want to expand the system show you a wish list of social needs that government might address through such things as workers' comp. But those who must watch the bottom line focus on two objectives: 1) preventing accidents and 2) getting the injured worker back on the job.

Most employers prefer to prevent injuries — rightly so. Loss prevention is the cheapest risk management. But no workplace can be wholly free of hazard; even the best accident prevention plans can't eliminate all problems. In physics, they use the word entropy to describe something similar: the incidence of disorder in a system, especially one undergoing change. In economic activity, change is a given, so disorder and hazard become givens, too.

The few who really need rehab

In short, accidents happen; you can't eliminate risk. What you can do is to limit your exposure to the *consequences* of accidents — by bringing an injured employee back to work. This often involves vocational rehab. (See Appendix Eighteen.)

Only a few injured workers need vocational rehab, but those who do, really need it. They have suffered serious injury, and without help they face the threat they will lead lives of dependency. Unfortunately, however, although good vocational rehab programs offer significant savings in cost and lives, the workers' comp system throws many obstacles in the way of the worker who seeks to overcome a disability and return to work. Not the least of these are the horror stories that circulate among workers themselves about people who lose their workers' comp benefits because they start vocational rehab.

This causes many injured workers to resist the idea. Their resistance mushrooms if they listen to the counsel of a workers' comp lawyer, who gains only if the injury brings cash in its wake in the form of a settlement from an insurer. The lawyer gets nothing out of any payments made by the insurer to a vocational rehab specialist.

In fact, the injured worker loses disability income only if rehabilitation succeeds and he or she returns to work. Employees need to know this, and the smart employer emphasizes it during safety programming.

Structural Problems

On the other hand, the workers' comp system presents real structural problems that may keep employees at home. Some low-wage workers resist rehab because they get almost as much in workers' comp benefits as from the job. This becomes all the more likely when an injured worker receives Social Security disability payments or some other form of public assistance. The safety net is supposed to catch those most vulnerable to the dislocation of workplace injury. But it ensnares some so effectively that it leaves them with no incentive to return to work.

The big insurers contribute to this problem. For one thing, most provide rehab services only if the law requires it, or only if rehab promises to cost the insurer less than a lump-sum settlement. For another, they fail to help the states identify workers who need rehabilitation. As a rule the states don't require insurers to recommend rehab until the injured employee has been out of work for some time, commonly six months, so insurers put off doing so until the last minute. By this time it's often too late for rehab to do much good. The injured worker has had too much time to grow accustomed to the disability checks.

Putting things off until the last moment

You can step in here. Make sure your carrier cooperates with state law respecting rehab services, and if your employee can benefit from rehab, you want the insurer to get on the ball.

Dismal Numbers

The longer your employee doesn't work, the less likely rehab will succeed. Conversely, the sooner it starts, the more likely the employee will return to a productive life. In a 1978 survey, the New York Workers' Compensation Board found that 82 percent of the injured workers who started rehab programs within four months of their accidents successfully returned to fulltime work. For those beginning rehab more than a year after their accidents, the success rate dropped to 50 percent.

After two years, only one out of 100 went back to work. The rest adjusted to dependency and to the prospect of spending the rest of their lives in its sad embrace.

Another structural problem stems from the cumbersome nature of the workers' comp bureaucracy. Some rehab counselors are so swamped with work — and so inefficient in handling their caseloads — that by the time they see an injured worker, the individual shows no motivation to return to work and instead concentrates on trying to win a large lump-sum settlement.

To combat this, some states send out information to an injured worker immediately following an accident. Some, however, insist on approving a rehab program before an insurer commits to paying the

Good but not good enough

bill, which only delays things. Florida employs nurses to oversee rehab programs for employees with long-term disabilities. The nurses get the cases in 34 days, on average — good, but probably not good enough.

Most states subsidize rehab for injured workers, either directly or through tax benefits. But few have any mechanism for identifying workers not referred by insurance companies.

Even when insurers do comply with state regs, it sometimes takes months for the state to process a vocational rehab case.

There's not much you can do about this, other than recognize trouble signs early. Make sure that your injured employee gets into rehab as soon as possible — so long as the employee can benefit from the effort. Otherwise, keep an eye on questionable claims and, if you can, put a stop to referrals that aren't likely to produce results.

According to the Massachusetts Rehabilitation Commission, which administers workers' comp rehab cases in that state, its services reach only one of every five disabled workers who legitimately need them. The miserable result: Of all workers referred to the commission for job placement or retraining, only 10 to 12 percent ever go back to work.[1]

Opting for the Lump Sum

Worse, many workers sign away their right to vocational rehab. Most states require that the insurer pay for rehab, but workers commonly waive the benefit when they accept a lump-sum settlement instead. One study of the Eastern industrial states indicated that almost 20 percent of all injured workers closed their cases with lump-sum settlements.

But don't be seduced by the idea that a lump-sum settlement solves everything. Once the injured employee gets far enough into the workers' comp claim process to consider rehab, his or her interests begin

---

[1]Other states do better, but only by comparison. California gets 33 percent back to work, Minnesota 34 percent, Oregon 54 percent, Wisconsin 30 to 35 percent, Florida 37 percent, New York 46 percent, Connecticut 48 percent, Kansas 30 percent, and Maryland 28 percent.

to merge with your own. Besides, a number of states (including Minnesota, Maryland, California and Connecticut) forbid the worker to sign away the right to rehab. So any lump-sum settlement to cover medical costs or lost wages doesn't cover rehab.

Your interests begin to merge

And don't think you can drop your guard once your employee begins a rehab program. Many—possibly half of all for-profit entities—operate only to handle workers' comp cases. Many charge big fees for doing little that helps injured employees.

A 1992 report issued by the Council on California Competitiveness[2] argued that most vocational rehab programs involved "costly schooling . . . of dubious value." The council proposed encouraging employers to accommodate injured workers in new jobs instead of sending them to rehab programs. The study also urged cuts in benefits for rehab.

One Step Farther

California Governor Pete Wilson went even farther, proposing to slash state subsidies by two-thirds and to require that injured workers contribute 50 percent of their permanent disability benefits, up to $10,000, to the cost of their retraining. Clearly, Wilson had in mind the high costs of rehab. Private programs, lightly regulated by the state, cost $8,400 on average and constitute 8 percent of the total costs of the state's workers' comp system. Wilson wanted to encourage workers and employers to use less-costly alternatives, shown to be effective in getting the injured back to work.

Critics, led by Ralph Nader, accused Wilson of "a consistent display of cruelty" toward injured Californians. "The cardinal sin of an elected official," Nader said, "is a consistent display of cruelty at the same time that a rational policy can make economic sense."

But it doesn't quite. Third parties gobble up big pieces of the workers' comp pie. Of every workers' comp dollar spent between 1990 and 1992, about 37 cents went to doctors, hospitals, and vocational re-

---

[2]See Chapter 13: The Myth of Reform

Third parties gobble up the pie

hab counselors, 33 cents to insurers, and only 26 cents to injured employees.

It's hard to pinpoint just how much goes specifically to vocational rehab. Some experts estimate that, nationally, vocational rehab takes as much as 10 cents of every workers' comp dollar.

From 1985 to 1992, vocational rehab costs in California rose about 25 percent a year. This paralleled a big explosion in stress injury claims.

"It's part of the same process," said a staffer on the state's Industrial Relations Board. "A lot of fortune hunters have moved into the market."

California law entitles injured workers to vocational rehab if their injury prevents them from returning to the job. The law allows the employer to modify the workplace to accommodate the physical demands of the worker, if possible, or to retrain the employee for a new vocation. But the system provides little incentive for cost-effective treatment. Injured workers receive state support for years while they enroll in long-term college programs that may not lead to a new job.

Little Good for the Worker

Other states do little better. Before Oregon restructured its workers' comp system, administrators blamed chiropractors and vocational rehab counselors for doing little good for injured workers.

Even so, vocational rehab can be a net positive investment for both employers and workers. The Ohio Bureau of Vocational Rehabilitation and the state Bureau of Workers' Compensation refer injured workers to Goodwill Industries. Goodwill assesses the abilities of the injured workers, places some directly into new jobs, and trains others, all for a nominal fee covered by the Ohio bureau. Goodwill describes itself as "the world's largest nonprofit provider of vocational services for individuals with these conditions and the world's largest private-sector employer of people with disabilities."

The successful rehabilitation programs of organizations such as Goodwill stand as paradigms for the

The paradigm of the good program

employer. If you must use the services of a private rehab firm, nonprofit or otherwise, judge its methods by comparing them to those used by Goodwill. The closer the better.

Goodwill's methods include:

1. Carefully analyzing the prospects for rehab. Is the injured worker young and resilient enough to find a new specialty or, if necessary, a new line of work? Is the injury so serious that rehab just won't help?
2. Beginning the rehab program as soon as possible, given the nature of the injury.
3. Training the injured worker for employment as close as possible to his or her previous job. This means keeping the injured worker at your own firm if you can, in identical or similar work.
4. Clearly defining goals from the beginning. Open-ended programs frustrate employers and injured employees alike.
5. Starting slowly, even if this means having the injured worker return to work only a few hours a day. Rehab is as much a psychological as a physical process.
6. Not forcing the rehab to a rigid time-frame. The process should be goal-oriented, not time-oriented. This doesn't mean it can go on indefinitely; but allow some flexibility.
7. Giving supervisors as much input as possible. They know better than anyone — even the rehab counselor — how much progress an injured worker is making.

Pay particular attention to the third and sixth points if you must use a private sector, for-profit rehab counselor. Have a plan in place before the program starts, so you can measure progress. And don't give the counselor more input than the injured worker's supervisors. The counselor knows therapy and rehab tools; your supervisors know your business.

The final goal, after all, is to get the injured employee back to work.

The final goal of rehab

Injury presents the employee — not to mention the employer — with subtle problems to overcome, and the smart employer pays as much attention to these as to the injury itself. As the following brief case study shows, injury itself can sometimes be so subtle that the *employee* has trouble acknowledging its seriousness, much less acknowledging that rehab is a must.

Averting Problems: A Case Study

Chizuko de Queiroz worked as an art teacher for the Palos Verdes Peninsula Unified School District in Southern California.

De Queiroz filed a series of claims involving back and soft-tissue injuries through the mid 1980s. The school district settled each claim but finally requested that she stop teaching and enter a retraining program for less strenuous work.

Citing numerous claims for emotional and physical injuries between 1983 and 1988, the district and its insurer claimed that de Queiroz was "vulnerable to significant reinjury in [the course of continued] employment."

De Queiroz argued that she was perfectly capable of staying on.

She said she'd stopped carrying and lifting and doing heavy repetitive work. Two art assistants did the lifting for her.

"I know my limitations . . . what I can do and what I can't do," she said, adding that the insurers and the district should not look at numbers but "look at me as a human being."

The school district wanted de Queiroz to enter a rehab program conducted by a trained counselor through the state workers' comp board.

De Queiroz wanted to keep on teaching. She flatly refused to enter rehab, saying she didn't need it. She insisted that she had modified her work habits so as to avoid reinjury.

A spokesman for the school district told the *Los Angeles Times* that "[there] always have been promises that she could change, that she would no longer do these things, would use assistants. That didn't happen."

Several physicians examined de Queiroz and recommended that she train for a new job to avoid reinjury and possibly permanent disability.

Faced with these recommendations, the art teacher countered that the school district's eagerness to remove her stemmed from a dispute over an art supplies account. She had pointed out a clerical error that overcharged her supplies allowance, and she suspected that someone wanted revenge.

In the end de Queiroz and the school district managed to avoid a showdown, however. Each side gave up a little and came away with something it wanted.

De Queiroz agreed to see a rehab counselor who worked out a regimen that allowed her to return to work as an art teacher. In effect she admitted the seriousness of the problem — an important concession.

The district, meanwhile, backed off from its insistence that she retrain for different work altogether. And life went on.

Done well, rehab saves money

Think Like an Ally

Reformers rant about fraud and abuse and offer vocational rehab as a cure-all for the woe of the injured worker. They don't realize that vocational rehab comes with its own complement of shenanigans and ripoffs.

The best thing for the employer to do when faced with a rehab case is to think like the injured worker's ally. Rehab will cost your insurer — or you yourself, if you self-insure — some money, possibly a lot; but done well, it saves you the employer and your insurer potfuls of money over the long run.

As the employer, it's your job to see that it gets done well — and to make sure that your insurer understands the long-term cost-effectiveness of a good rehab program. You don't want trouble from your insurer just when you see your injured worker turn a corner and make important progress toward recov-

Judge the costs carefully

ery. Prepare to act as your employee's advocate if necessary.

Keep an eye on cases threatening long-term disability in particular — specifically, on the costs of permanent disability. You want to judge these costs very carefully; they can be astronomical. But the higher these costs threaten to go, the more cost-effective a successful rehab program becomes.

If rehab is a viable option, keep close tabs on the process in the same way you keep tabs on medical costs. Identify the legitimate providers — and the quacks — in your area; make sure your injured employee doesn't fall into the hands of the quacks. Remember that some rehab counselors hesitate to call a case closed. Monitor progress carefully, and steel yourself to put a halt to things if your injured worker stops making progress.

Pulling the Plug

If you can't be sure, intervene personally, encouraging the injured worker yourself when it will do some good — and pulling the plug when it won't.

In fact, count on doing this as a matter of course, especially when your employee has suffered a serious injury. By its very nature, workplace injury threatens the livelihood of the worker — a fearsome and depressing thing. Indeed, injured workers struggle just as hard with fear and depression in recovering from injury as they do with the physical effects of the injury itself. Don't hesitate to do some hand-holding with your injured worker and with his or her family.

Keep in mind that you and your injured worker have the same end here: to get the injured employee back on the job. Don't harass the worker unless you think it will do some good. Be a coach.

And remember that you want the worker back in your employ, not in somebody else's. In the best of all possible worlds this means getting the worker back into his or her old job. In the real world it may mean modifying a job to fit the injured worker's new skills.

Don't pooh-pooh the benefits that flow from this.

Your end of the old bargain

Every employee you have will know what you have done — will know, that is, that you have kept up your end of the old bargain between employer and employee with respect to workplace injury. And they won't forget.

Chapter 9: Insurance

The beast itself

Most employers buy commercial workers' comp insurance to meet the requirement that they stand responsible for the cost of workplace injury. Few, however, ever read their workers' comp policies, much less understand how they can turn the ins and outs of commercial coverage to their advantage.

But it pays to become a good insurance buyer, especially if you have no choice but to cover your workers' comp exposure with commercial insurance.[1] As we have already seen, you can attack your workers' comp problem by grappling with classifications, cost control, cost containment and a variety of other techniques. You can also grapple with the beast itself — your workers' comp carrier and the policy it sells you.

The Tricks of the Trade

The carriers in the workers' comp marketplace use tricks you find nowhere else in the insurance industry. Much of what they do seeks to deter the cost-conscious employer, and they act with the tacit approval of the regulatory apparatus. Insurers want things to appear automatic and routine. They want you to ignore the mechanics that go into setting premiums so you won't complain much when they "adjust" your premium next year.

Don't fall into this trap. The insurance establishment wants you to think its policies are all the same. They're not. Smart buying makes a difference — in the premium you pay and in the service you get before and after you make a claim. For that matter, it

---

[1]Some states (six, to be exact: Nevada, North Dakota, Ohio, Washington, West Virginia, and Wyoming) give you no choice in the matter, unfortunately. Known as monopolistic states, they operate pools that act as sole supplier of workers' comp insurance. Commercial carriers don't sell in these states at all.

A good place to start

makes a difference when you set out to control losses or contain costs. Some carriers know more about safety programming and cost containment than others. Some don't seem to care.

In all, different carriers offer different blends of opportunity and exposure to the employer who takes control of the workers' comp problem. It pays to find a carrier who thinks like you do.

The Standard Policy

What can you expect from a plain vanilla workers' comp policy? Plain vanilla — a good place to start. The shenanigans come a little later.

Most workers' comp policies follow the short standard form published by the NCCI (See Appendix Twenty-Four). It warrants a look, starting with the data on the information page. Check the details, including your locations if you operate in more than one state. Check your classification, of course. Note that all the information is "subject to verification and change by audit." Among other things, this means that the insurer can change its mind as to the classification of your business, for example, and send you a new premium notice.

Check the section explaining the scope of the coverage as well. It speaks in a bureaucratic monotone, but it's important:

> *This workers' compensation insurance applies to bodily injury by accident or bodily injury by disease. Bodily injury includes resulting death.*
>
> 1) *Bodily injury by accident must occur during the policy period.*
>
> 2) *Bodily injury by disease must be caused or aggravated by conditions of your employment. The employee's last day of last exposure to the conditions causing or aggravating such bodily injury by disease must occur during the policy period.*
>
> *We will pay promptly when due the benefits required of you by workers' compensation law . . . this includes any amendments to the law which are in effect during the policy period.*

The key to this language lies in its requirement that workplace conditions cause or aggravate the injury. This accurately reflects the old bargain between employer and employee that the employer assume responsibility for workplace injury in exchange for the employee's promise not to sue.

New guests at the table

On the other hand, the policy turns immediately to quite another matter when it speaks of "the benefits required of you by workers' compensation law." This may sound innocent enough, but it isn't. Indeed, it taketh away what the phrase about workplace conditions giveth. It brings new guests to the table, notably your legislature and the courts, and leaves it up to them to decide what's on the menu.

The Essential Elements

In fact, these new guests control the essential elements of your bargain with your employees. They hold the right to distort the simple justice of that bargain to suit themselves. They decide exactly what benefits you must pay and under what conditions. They decide what happens in the real world.

Thus the NCCI's standard policy makes explicit your vulnerability to people who have no interest in your bargain — people who, for their own ends, exploit the fact that they can define workplace injury as they see fit.

This section of the policy does something else with greater subtlety. It makes it clear that your insurer pays claims, not you. This sets you up for another section of the policy which reserves to your insurer the right to decide when to fight a claim and when to pay:

> *We have the right and duty to defend at our expense any claim, proceeding or suit against you for benefits payable by this insurance. We have the right to investigate and settle these claims, proceedings or suits. . .*

You may think this all and good; after all, what's an insurer for if not to take on some of the bother of a workers' comp claim? But in fact this language gives your insurer, not you, the power to police claims — and most insurers don't police claims at all.

The slam dunk claim

Instead, they settle them. They follow strict guidelines, formulated with the blessings of the regulatory apparatus, to limit the time and effort they spend reviewing claims. As a rule, this means that they settle claims of $25,000 to $30,000 without batting an eye.

Every workers' comp lawyer in the country knows this. They seek out people with claims under these limits because they want the easy money. They advertise on television and troll their state unemployment offices and their local hospitals looking for people whose claims fall within these limits. They don't file claims for anybody else; they want cases that insurers settle without dispute. Some limit themselves to insurers that don't investigate claims at all. One Los Angeles lawyer uses a computer to track his claims. His software looks for red flags indicating trouble with an insurer, so that the lawyer can change tactics or abandon the claim altogether. He says: "The strict methods insurers use to settle claims act like a blueprint for us. We keep our claims within their limits, and every one is a slam dunk."

You Pay

Your insurer factors these slam dunks into its premium-setting formulas. You pay for them — those that hit you and those that hit every other employer insured by your carrier. Some reasonable reckonings put the cost of these subsidies at more than one-third of total workers' comp costs.

Worse, the regulatory apparatus encourages the insurance industry's practices in settling claims. For one thing, the faster your insurer settles a claim, the nearer it comes to the law's mandate that the injured employee receive just and speedy compensation. For another, a speedy settlement makes it less likely that the claim will end up as a costly lawsuit. For yet another, the states keep constant pressure on workers' comp premium rates, so insurers just don't have the money to investigate small claims.

They have every incentive to settle — and no incentive to police anything but the most egregious claim.

The NCCI standard form offers insurers an escape clause against the big claim, too. It says:

Hedging the big claim

You are responsible for any payments in excess of the benefits regularly provided by the workers' compensation law including those required because:

1) of your serious and willful misconduct;

2) you knowingly employ an employee in violation of law;

3) you fail to comply with a health or safety law; and

4) you discharge, coerce or otherwise discriminate against any employee in violation of the workers' compensation law.

If we make any payments in excess of the benefits regularly provided by the workers' compensation law on your behalf, you will reimburse us promptly.

and:

We have no duty to defend a claim, proceeding or suit that is not covered by this insurance. . .

We will not pay more than our share of benefits and costs covered by this insurance and other insurance or self-insurance. Subject to any limits of liability that may apply, all shares will be equal until the loss is paid. If any insurance or self-insurance is exhausted, the shares of all remaining insurance will be equal until the loss is paid.

and:

We will also pay these costs, in addition to other amounts payable under this insurance, as part of any claim, proceeding or suit we defend:

1) reasonable expense incurred at our request, but not loss of earnings;

2) premiums for bonds to release attachments and for appeal bonds in bond amounts up to the amount payable under this insurance;

3) litigation costs taxed against you;

Some truths about insurers

4) *interest on a judgment as required by law until we offer the amount due under this insurance; and*

5) *expenses we incur.*

Don't think for a minute that your insurer does all these things for your benefit. It does them for its own benefit.

Underlying this language are some important truths about insurers: They don't like to think about settlements, and they don't like questions. They don't want to cut the costs of settling claims; they want to pay them and get on with things. They loathe the messy details: investigations, mitigating circumstances, employers who fight the nickle-and-dime claim, and, above all, lawsuits.

And they want to make sure that the onus falls on the employer if unforeseen circumstances arise. If your insurer really wants to, it could probably make the case that you have engaged in wilful misconduct or, at the very least, have discriminated against an employee in violation of workers' comp law. As a rule insurers don't fall back on such arguments. But they can if you present them with a claim they really don't want to pay. About one time in four, insurers pay only part of claims exceeding $1 million.

Experience Rating

Experience counts when it comes to buying workers' comp insurance: the better your experience, the lower your premium, and vice versa. But it doesn't count for much.

Insurers bring experience rating into play when your premium reaches a set amount, usually $6,000 to $10,000 annually. The idea is a good one—i.e., that a favorable claims experience puts money in your pocket. But it only goes so far. As a rule, insurers limit their ex-mods to 20 percent, so that the employer with good claims experience pays 80 percent of the ordinary premium and the employer with poor claims experience pays 120 percent.

This gives the former a slight break, but it gives the latter a bigger break. You can cut your claims experience by far more than 20 percent once you set out to master your workers' comp problem. But your insurer doesn't help much if it cuts your premium only 20 percent.

Shielding a poor safety record

Conversely, you can ignore your workers' comp problem altogether and suffer no worse than a 20 percent ex-mod penalty.

Of course, insurers offer ex-mods with the blessings of a regulatory apparatus not known for understanding how things work in the real world. Even so, insurers don't like to use ex-mods extensively. They look too much like merit-based refunds, so employers get a little too insistent about receiving them. They also resist their penalties. A lot of litigation can follow.

The bottom line: You don't have the upper hand here. Experience ratings don't really reflect good experience; more often, they shield poor experience. They allow your insurer to *appear* to reward your safety efforts without really doing so.

Dividends, Retros and Other Devices

The relationship between workers' comp insurers and the regulatory apparatus isn't so much cosy as it is odd. On the one hand the regulatory apparatus squeezes insurers by keeping a tight lid on premiums, ostensibly to the benefit of the employer. On the other it allows insurers to play games with experience ratings, dividends and retrospectively-rated policies, often at the expense of the employer.

In all likelihood the regulatory apparatus believes that it follows its original mandate — to protect the public — in squeezing premiums. It may believe the same with respect to experience rating, dividends and retros; after all, properly structured, all of these really would benefit the public. But the ordinary mortal scratches the chin with wonder at these practices, because in the real world they benefit the insurer. They hurt the unwary employer.

Commercial insurers trot out dividend plans and retros when they run out of other blandishments to try out on you. Lend them a skeptical ear. The theory

Some insurers play the dividend game

behind dividend plans is that you get part of your premium back if you make no claims — a reward for good behavior. Life insurers make broad use of dividends, with reasonable success. But workers' comp insurers don't do so well. Some play games with their dividends at the expense of the gullible employer.

Off the record, insurers admit that they rarely pay dividends of significant magnitude even on big policies. Commonly they offer them only on big policies in the first place, so the small employer doesn't stand much of a chance.

"The odds are that if you've got more than a dozen employees, you'll get a workers' comp claim in a given year," says an executive with a large East Coast carrier. "And if you have less than a dozen employees, you're not going to get a dividend policy. Probably not even if you have two dozen employees."

He admits that smaller insurers hungry for business might offer a dividend policy to a smaller employer. But, he says, "they'll charge more for it and then find some way not to make the dividend."

A Drop-Dead Rate

All too often, the same goes for retro policies. The insurer shows you a drop-dead rate and leads you to believe that, although the fine print allows the insurer to increase your premium later on if you show poor claims experience, in all likelihood the insurer won't do so because you, of course, show such good claims experience.

Look out for the smoke and mirrors. Insurers play a cynical game with dividends and retrospectively-rated policies. Back-end cost reductions don't work because they don't happen.

Back-end cost *increases*, on the other hand, work very well for insurers. They conceal these increases in a fog of technical language, calling them "premium surcharges" to "enforce minimum premium requirements" and such like.

They're just another hedge. Your insurer can't drop you during the term of your policy, but it may very well "adjust" your premium at the end of the term. In theory these adjustments reflect your claims experience and give you an incentive to improve it. In reality, since few employers avoid claims altogether, insurers use them to cover a multitude of sins, including some of their own doing (for example, dumb moves with their investment portfolios). Some insurers buy their way into a market by showing you rates you can't refuse — knowing all the while that they can make up the difference at renewal time. Insurers can't pull this kind of ploy in any other line of coverage, but in workers' comp, the regulatory apparatus doesn't bat an eye at the practice.

Covering their own dumb moves

Smaller employers may try to negotiate retros or dividend policies if they believe their claims experience justifies doing so. In most cases, though, premium adjustments work against you, not for you.

They're best left alone.

The Legal Wherewithal

Experience ratings and dividends came out of some heated legal battles during the 1950s and 1960s — when workers' comp law really grew and when insurers and the regulatory apparatus formed their odd ties.

One California case, in particular, codified the relationship between the two parties.

In the late 1950s, California's insurance commissioner, Britton McConnell, launched one of the first attempts to introduce dividend-paying policies to the workers' comp marketplace.

The establishment objected almost immediately, starting with the California State Compensation Insurance Fund, which feared that dividends in the commercial market would put it at a disadvantage. SCIF sued, calling the commissioner's plan an illegal attempt to fix prices.

The courts sided with McConnell almost from the start. They couldn't deny the reality of the state fund's position in the marketplace. They sensed that, as the state fund took on more and more employers, it, too, would greatly influence rates in the commercial marketplace.

The state Supreme Court affirmed that McConnell held power to adjust rates. The law, the court said, gave McConnell authority to do more than group employers by hazard and match classifications with premiums. It ruled that the legislature had not intended, when using the words "classification of risks and premium rates," to restrict the commissioner to any particular rate-setting method. It said:

> *Rate-making involves a consideration, not only of the particular hazards of various occupations, but also of losses (pure premium) and of expense (expense loading). Expense is, therefore, not only a relevant, but an essential factor to be considered.*
>
> *It is true that the commissioner in the past has always reflected this expense factor in the rate by means of a flat percentage loading. But there is nothing in the statute which expressly or impliedly restricts him to that [method].*

and:

> *. . . the effect [of McConnell's plan] will be to promote competition between all types of workmen's compensation insurance carriers and to reduce rates charged to the public.*

and:

> *Legislation must be given elastic operation if it is to cope with changing economic and social conditions.*

The regulatory apparatus understood what this meant. So did insurers. It meant that they could get in bed together.

Unintended Consequences

SCIF v. McConnell didn't promote much competition, as the court expected. It did the opposite. It gave practical power to the regulatory apparatus — which had been powerful only in theory — to govern what insurers did in the workers' comp marketplace. It gave insurers the freedom to bedazzle employers with dividends, retros, experience ratings and other gimmicks that don't work well.

Above all, it allowed the regulatory apparatus and the insurers to form their odd relationship.

It was at this point that someone might have done something to change the parameters of workers' comp in America. No one did. Commercial insurers, the state funds and the regulatory apparatus didn't fight again. They accommodated one another in such a way as to allow insurers to charge employers more money, and offer less service, for workers' comp insurance than they do for any other insurance line.

Where woe betides all

The Residual Markets and Other Bad Ideas

If all this makes you think that the commercial marketplace for workers' comp insurance means nothing but trouble, consider what happens to the poor souls who can't get commercial coverage at all.

These luckless people must venture into the residual market, where woe betides all.

The states require that employers cover their workers' comp exposure, but they make it next to impossible for employers and insurers to do business with one another in a rational way. The states intervene in the transaction themselves, and they allow too many others to do the same — lawyers, doctors, you name it.

Inevitably, employers find themselves unable to buy workers' comp insurance at a reasonable price, so they complain to the states. This is reasonable enough, since the states distort the marketplace in the first place.

The states respond by making themselves the insurers of last resort (or, in the case of the six monopolistic states, the insurers of only resort). They set up state-run insurance pools to cover those employers who can't get commercial coverage.

And they bring to grief anyone who dips a toe into the waters of these pools. Government knows how to distort marketplaces, not how to run them. Almost none of the state-run mechanisms functions well.

No fun in the state pools

The most common mechanism is the state pool. The state requires all commercial insurers doing workers' comp business in the state to join the pool; each must accept otherwise unacceptable employers to a degree commensurate with its share of the commercial market.

Employers have no fun in these pools. The states set premiums for pool business, and they are never cheap. Employers in the pools pay as much as two or three times what they would pay for commercial insurance. Worse, when the pools fall into deficit, the states commonly assess commercial carriers in proportion to their market share to make up the difference.

The insurers, of course, pass these assessments on to employers in the voluntary market in the form of higher premiums. These employers subsidize the state pools, and the employers in them who make no effort to keep the workplace safe, whether they like it or not.

Some states — notably California and Idaho — operate funds that compete with commercial carriers. Oregon runs a discrete corporate entity called SAIF that insures all risks. Almost alone among the state-run enterprises, SAIF succeeds. It runs so efficiently that it has chased most commercial carriers out of the state.

Easy Promises

In other states, when politicians and the workers' comp bureaucracies set these funds up, of course they promise to make them self-sustaining. The pools almost never are. They don't underwrite the business they get; they simply accept it. Business gravitates to the pools, and commercial carriers abandon the marketplace. The trend accelerates, and sooner or later it threatens to overwhelm everybody. Most state funds teeter on the brink of disaster year after year.

Employers fall into the pools because they have no choice. Some can't get commercial coverage because they show high rates of workplace injury. Some can't get commercial coverage because they're small and the big insurers don't want to bother with them. Some have no choice because their state fund acts as the sole provider of workers' comp insurance and commercial carriers just don't sell the coverage at all.

Don't go near the water

Whatever the cause, the grim certainty for the employer who falls into a state pool is that workers' comp coverage will cost more next year than it did this, and more the year after that, and more the year after that.

The better idea is not to fall into the pool in the first place. But if it happens, don't think the game over. Every employer has the means at hand to solve his or her workers' comp problem by using the techniques analysed in this book. The state pools may indeed represent the very worst that can befall an employer; to be sure, with their deficits and assessments and bailouts, the funds do nothing to solve anybody's problem, even in the short run. But the employer who wants to solve the problem can do so irrespective of anything the state may throw in the way, including the state funds.

The Employer's Best Bet

What can you do? Assuming that you stay in the voluntary market, you pester your insurance broker and your workers' comp carrier about your coverage. How aggressively does the insurer defend itself—and you—against abusive, if small, claims? To what point does it just pay claims without questioning them? What triggers an investigation?[2] Exactly what does it do when investigating? Can it show a track record in fighting abuse — claims denied, maybe abusers arrested?

What does the carrier do about doctors and other health care professionals who milk the system? Does it even know who the bad guys are in your area? What does it do about cost containment in general?

---

[2]You make sense of your carrier's answers to these questions by looking at some numbers of your own. For example, you know you need a new carrier if yours never investigates a claim costing less than $15,000 and all of your claims come in at $14,500.)

Small insurers fight hard

What about loss control and safety programming? Exactly how much of these services does your premium buy?

A rule of thumb: Small carriers fight harder than big carriers, for good reason. They can't afford big claims any more than you can.

This may run counter to your intuition about insurers, but it's true. A smaller, nimbler, more aggressive, less well-capitalized carrier may well prove the better choice when it comes to workers' comp insurance. Even big employers like small workers' comp insurers. In a deposition for litigation against an employee unhappy with his settlement, the president of a California-based defense subcontractor said:

> *. . . we sought out a smaller carrier. And we did it intentionally.*
>
> *We'd used a number of larger carriers in the past, including Chubb and Liberty Mutual. And we weren't happy with their willingness to settle just about every claim anyone filed.*
>
> *We complained about what we thought were several bogus claims. They didn't respond.*

As this employer understood, scrappy carriers pressure workers' comp costs downward, especially in states which allow insurers to compete on price.[3] Where they don't compete on price, the scrappers earn their keep by fighting abusive claims.

Bags of Tricks: A Case Study

It's tough to fight an insurer's tendency to settle quickly. It's even tougher to fight your insurer when it tries some other trick on you. You lose if you don't keep your eyes open; insurers fill bags of tricks just for the workers' comp marketplace — as one small New Orleans employer discovered when its insurer changed the terms of its policy upon renewal, without doing much to inform the client. The change cost the employer, tugboat operator Mike Hooks, Inc., a pot of money.

Hooks operated along the Mississippi River, employing over-the-water and yard workers. Its argument with the insurer stemmed from technicalities in the

---

[3]Not all do. Indiana, for example, allows competition only in theory; in reality the state fixes prices, so employers don't get much help.

workers' comp policy that might have escaped the notice of another employer.

Proper notice in the policy

In 1973 Argonaut-Southwest Insurance — without explanation — issued two separate policies on Hooks' operations containing technical clauses governing the experience modification upon which the insurer calculated Hooks' premium.

Hooks complained. Checking its books, it discovered that Argonaut had applied an ex-mod of 66 percent only to Hooks' land operations, not to its over-the-water operations. Hooks thought the ex-mod should apply to both. It sued Argonaut in late 1975.

The Authority to Apply

Argonaut blandly answered by citing the rules of the Southeastern Compensation Rating Bureau (SCRB), to which all regional insurers belonged and to which they reported their losses for rate-setting purposes. Argonaut said it wasn't sure whether the rules gave it authority to apply the ex-mod to all of Hooks' operations.

Hooks persisted. Argonaut responded by raising the rates for Hooks' over-the-water coverages in an amount that nullified what Hooks might have saved with the ex-mod credit.

In court, Hooks argued on two grounds: that the ex-mod should apply to all of its operations, and that the insurer had slipped the technicalities into its policy without informing Hooks in proper fashion.

Hooks won the first round; the trial court ruled Argonaut just plain wrong. But the tugboat operator lost on appeal.

The appeals court ruled that the policies themselves clearly specified the basis on which Argonaut calculated premiums. And it tossed out the procedural argument on the grounds that Hooks, after all, had the policies, and they unambiguously contained the (vague) technicalities in question.

As Hooks learned to its sorrow, the bottom line here is that an insurance policy is a contract, and you'd better learn what it says. You can't plead ignorance,

Find an insurer to fit your needs

and you can't demand that your insurer interpret the policy for you.

A Fog of Words

You'll have a tough time finding a workers' comp insurer you like. But don't give up when you run into the fog of words with which insurers envelop their policies.

Instead, think of the process as something akin to evolution, or maybe a good marriage: It doesn't happen overnight. Take a step here and a step there, and never forget that your goal is to solve your own workers' comp problem, not somebody else's.

Look for a small, aggressive insurer willing to challenge the marginal claim. Get to know your carrier. Check into its practices in settling claims; some states keep files on these things. Pay attention to the insurer's underwriting of your company, especially to its methodology in calculating your premium.

Different insurers operate differently, so match the practices of your insurer with the needs of your enterprise. Small differences are important — for example, the insurer's flashpoint for investigating claims.

Read your policy. Be skeptical but not completely dismissive of dividend plans. Consider the dividend a bonus; don't count on it to make your premium affordable. Look long and hard at the cost containment tactics suggested elsewhere in this book, because if you want your insurer to play straight with you when calculating the dividend, you must muster the best injury avoidance efforts possible. The challenge may do great things for your company, but don't count on this alone to guarantee a dividend from a reluctant insurer.

You avoid a lot of trouble if you hook up with the right carrier. They're hard to find, but they're out there.

Chapter 10: Self-Insurance

If the toil and trouble of the workers' comp system produces any good at all, it is without doubt the trend toward self-insurance. Every employer should give serious thought to the idea because, to the degree that each embraces it, each solves the workers' comp problem once and for all.

Solving the problem once and for all

Not everyone can self-insure; some states don't allow it at all, and where they do allow it, not all employers have the resources to take advantage of the option. But where they can, they should — because self-insurance gives the employer the opportunity to put the workers' comp problem to rest for good. It allows the employer to take control, to pre-empt those who contort the workers' comp system for their own ends, and to reestablish the old bargain between employer and employee with respect to the cost of workplace injury.

In setting up a self-insurance program, the employer commits to doing many of the things an insurer does: accumulating and managing cash reserves, administering claims, setting up loss control programs, and dealing with lots of paperwork.

Big Firms Take the Lead

Large companies make the process work most effectively, but this doesn't leave small employers out in the cold. A number of techniques lie at hand to enable the small employer to accomplish the same end.

Few employers regret the undertaking. The payoff is just too big.

In the short run self-insurance allows the employer to escape the high premiums of workers' comp insurance and the dead certainty that, no matter what one's claims experience, premiums will go up next year. In the long run self-insurance allows the employer to gain complete control over all workers' comp costs ranging from premiums to claims.

The decisive factor: cost

Cost control lies at the heart of any good self-insurance program, and cost control helps any employer. Self-insurance doesn't come cheaply, however; it costs money and time. But the workers' comp system costs money and time anyway. Worse, whatever it costs now, it will cost more in the future unless employers take matters in hand. No one sees an end to the spiralling increases in insurance premiums, for one thing. No one expects that the legislatures will embrace real reform, or that honorable work will lure lawyers and doctors away from the spoils of the workers' comp system, or that workers will cease abusing the system.

But against all this, the trend to self-insurance emerges as a positive. More and more employers turn to it every year, big and little, private and public. They turn to it because they have no alternative. They turn to it because if they don't, the problem threatens to overwhelm them.

In doing so they seize the initiative from parties who have no real interest in solving the problem: insurance bureaucracies, politicians, lawyers, doctors, and workers. All of these people fish in the vast and unseemly tides of money flowing through the workers' comp system. The employer who self-insures leaves these parties with one less fish to fry. The employer who self-insures reforms the workers' comp system without the "help" of people who don't want it reformed.

The Mechanics

You really have two options when you consider self-insurance. You can self-insure your workers' comp exposure from beginning to end, shielding yourself only from massive loss with excess insurance coverage, or you can shoulder only part of the problem with a large deductible. Seen correctly, these options become variations on one theme, the difference between them being only the degree to which you shoulder responsibility.

A third alternative — joining a risk pool — transfers the risk to the group, so it qualifies as self-insurance only insofar as it cuts commercial insurers out of the picture. Still, risk pools give the employer a greater degree of control over the workers' comp problem than, say, commercial insurance or, worse, the state pools, so we consider them here in this light.

It cuts insurers out of the picture

If you shoulder all of your exposure, you take the more expensive of the two main options — and you give yourself the greater chance to solve your problem in its entirety.

You start by steeling yourself to deal with your state regulators on your own. They don't make it easy to set up a self-insurance program. They have rules for the employer who self-insures, and they make sure that everyone follows them. Some states require that the self-insurer back his or her claims-paying ability with cash reserves to strict limits. Some require $500,000 to $750,000, set aside as a so-called "stand premium." Some require a surety bond, some letters of credit. Twenty-six states require that self-insurers contribute to a guaranty fund, designed to pick up the pieces should a self-insurer go belly up. The states impose numerous other regulations as well, including lots of paperwork. A state-by-state rundown of these requirements appears in Appendix Twenty-Five to this book.

A Lengthy Process

Even when you have all your ducks in a row, the states can take months to approve an application to self-insure — sometimes as long as four months. You muster all the patience you have when you begin this process, because you'll need it.

But don't let your efforts flag. Look on the obstacles the states put in your way as the price you pay for solving your workers' comp problem. And remember the alternative: *not* solving your workers' comp problem.

In establishing your program you become your own insurer. You set up your accounting and administrative services, and you reserve for yourself the right to figure out the fairest and least costly way to handle claims, not to mention the right to decide which claims to fight and how hard to fight them.

Farming some services out

You tailor your loss control services to fit your own needs. You find the best way to impose cost containment on the health care professionals who treat your injured employees.

You may decide to contract some of these services out. If you do, however, you must give the providers of these services a stake in the outcome — in the same way that you would give an employee a stake in the outcome of a successful unit within your enterprise. You don't want an outside claims administrator, for example, who merely adds up the cost of your claims, tacks on overhead and profit, and sends you a bill. That's what insurers do, and they have in mind their own bottom line, not yours.

Don't make light of the costs of administering your self-insurance program. Administration, claims handling, loss control, and accounting and actuarial services can eat up as much as one-third of the total budget for your self-insurance program. Go about setting up these services carefully. Keep your bottom line in mind.

Most self-insurers buy excess workers' comp coverage to shield themselves from the catastrophic claim. To their surprise, they find an active marketplace for this kind of coverage: plenty of insurers willing to do business with them at reasonable cost. Why? Insurers fear the commercial workers' comp marketplace because, like employers, they cede control to others when they enter it. They love the excess workers' comp marketplace, on the other hand, because they know that somebody they can trust — the employer — exercises control over the basic forces that distort the commercial marketplace.

The Large Deductible

For the same reason they make themselves reasonably available to the employer who wants to buy commercial workers' comp insurance with a large deductible.

This form of self-insurance appeals to the employer who doesn't have the resources to take on sole responsibility for the workers' comp exposure. The employer buys a commercial workers' comp policy with a deductible running somewhere over $100,000 per claim. Many carriers write deductibles ranging to $500,000. Big carriers — for example, Travelers Corp. — write deductibles as high as $2 million per claim.

As much control as possible

The idea here is that the employer self-insures to the limit of the deductible. Commonly the employer pegs the deductible to his or her own claims history. If yours shows claims averaging $100,000 in the aggregate over the last three years, talk to your insurer about a deductible in that range. If you show claims aggregating $500,000, go for that. Better yet, go for a deductible slightly higher than your aggregate so as to give yourself as much control as possible.

If you have limited resources, the payoff is that the big deductible allows you to police the people who abuse the system exactly to the extent that you can afford to. As they get into it, many employers find that they have a greater ability to police these people than they expected themselves. Big deductibles work.

Big Cuts in Premiums

Insurers don't impose stringent requirements on employers who want big deductibles, so those with tight capital constraints still qualify. Small employers find that they cut workers' comp insurance premiums by as much as two-thirds. Better yet, they don't take on the administrative burdens that self-insurance plans require. In most states, the employer doesn't need regulatory approval for a big deductible.

The employer thus gets most of the benefits of true self-insurance without the big headaches.

As the deductible gets really big, the underlying insurance policy comes to resemble the excess coverage that employers buy when self-insuring. A policy with a $500,000 deductible requires the employer to absorb all of his or her workers' comp claims to that limit — which is to say, most claims altogether. Even better, most commercial insurers offer loss control and cost containment services that excess lines carriers don't provide. So you don't have to go without; insurers make these services

Pool members share the risk

readily available to the employer with a big deductible.

The downside to the big deductible: The underlying policy remains a commercial insurance policy from a commercial insurer. The employer thus remains in the clutches of the commercial insurance marketplace and so cedes control over workers' comp in important ways. As the marketplace erodes, the employer pays the escalating premium of the underlying coverage and runs the risk that the insurer will abandon the marketplace.

Spreading the Exposure

Employers flock to risk pools when they can't get big-deductible workers' comp insurance or qualify as self-insurers. Risk pools consist of employers who set up a sort of co-op insurer to spread the workers' comp exposure among themselves. The members of the group share and self-insure their risk.

Risk pools emerge as the alternative mechanism of choice for the small employer as the commercial workers' comp insurance marketplace deteriorates. Risk pools insulate the small employer from the vagaries of the commercial marketplace and, properly structured, give the small employer much of the cost-fighting flexibility of the big deductible.

The employers form a trust with reserves capitalized by the members. The trust insures the members' workers' comp exposure to limits commonly set by state law, with excess coverage for anything beyond that. The trust provides such services as claims handling and loss control on its own or else secures them from third parties.

The trust must abide by all regulations applying to self-insurers — which means that it goes through the same obstacle course that taxes the patience of the employer who goes it alone. Many states require that risk pools acquire excess coverage against catastrophic loss. Some want to see a bond covering the administrator of a risk pool.

Risk pools commonly require the new member to pony up a contribution to capital. Over time, members fund claims and ongoing expenses with regular payments, much as they would pay premiums to a commercial insurer. These contributions change with the fortunes of the risk pool; good times mean low contributions, and big claims mean big contributions.

Benefits come from the employer

Risk pools commonly allow the employer to retain a considerable part of the risk — in effect, a big deductible. From this flow many benefits, ranging from cash flow to the opportunity to control losses and medical costs.

A Vital Step

You don't dilute your responsibility by joining a risk pool; you take part in running your own insurance company. And when an injured employee makes a claim, the pool settles through the employer. This is important. A risk pool gives its members direct say in defending and settling claims — maybe the single most vital step in employer empowerment. The injured employee sees money coming from the employer, not from the deep pockets of a faceless insurer. The transaction promotes the bond between employer and employee and makes it harder for either to abuse the other.

Meanwhile the employer benefits from the financial leverage of the group. This helps in purchasing excess coverage and in contracting for (or staffing) administrative and claims handling services, not to mention loss control and cost containment programs. The leverage extends to investment income as well; a larger capital base means bigger income for the risk pool. Last but not least, a risk pool doesn't pay commissions to insurance brokers.

In short a well-run risk pool covers the workers' comp exposure far more efficiently than commercial carriers or the state pools possibly can. It brings the tight-fistedness of true self-insurance to employers who can't get it otherwise. Risk pools don't just talk of reform; they give the employer hands-on control. But they aren't always perfect solutions, especially if the members don't join together at arm's length to operate the pool.

It isn't easy to underwrite the businesses of the members if they vary greatly in size and business,

Pools must treat members equally

for one thing. For another, it's all too easy to dispute costs and other day-to-day things. A well-run risk pool treats all members equally and favors none — hard to do when one or two members of the pool dominate its affairs.

Risk pools present the employer with long-term obstacles, too.

Joining a risk pool usually locks the employer in for extended periods of time. This limits the employer's flexibility if the future changes the employer's insurance needs. This becomes especially problematic when a company grows quickly or changes its profile.

In most states the pool must comply with the same requirements that apply to individual self-insurers. In some cases this can mean divulging proprietary information the members may not want to share with one another.

Joint and Several Liability

Worst of all, the members of a pool take on joint and several liability, so a series of big losses can deplete the pool's assets and require sudden new contributions to capital. If one member goes bankrupt, the others foot the bill for the workers' comp exposure.

This liability presents the biggest disadvantage in a risk pool. It's like a marriage; a good one's great and a bad one's hellish, but good or bad, while you're in it, you share everything.

In addition, like a bad marriage, a risk pool can collapse quickly, and you don't want yours to fold just when you get a claim from an injured employee.

The bottom line: Join a risk pool with your eyes open. Make sure the pool does its homework — on the members as well as on their workers' comp exposure. The pool must be sound, so the members must be sound, too. The group must qualify them carefully; it must underwrite membership with all the meticulous care of a picky insurer.

A well-run risk pool should save its members 30 percent of their workers' comp costs, maybe as much as 40 percent.

One example: The members of Greater Portland V, a group of small to mid-sized employers in Maine, cut their workers' comp premiums more than 40 percent upon joining the pool. All had bought coverage from Maine's basket-case state pool. The group attributes its success to its safety and cost containment programs.

Big savings on premiums

Another: The Archdiocese of Boston formed a group program in 1990 for Catholic business entities in Massachusetts. This pool saved its members well over 20 percent, on average, by streamlining administration and eliminating insurer overhead and profit.

The Statistics

No one doubts that the problems in workers' comp around the country lie behind the boom in self-insurance. The states have helped by liberalizing their insurance laws to allow a broader mix of employers to form risk pools.

The dramatic results: According to insurance giant Johnson & Higgins, risk financing alternatives accounted for 33.6 percent — or $62.3 billion — of the $185.2 billion in the total workers' comp market in 1991. Johnson & Higgins expected the share to hit 34.3 percent in 1992. By way of contrast, alternative financing took less than 10 percent of the insurance market in the 1970s.

The study defined risk financing alternatives as self-insurance, high-deductible policies, risk pools and mechanisms such as captive and policyholder-owned insurers.

Without doubt, workers' comp was the engine that drove this trend. Most employers in high-risk industries — for example, chemical and drug manufacturers — bailed out of the commercial workers' comp insurance market long before 1990. In 1991 alone, self-insured workers' comp programs produced the equivalent of $19.4 billion in premiums, up 27 percent from 1990. In 1992, industry experts expected the number to jump another 15 to 20 percent.

For the first time ever, short-term savings — i.e., the thought of next year's premiums — motivate em-

Hands-on loss control program

ployers to self-insure. Commercial insurers can't compete any longer. Self-insurers save money from the first premium dollar. They avoid the exorbitant costs of the basket case state pools. They eliminate the costs of insurer overhead and profit, not to mention broker commissions. They benefit from the income generated by their own investments. They reduce claims with hands-on loss control programs and claims management.

The Smarter Idea

And, once in a risk pool, they do almost anything to stay in, as the case of Smitty's Super Valu, Inc., shows. The company operates 24 grocery stores in the Phoenix, Arizona area. A unit of the Canadian conglomerate Steinberg International, it has self-insured its workers' comp since 1976.

But it went through shaky times, making Arizona regulators nervous and putting its self-insurance program in jeopardy.

Steinberg International put Smitty's up for sale in 1988 but couldn't find a buyer. In 1990, Smitty's cut 300 jobs. It was the second most popular grocery chain in Phoenix, but it lost money — $12.1 million in 1990 and $5.3 million in 1991, according to Arizona's Industrial Commission, which regulates self-insurance programs.

This brought trouble from the Food and Commercial Workers Union when Smitty's applied to renew its self-insurance program in 1992. The union had sought to organize the company's workers for more than one year, with mixed results. It objected to the grocer's shaky finances, leading regulators to consider new conditions that would mean higher reserves for Smitty's.

More specifically, the union charged that Smitty's had discouraged workers from filing claims. The union offered up one employee who had suffered an injury in June 1991 but filed no claim because she'd been told that it would cost her job. The union wanted the commission to revoke Smitty's self-insurance program.

But Smitty's executives knew that if they couldn't self-insure, their workers' comp costs would become prohibitive. They would have to consider downsizing or closing completely.

The Arizona Industrial Commission took the middle road, ruling that Smitty's must increase its reserves from $489,000 to $980,000.

Smitty's quickly agreed; despite its overall losses, the company considered the extra $500,000 cheap compared to the cost of getting workers' comp coverage from the state pool. The company happily agreed even to send its managers to training courses on handling claims.

Like other employers who join pools, Smitty's knew that its position would significantly worsen if it didn't go along with the change. An increase of 100 percent in its reserve requirements was bad enough. The alternative was worse.

A private solution to a public problem

How Politicians and Regulators React

If employers love risk pools, politicians hate them. So do insurers, and for the same reason. Like self-insurance programs, risk pools allow the employer to take the workers' comp problem into his or her own hands; they allow the employer to solve a public problem by private means. This, of course, leaves the public problem in the hands of those who have no interest in solving it — politicians and commercial insurers. And it only worsens the conditions they face. Like self-insurance programs, risk pools skim the cream off of the top of the insurance market, leaving commercial carriers and the state pools with employers they would rather not cover.

Politicians respond by trying to force employers back into the marketplace for commercial workers' comp insurance. More specifically, they want to tax risk pools as they tax insurers. They haven't succeeded just yet, but they'll be back.

They started trying to curb self-insurance as early as 1987. With a little help from lobbyists for the plaintiffs' bar and some larger insurers, the House Ways and Means Committee proposed to tax capital reserves set aside for settling workers' comp claims. Hundreds of firms across the country had begun forming risk pools. The pols smelled the chance to make some money.

The pols smell money

Among those who fought back was the Detroit Tooling Association, which represents more than 700 high-risk machine tool companies and 40,000 workers in Michigan. The association figured that it would owe the government $18 million if the Ways and Means proposal became law. Richard Moore, who administered the group's fund, testified that the proposal threatened the jobs of hundreds of Michigan workers and thousands more in other states.

'Unfair' to Commercial Insurers

Until 1986, the Internal Revenue Service had ignored self-insurers, by and large. Then it audited several funds in Michigan — notably the Detroit Tooling Association's — and found more treasure than it had imagined.

It decided to pursue the matter.

A special assistant for tax policy at the Treasury Department told the Ways and Means Committee that the government considered the current state of things unfair to commercial insurers.

Rep. John Dingell, the powerful Michigan Democrat, intervened on behalf of employers. He sponsored legislation that temporarily prevented the IRS from taxing risk pools. His fellow Michigan Congressman Guy Vander Jagt followed with a bill giving self-insurance reserves permanent tax-free status. After some bickering, it became law in 1988. The legislation allows the employer to exclude contributions to self-insurance reserves from earnings as "non-cash charges." This reduces net income, on which the employer figures taxes.

But self-insurance continues to worry regulators.

By the early 1990s, so many employers self-insured that the state systems started looking for ways to get in on the action. In 1992, for example, the Iowa legislature considered a bill to force self-insurers to shoulder part of the responsibility for deficits in the state pool. Other states will doubtless follow suit.

The backers of such ideas complain that, as good employers flee the commercial markets, the remaining risk base shrinks and becomes volatile — a flight of quality. They portray those employers who remain as the victims of this flight.

All of which is true enough.

But those employers who flee show themselves willing to solve the workers' comp problem. The employers they leave behind show themselves incapable of doing the same. So do the pols and insurers.

In the best of all possible worlds the pols and insurers would just get out of the way. But they possess the means of imposing their will on those who know how to solve their own problems, so the smart employer figures that they will assault self-insurers again, given the chance.

A Formidable Alliance

Will they succeed? Probably not, because they would encounter fierce opposition from local government.

Public entities didn't invent self-insurance, but they surely gave the idea currency. In the 1980s, commercial carriers either declined to write workers' comp coverage for local government altogether — cities, counties, schools — or else wrote it only at prohibitive cost. In this they did not act arbitrarily, of course. The plaintiff's bar had discovered a rich lode in liability litigation against small government, and the market responded.

Liability coverage simply became too dear. Small government couldn't afford it.

This forced public entities into self-insurance. They had no choice — just as increasing numbers of private employers have no choice. Forced to rely on themselves, public entities found a solution in self-insurance and risk pools — just as employers do.

The bottom line: The employer who opts for self-insurance won't stand alone when the pols attack self-insurers again.

The pols surely will attack, but when they show up they will find a powerful alliance arrayed against them: private and public employers who, finding themselves locked out of the marketplace for com-

Benefits for dubious injuries

mercial workers' comp insurance, solved the problem on their own.

A Public Sector Case Study

In February 1989, elected officials in Gloucester County, New Jersey — called freeholders — approved a plan to make their workers' comp exposure self-insured by the end of that year.

The plan didn't just sail through, however. Indeed, it caused county officials to give a hard look at employee safety. One longtime freeholder (the equivalent of a county commissioner) cautioned that, if the county wanted self-insurance to work, it would have to improve employee safety markedly.

That would take some doing, county officials knew.

In 1987, Gloucester County had spent $595,671 for workers' comp insurance written by Philadelphia-based Crum & Forster, which had insured the county for more than 30 years. For years, county officials had privately criticized the firm's claims handling. They went public after learning that in 1988 Crum & Forster had approved payments for injuries as dubious as flea bites.

How much oversight did their premium entitle them to, they wondered. Couldn't the county do better on its own?

It could hardly do worse. Through 1987, Gloucester County had paid the highest rates for workers' comp insurance in Southern New Jersey: $460 per employee. Eight nearby counties spent $257, on average. Alone among the group, Gloucester County bought commercial coverage.

The county's insurance broker had favored self-insurance for some time. He, too, warned that the county must improve job safety. He pointed out that county employees showed a history of expensive claims; in 1988 alone, just six injuries had cost some $276,000—and that didn't count $75,000 for the death of a county engineer whose car was hit by a tree that had been struck by lightning as he drove home from work.

So Gloucester County had a way to go. It found, however, that its safety record improved markedly once the county embarked on a systematic effort to live by the discipline of self-insurance.

Safety record improves

By 1991, Gloucester had implemented a safety program that reduced its workers' comp claims by more than 20 percent. Its settlements still exceeded those in other counties, but the county paid attention now, and the differences weren't so wide as they had been.

Virtually no one in county government regretted the decision. One of the freeholders summed up the improvement: "We needed a system that forced us to be more efficient. And the best way to do that was take care of workers' comp ourselves."

Amen.

Taking the Abusers Out of the Game

Self-insurance dries up the tides of money that entice lawyers and doctors and workers into abusing the system. It takes these people out of the game. It makes it impossible for them to take advantage of the old bargain between employer and employee with respect to workplace injury.

In the short run, self-insurance promises to lower the employer's monthly costs.

But self-insurance has a different, and more profound, effect on those employers who undertake the venture. It forces them to do what others just talk about with respect to worker safety and cost containment.

It forces them to pay attention. And in paying attention they discover all the ways of solving their workers' comp problem presented in this book, quite on their own, without the help of government or commercial insurers.

And in discovering these techniques, they solve the workers' comp problem once and for all.

In short, the employer who self-insures imposes discipline on a marketplace that now operates with-

Great woes

out it — the discipline of the employer who knows whose money it is that disappears into the system.

As time passes and more and more employers turn in desperation to self-insurance, they do indeed leave behind those who cause the problem. With any luck, the woes of these people will become so great that they, too, will see that they have no choice but to assume all of their own exposures but no one else's.

CHAPTER 11: OTHER TOOLS

The choices buy some time

Two drastic options remain open to you if you find no other way to solve your workers' comp problem. You can move your operations to another state, or you can stay where you are and lease your employees.

A moment's thought shows that these options give you only short-term solutions. You merely run away from your problem if you move your operations to another state, because in all likelihood the problem will catch up with you sooner or later. If you lease your employees, you shift the problem onto somebody else's shoulders, maybe illegally and, once again, probably only temporarily — unless you address the underlying forces that drive your costs upward.

In either case, however, you buy some time and the hope that, just maybe, government will solve the workers' comp problem for everybody.

After all, time is money, and some employers find their workers' comp problem so intractable that they turn to one or the other of these two options as their only way out.

Go East, Young Man — or Somewhere

When America was young, the frontier always beckoned the individual caught up in "sivilization," as Huck Finn called it. The frontier lay over the hill, across the river, beyond the mountains. It promised a second chance, and government made it a matter of policy to entice settlers to pick up and go.

Government still does, only this time the settlers are employers. Sometimes government makes it a matter of policy to get employers to move *in* from other states. Sometimes government entices employers to pick up and move *out* by making life so miserable that they really don't have much choice.

Employers flee the big states

California falls into the latter group. Employers began fleeing the Golden State in alarming numbers as the decade began. In 1991, Gov. Pete Wilson and the Democrats in the legislature hit Californians with the biggest tax increase in the state's history, and employers grew restive.

When someone asked one Democratic legislator whether the new taxes might drive employers elsewhere, the legislator laughed. "Oh sure," he said. "They're going to take all those yachts from Newport Harbor and move them to Nevada."

As it happened, the legislator had it wrong. Employers didn't take their yachts to Nevada. They took their businesses. They left their yachts behind so that they might have a reason to come back to California for a visit.

The Pluses and Minuses

And they left in droves. According to one study, in five years 668 employers either moved elsewhere or cancelled plans to expand operations in California. Hughes Aerospace Corp., for example, moved a missile-building operation and 4,500 jobs from Southern California to Yuma, Arizona, in 1992. The big defense contractor added up the pluses and minuses between Arizona and California, and California came up short. It studied taxes, the regulatory burden, utilities, labor costs, housing and — high on the list — workers' comp costs. Arizona came out better in almost every instance.

Hughes Aerospace left behind a government that puts as many obstacles as possible in the way of the employer who wants to open a new business. An angry Wilson chanted that employers needed some 80 permits to get a business going in Los Angeles, and if they survived the ordeal, they still had the state's dizzying workers' comp system to contend with.

California wasn't alone in its troubles. The early 1990s saw businesses flee such states as New York, Florida and Illinois to set up shop in North and South Dakota, the Carolinas, Arkansas and Arizona.

Small states compete actively to recruit business, and the big states don't stand a chance in this game.

The small states know very well that employers get itchy when they spend more time complying with state and local law than they do making and selling product. They also know which states make life uncongenial, and in what ways.

Knowing just what to say

So they know exactly what to say about your problems when they come to visit with you about your plans for the future.

Indeed, the small states spend millions of dollars to entice employers to pack up and leave the big city. They keep business recruiters on the road beating the bushes for employers who will listen to their pitches.

Iowa touts itself as "the smart state for business." It offers a range of incentives for employers, starting with workers' comp insurance rates that undercut those in California and New York by as much as 50 percent. The state maintains a venture capital resources fund with $11 million targeting young, growing businesses. It keeps another $4.6 million in a community economic betterment account for companies that come in and create jobs.

The state's business information center, near Des Moines, fielded 6,000 calls from business owners in 1991.

Low Taxes

Nevada, meanwhile, levies no personal income tax, no corporate tax and no inventory tax. Its workers' comp costs rank among the lowest in the country. And like other small states, it doesn't care how small your enterprise is.

"We target businesses with about 10 employees," boasts Jim Spoo, executive director of the Nevada Economic Development Commission in Carson City. "Moving small companies is easy."

About half of Nevada's new businesses move in from California. In 1991 and 1992 alone, some 65 employers moved to Nevada, bringing more than 2,500 jobs with them. The state has become a mecca for warehouses and distribution centers.

Arizona, Idaho, the Carolinas, Georgia and even Michigan all run successful recruiting operations.

The bond between employer and employee

Every week, recruiters from these and other states travel across California, enticing employers to move. They emphasize California's steep workers' comp insurance rates, high taxes and stringent air-pollution and environmental control laws.

Time and again, the workers' comp system comes up as a decisive factor for the small employer. In 1991, Russ Cosby, president of a carpet manufacturing company called Artistic Sample, told California lawmakers that he had cut his workers' comp costs from $300,000 a year to a mere $20,000 by moving his operation — and 60 jobs — from California to Georgia.

"My sales were $2 million a year. So California's workers' comp cost was 15 percent of my sales." Cosby said. "I just couldn't make it."

He couldn't resist when recruiters from Georgia described their lower workers' comp rates and the package of tax benefits they could offer. He kept only a small sales office in California and didn't look back.

Overcoming Inertia

You can't know what lies ahead when you pick up and move from one place to another. What you can know is that you leave your workers' comp troubles behind, at least for a while. For countless employers, that's enough. It comes down to a question of short-term dollars and cents.

But you leave your workers behind, too — usually jobless. You sever the bond between employer and employee, and you add some bodies to the line at the state unemployment office. It's hard to do this without mixed feelings; as an employer, you enable others to provide for themselves and their families, and when you go elsewhere, you leave these people and their families to their own devices.

It will come as no consolation whatever to discover that some of your employees file workers' comp claims as you hit the state line. Indeed, as you plot the pros and cons of moving, you must take into account the fact that some will file and that, in the very short term, you worsen the workers' comp problem by leaving. You make it a dead certainty that one or more of your employees — angry and frustrated, no doubt, at your departure — will seek benefits from the very system whose woes you seek to flee.

Paydirt for lawyers

The lawyers who troll the unemployment offices don't care where you go or why. Indeed, some of them specialize in signing up people whose employers leave them in the lurch. They fly into towns facing factory closures, and they sign up everybody they can reach. Factory closures make for perfect stress claims; sometimes they make for good class-action suits — paydirt for the plaintiff's lawyer.

Somebody else picks up the pieces for you when this happens, namely the employers in your old state, along with their insurers, so that in this sense you solve your own problem but you add to the problems of others.

You also present yourself with a host of obstacles. You must scout a new location. You must plot out your costs in great detail, taking into account what you will spend winding down your business in the old location and getting it started again in the new. You must tally the money you won't make in the interval. You must move yourself and, in some cases, your key people. You must make contact with people and businesses in your new location — local officials, suppliers, utilities. You must hire and train new employees.

Does this mean that you should stay put? Of course not. Employers move from one state to another when it makes financial sense, and it makes financial sense when the employer sees no way to exercise control over the forces that distort the workers' comp system — and when the state to which you move makes you an offer you can't refuse.

Employee Leasing

Not surprisingly, many employers turn to employee leasing before they up and move away.

Employee leasing builds on the idea of the temporary worker farmed out by a temp agency for a week here, a week there. In the past such agencies specialized in low-skill workers such as filing clerks, receptionists and the like — people who could fill in for

An escape from high rates

vacationing employees, for example. As the workers' comp crisis ripened, however, such agencies saw an opportunity. At the moment more than 1,300 employee leasing companies farm out roughly 1 million employees nationwide, according to the Aegis Group, a California-based consulting firm that specializes in employee leasing. Most of these companies operate in the Sunbelt. Aegis expects the industry to expand by about 20 percent a year throughout the decade.

The employee leasing organization essentially hires the employer's workforce and then leases the same people right back to the employer. The workers become employees of the leasing organization, not the original employer.

Leasing companies usually charge a fee of 1 to 5 percent of the client company's payroll for administrative services such as payroll processing. Premiums for health and workers' compensation benefits go on top of this fee.

But the payoff is that the employer often saves a bundle on workers' comp costs. Here's how:

Unlike health insurance, workers' comp doesn't come with volume discounts. You don't cut your premium by showing your carrier a big payroll; you cut it by improving your accident record.

Alternative to the Pools

Good record or bad, however, many small companies must buy their workers' comp insurance from the state pools, commonly because the employers can't interest an insurer in their business. And as we have seen, the state pools charge high rates.

But even employers with poor accident records can cut their workers' comp costs through employee leasing. The key is to give the leasing firm free rein in improving safety and containing costs. Good leasing companies gain expertise in these matters because they know that their own profits depend on it. Many conduct safety inspections of client companies and require them to appoint a safety manager. Once an accident occurs, the leasing company oversees treatment. It steers the injured worker to specialists who treat injured employees for discounted fees. It keeps tabs on the treatment, maintains contact with the injured worker, and gets the worker back on the job.

The leasing company, in short, does nothing more than the employer does who decides to take control of the workers' comp problem. It ensures that employers maintain a safe workplace, that doctors don't get greedy, that lawyers stay out of the picture, and that injured employees don't malinger.

Do your homework first

Does this mean that you should sign up with the first employee leasing company that comes knocking on your door? Absolutely not. Employee leasing is a good idea, and it works for growing numbers of employers. But the better idea is to seize control of the problem yourself. If you can't, or if you consider it wiser to pay a leasing company to do it for you, keep your eyes open.

Before signing up with any employee leasing company, make sure that you get the details on its workers' comp coverage. Is it commercially insured or self-insured? Does it carry a high deductible? If so, what relationship exists between the deductible and the firm's aggregate claims over the last three years? What about its safety record? Its settlement history? Its cost containment practices?

The good leasing companies help employers cut costs by screening job applicants, by establishing effective workplace safety programs, and by actively managing claims once an injury occurs. Check into all of these in detail.

Beware of new leasing companies that manipulate the system to slash premiums.

Two Caveats

For the very small employer, the switch to leasing means giving up your exemption from certain state and federal regulations that apply only to larger employees.

The Americans with Disabilities Act, for example, applies to employers of more than 25 people. The employer of fewer people becomes subject to this

'The next guy up the ladder'

law upon entering into a leasing arrangement because the workforce becomes part of the leasing company's larger group.

The other big pitfall: You pick up the pieces if your employee leasing company does a disappearing act.

Since 1989, half a dozen large leasing companies employing some 36,000 workers have collapsed, leaving hundreds of small employers and their workers responsible for millions of dollars in health care and workers' compensation claims. CAP Staffing, a North Carolina-based leasing firm, closed its doors in 1989 after less than a year in operation. It left behind some $2.2 million in unpaid health claims in eight states. Company officials allegedly drained money from company accounts to pay personal debts. The company's president pled guilty to multiple counts of fraud and went to federal prison.

If your leasing company folds, your employees get stuck with their unpaid health insurance claims. You get the tab for workers' comp (and maybe the health care costs, too, if your employees come after you in court).

Paragon Industries, Inc., an Oklahoma-based manufacturer of oilfield pipe employing more than 125 workers, took a hit of $350,000 in unpaid claims after its leasing company, Alliance Temporary Services, Inc., failed to purchase workers' comp coverage and went belly up.

Paragon remained liable even though its contract with the leasing company promised coverage. "The state goes after the next guy up the ladder," says a company spokesman.

Budding Regulation

In the worst-case scenario you break the law if you lease your employees from a crooked organization.

How? The scam occurs when the leasing organization pulls a fast one on its own workers' comp insurer. The organization may misclassify the workers, fudge their claims histories (which is to say, your claims history), or otherwise defraud the insurance carrier.

In some cases, employee leasing companies disappear one day only to reappear the next under another name. This presents the insurer with what appears to be a new business with a new staff — hence no claims history, hence a low premium for workers' comp insurance. The employee leasing company pulls another phoenix act as soon as it starts posting claims.[1]

The states want to clamp down

Regulators investigate when they think that employee leasing companies finesse classifications and insurance rates. And when they can, they go after the original employer, too.

"We think there's a lot of this going on," says an Ohio workers' comp official. "They're pressed hard to offer competitive costs. And it's relatively easy for them to do. A lot of them can't resist telling a few lies."

On the Way

Employee leasing provokes much heated discussion in the insurance industry, and regulation is on the way. Some proposals would require that employee leasing companies submit to regulation by the state insurance departments. The NCCI has proposed a model regulation system, specifically aimed at eliminating the cost advantages of employee leasing. This plan is being studied in 37 states, including Missouri and Illinois. The National Association of Insurance Commissioners has incorporated some of these ideas into model laws it recommends for state adoption.

Since 1991, four states — Florida, Arkansas, Maine, and Utah — have passed laws regulating the industry. At least seven more have legislation under consideration. Florida requires that leasing companies obtain licensing from a state board and show a tangible net worth of $50,000 each year and positive working capital. The Arkansas statute calls for licensing fees of up to $5,000 a year plus a $50,000 bond, or equivalent securities, or a financial statement showing a net worth of $100,000.

---

[1]See Chapter 6: Fraud and Abuse

Hot on the trail of the scammers

Good, well-capitalized employee-leasing companies take the lead in promoting federal and state laws to protect employers. Industry leaders want Congress to give state and federal regulators greater enforcement powers and to clear up the confusion about who holds responsibility for regulating leasing companies — the states or the federal government. Congress hasn't acted so far, but it may.

Not surprisingly, the NCCI has been hot on the trail of leasing scams. The NCCI cooperates with a group of workers' comp insurers to crack down on premium fraud from all sources. In one case filed by the NCCI, a Texas judge approved a settlement requiring a Louisiana leasing company to pay a group of workers' comp insurers $18 million plus interest. The insurers alleged that a Louisiana trucking firm formed the leasing company just to cut its workers' comp premiums.

This case illustrates the central weakness of employee leasing. A new leasing company starts with a clean safety record and, hence, low premiums. This lures employers with poor safety records and high premiums to switch to the leasing company for a big discount. But without good safety programming and cost containment, the big discounts don't last. Soon the leasing company's experience rating goes into meltdown. Its premiums skyrocket, and the leasing company closes down and starts up under a new name, beginning the cycle again but solving nobody's problem.

The Upside: A Case Study

It doesn't have to work that way. In 1989, Texas entrepreneur David Hinds, a maker of food flavoring extracts, faced a hike of nearly 100 percent in his workers' comp costs — this, on top of increases averaging 20 percent annually for his health insurance. Hinds wasn't sure that his firm, Van Tone Co., would survive.

Hinds looked desperately for a new carrier. He employed 24 people — too few for many commercial insurers to consider. On the advice of a fellow employer, he turned to employee leasing. He saw it as a chance to cut benefit costs and get out from under the mountains of payroll and administrative paperwork.

Hinds settled on Employers Resource Management, an employee leasing company based in Boise, Idaho. The leasing company offered him access to cheaper, pooled health insurance rates not available to small employers. And it cut his workers' comp costs because it showed a better safety record than Hinds did on his own.

A better safety record

The leasing arrangement made it possible for Hinds to expand the benefits offered to his workers, even as he cut costs. The leasing company's health plan added dental and vision care as well as yearly physicals, and it offered a lower deductible and out-of-pocket annual maximum. It gave Hinds' workers access to a credit union.

All in all, Hinds counts himself a satisfied customer. He attributes 70 percent of Van Tone's 1991 profits to savings derived from employee leasing. If it weren't for employee leasing, he believes he'd be out of business.

The Costs Come Back

Hinds did well in leasing his employees, and so do many other employers. Countless others improve matters, at least temporarily, by moving their operations to another state.

But moving and employee leasing don't eliminate the burdens of the workers' comp system. At best they reduce costs temporarily, or deflect them to someone else. At worst they heap more trouble on the workers' comp system as a whole. And in one form or another, the costs come back to the original employer.

The better idea, as we argue throughout this book, is to take matters in hand and solve the workers' comp problem inside the walls of the castle. Don't run away from the problem, and don't foist it off on somebody else. Solve it yourself.

CHAPTER 12: REGULATION

When to fight, when not

We've spent most of our time so far talking about what you can do to limit your financial exposures in the chaotic world of workers' compensation. This chapter helps in another way by taking a look at the regulatory system: the state insurance commissioners, the regulators who work for them, and the state-run dispute resolution processes.

The smart employer avoids these parties when possible, and knows what to expect when it's not possible to do so. The regulatory system presents you with some pretty big odds, and no general goes into battle against such odds unless some high duty — to principle, say — demands it. The regulatory system doesn't yield to surprise attack, it recognizes no bigger bully, and it cares nothing for principle. But don't let that discourage you. You need to know how the system works — why it does some things more nonsensically than others — so that you understand when to pick a fight and when to retire to fight another day.

The Commissioner as Political Animal

In state after state, the workers' comp problem proves so intractable that most governors happily steer clear of it. They recognize that no consensus exists to reform the system one way or another. So they see no point in expending political capital on it. Instead they leave matters to their insurance commissioners, the officers with direct responsibility.

Until recently most states made the office of insurance commissioner appointive, and most of the time the holder of the office came from the local insurance establishment and reflected the views of the industry. It was an administrative post in the truest sense. The commissioner suggested policy and implemented whatever the governor and legislature approved.

The stepping stone

But as the workers' comp problem deepened in the last decade, and as insurance costs in general skyrocketed, the post changed. A number of states made the insurance commissioner an elected official. This gave ambitious pols the chance to use the position as a stepping stone to higher office.

No discussion of the insurance commissioner as political animal goes far without a look at John Garamendi of California. Garamendi is the paradigm of the new commissioner: ambitious, shrewd, commanding, articulate, mediagenic, and not to be taken lightly. Garamendi sees his office as a doorway, and he does almost nothing not designed to get him on to bigger and better things.

Early on in his tenure, Garamendi seized on the junk-bond troubles of Executive Life Insurance to get himself onto the evening news month after month. The brainchild of a former mutual fund salesman named Fred Carr, Executive Life did business with Michael Milken in the heyday of the junk-bond market in the 1980s. The insurer posted impressive returns on its investment portfolio, outdoing virtually all of its rivals and in the process changing the way most of them operated. Then the government, alarmed at the massive changes wrought on corporate America by the junk bond, intervened and sent the market for unrated bonds into freefall. Like many another life insurer, Executive Life saw its portfolio shrink rapidly. It went into receivership, and its policyholders faced millions in losses.

The able Garamendi salvaged more of the company's assets than most people had thought possible. Executive Life's policyholders by and large hailed him, and the media gave him lavish attention.

Making the Most of Things

It was an auspicious start, and Garamendi made the most of his prominence. In late 1991, he slashed an NCCI request for increases in workers' comp insurance rates from 11.9 percent to 1.2 percent. This time employers hailed him, but insurers charged that Garamendi acted at their expense. He shrugged off the charges. "These are tough times for businesses," he said. "And an increase of 11.9 percent could be the straw that breaks many of their backs. Government should be the caretaker for the people, not the undertaker."

One act didn't tell the story

Garamendi sounded like the friend of employers. But one act didn't tell the whole story.

In 1992, workers' comp insurers collected more than $10 billion in premiums from California employers, making the state by far the biggest workers' comp market in the nation. Even so, claims dwarfed premiums; as a whole, insurers posted big losses on workers' comp business.

Existing state law required that workers' comp insurers charge minimum premiums. It allowed carriers to claim expenses of 32.8 percent of premiums — regardless of what their true expenses might be — when seeking rate increases.

True Expenses

Garamendi claimed that the insurers' true expenses were far lower, closer to 20 or 25 percent of premiums. This, he said, justified slashing the insurers' request for rate increases. He suggested that insurers reform themselves and crack down on fraud.

But fraud isn't the only problem in the workers' comp universe, or even the biggest. Lawyers and medical costs sop up far more money than fraud artists. Fraud accounts for about 10 cents of every benefit dollar in California. But between 1982 and 1992, litigation costs around the country increased more than 100 percent. Stress claims went up some 700 percent. Vocational rehabilitation claims went up almost 300 percent.

Garamendi kept his focus on fraud even so. He pushed legislation to give his department and local district attorneys more resources to combat fraud. He boasted to the *Los Angeles Times* that he'd "go after the professionals — the doctors, attorneys and other medical care workers — who are involved in fraud and put them out of business."

Garamendi's posturing led several newspapers to misreport that California's four biggest workers'

A focus on the wrong target

comp carriers had paid handsome dividends to shareholders. In fact, they'd paid dividends to policyholders whose claims experience justified them.

An Uncertain Grasp

Insurers questioned whether Garamendi grasped the fundamentals of the business he regulated, but the commissioner didn't break stride. A few months later, in early 1992, he endorsed a reform plan pending in the legislature. Like Garamendi himself, the plan concentrated on curbing fraudulent and unwarranted claims, not on the burden of litigation and increasing medical costs as a whole. Among other things it gave Garamendi discretion to create new units to investigate workers' comp fraud. (Governor Pete Wilson refused to go along. He used the line-item veto to deny funding for the investigative unit.)

Garamendi fed more sound bites to the media. "California businesses are being strangled by exorbitant workers' compensation insurance premiums," he said. "Workers' compensation costs have gotten out of control, especially in the areas of insurer expenses and fraud."

In July 1992, he approved a 6.7 percent hike in workers' comp insurance rates. Insurers wanted more, but they liked 6.7 percent more than the 1.2 percent they had received the last time around.

To cover the increase, Garamendi loudly renewed his call for reform. "There are simply too many pigs feeding at the trough," he said. "We must stop the special interests from unjustly profiting from an increasingly costly workers' compensation system."

Little Progress in the Legislature

Reform, however, had made little progress in the legislature. At the bidding of his friends in the plaintiff's bar, the powerful speaker of the California Assembly, Willie Brown, emasculated the effort. The legislature passed a weak bill and convinced no one that the legislation would reform anything at all.

Meanwhile employers — especially in the Los Angeles area — pulled up stakes and left for fairer climes in such states as Nevada and Arizona or, worse, closed down. They could not bear up under the strain of a local economy in deep recession and the burden of workers' comp costs spinning out of control. The spokeswoman for a San Bernardino County manufacturer told a newspaper that Garamendi's hike in workers' comp insurance premiums would chase employers out of the state. Her company, whose annual premiums would rise at least $20,000 with the hike, would consider moving to Nevada, Arizona or "anywhere else."

Off for fairer climes

In December, Garamendi denied insurers a 12.6 percent rate increase, estimated to cost employers some $1 billion in 1993. He said insurance industry documents contained "wild and unexplained" variations of operating costs and "rotten data" to support the increase request.

Another Attempt

Garamendi urged the legislature to make another attempt at workers' comp reform. And he bashed the insurers. "The industry cannot be allowed to live off the fat of a dysfunctional system while so many California employers are forced to live on starvation diets."

After all this, even Garamendi's partisans admit that the long-term problems of the workers' comp system fester. The unchanged facts: California employers pay some of the highest workers' comp premiums in the nation, but the benefits to workers rank among the lowest.

Even a forceful and ambitious commissioner like John Garamendi cannot realign the forces that bear on workers' comp — lawyers, medical professionals, insurers, employers, workers. For all of these except employers, workers' comp is a lucrative problem. None wants to break the lock and start serious reform.

New Hampshire's Experience

Other states fare no better. In 1990 New Hampshire, for example, allowed workers' comp insurance premiums to increase by 9.3 percent, on average. For employers, this translated into $28 million more

A long phase-in period

than they paid for workers' comp insurance in 1989. In all, their bill hit $328 million.

Things could have been worse. The NCCI had recommended a hike of 27.1 percent, but Insurance Commissioner Louis Bergeron — an appointee — rejected the recommendation outright. Bergeron considered it his responsibility to set rates high enough to keep insurers in the market without unduly burdening employers. On these grounds he believed 9.3 percent a "fair and reasonable" solution.

But 9.3 percent was the average. Some lower-risk employers, among them machine shops and some printing firms, got rate *decreases* of as much as 5.9 percent. Higher-risk operations got hikes reaching to 27 percent.

The legislature had enacted a compromise reform bill to stabilize insurance rates and, with a little luck, to effect changes in workers' comp law. But the legislation phased in many of its most important reforms over three or four years. Opponents of workers' comp reform love such phase-in periods. They agree to changes and then renege on the grounds that "new" conditions "dictate" doing so.

Thus the effort at reform didn't attack New Hampshire's real problem: a system skewed to benefits, handing them out willy-nilly in ever increasing amounts. The legislation traded increases in premiums now for "reform" later on. Bergeron tried to find a way through this morass, but the benefits awarded by workers' comp referees and the courts outstripped whatever good might come from reform.

The Goodness of Insurers

Employers dare not trust to the goodness of their insurers, either, when it comes to dealing with the regulatory apparatus. (See Appendix Fifteen.)

In Arizona, workers' comp carriers followed the NCCI in seeking increases averaging 1.6 percent in the summer of 1992 — one of the smallest increases in years. In setting their sights so low the carriers and the NCCI took a new tack, pursuing smaller, more certain rate hikes instead of bigger hikes guaranteed to make employers squawk.

The Arizona Department of Insurance reviewed the request and quickly approved it. Employers breathed their relief; the year before, insurers had asked for 15.5 percent and won 9.9 percent.

This year's numbers — or next year's

No one seemed to notice that, in seeking 1.6 percent, the NCCI was projecting increases in medical costs for the coming year. The numbers for the preceding year showed modest *decreases* in claims. In fact the state had instituted cost controls that bore fruit. In addition, a number of large insurers had expanded their own cost containment programs.

Still, the NCCI said it expected increases in medical costs in the coming year and wanted to prepare for them. When asked why lower claims meant higher premiums, the insurance group pointed to other states where increases of 25 to 30 percent were "distressingly common."

This illustrates a common tactic used by insurers to win rate hikes: Use this year's numbers when you (the insurer) have done badly; use next year's projected losses when you've done well.

The Dispute Resolution Systems

Every insurance commissioner in the country works with a bureaucracy in place that sometimes daunts the best efforts at evenhanded administration. Run well, the states' dispute resolution systems offer you at least a fighting chance of seeing a difficult claim through to conclusion in circumstances that give you and your worker a chance to state your cases. But the systems don't always run well, as employers in Pennsylvania, for example, can attest.

In 1986 a committee of the Pennsylvania legislature issued a report on the state's dispute resolution system that set a standard for clarity of analysis that remains unequalled.

In a nutshell, the study argued that Pennsylvania's system was so cumbersome, so slow, so poorly run as to corrupt the whole idea of workers' comp. On average, the state Department of Labor and Industry took nine and a half months to settle a contested workers' comp claim. The state's appointed referees, who rule on workers' comp disputes—and who often refer to themselves as judges—took more than thirteen months to decide contested claims.

The Average Case

The study found that it took 63 days for the average case to come up for an initial hearing, mandated by state law to occur within 35 days. One case had hung fire for more than 125 days. It took 14 months for appeals to come up for review. The state routinely failed to require self-insured employers to post sufficient security to cover their workers' comp liabilities. The state failed to enforce a law requiring employers to file injury reports within 10 days. The state failed to police the many employers who went without workers' comp insurance altogether. An advisory council created to advise the state on workers' comp programs had not met for nearly three years.

Reform bogged down in partisan strife. Labor groups wanted to expand workers' comp coverage regardless of cost. Employers wanted to reduce costs regardless of their obligations to injured workers.

State officials defended the status quo, arguing that they already had the issues raised by the report in hand, or that the problems weren't as serious as portrayed. They said staff vacancies were being filled and they launched a two-year effort to computerize case records and enforce new work rules for referees. In this last effort they encountered opposition from the referees themselves, who belonged to a union.

Employers Without Coverage

As for the employers who went without insurance, the state checked on almost two thousand cases cited by the auditors and found that only three employers might have violated the law.

One anxious state senator said the report confirmed his belief that the workers' comp system was a "disgrace" and that a nine-and-a-half-month delay was too long for an injured worker to wait "when he has no money to buy food or pay the rent."

What happened, in the end? Very little. The report generated some publicity and prompted some legislators to speechify on the wisdom of doing something. But that was about it. The troubles in Pennsylvania went on, twisting the system into the antithesis of itself.

The Lockheed Case

California, more than most other states, treats its workers' comp referees like judges. In some ways this works for the state, since the referees can't join a union as Pennsylvania's referees do.

But what happens to employers and employees in the California system isn't much different from what happens in states like Pennsylvania. The system grinds on slowly and sometimes erratically, and the deserving injured worker waits and waits. The lawyers, meanwhile, see time as an investment; the more they spend litigating a workers' comp case, the more they stand to make.

In 1989, some 225 Lockheed Corp. workers alleged that their health had suffered while they worked at the company's top-secret Burbank, California, aerospace plant. They claimed that their work exposed them to composites — materials used to elude radar in stealth aircraft — and to other exotic materials that caused illnesses ranging from headaches to cancer.

They sought compensation for illnesses and even death, although California law limited each claim to $80,000 plus lifetime medical payments.

Easing the Logjam

The state normally handled workers' comp claims case by case, but the Lockheed claims overwhelmed the Workers' Compensation Appeals Board. To ease the logjam, the board appointed a special judge to hear all cases dealing with Lockheed workers.

George Deukmejian, then governor, and other state officials already faced a class-action lawsuit seek-

Backlogs in hearing cases

ing to speed up the claims process. The suit challenged Deukmejian's authority to veto money appropriated to expand the staff of the state workers' comp courts. The lawsuit was filed on behalf of some 200,000 workers whose claims were held up by a "bureaucracy run amok."

Backlogs existed in the 22 compensation courts scattered around the state. Many claims languished for as long as 10 months before coming up for hearing, despite a state law mandating that the state schedule a hearing within 30 days and resolve a contested claim within 60.

The suit accused Deukmejian of breaching his "constitutional duty to see that the law is faithfully executed." Each year since Deukmejian took office in 1983, the state legislature had appropriated additional moneys to run the courts. Each year Deukmejian vetoed the extra funds.

The suit asked the court to order the state controller to ignore Deukmejian's veto of the additional funds.

The lawsuit didn't achieve its goals, but it did highlight the fact that workers' comp afflicts even states with conservative governors; it's a nonpartisan problem.

A Special Judge

Lawyers for the Lockheed workers agreed that the special judge could dispense with repetitive evidence so as to speed up the processing of the claims. But, as Lockheed contested the claims, they predicted that resolution could still take as long as five years.

Lockheed self-insured its workers' comp. Facing an exposure of at least $20 million, the company determined to fight the claims as long as possible. The company wanted a settlement of far less than $20 million. And with billions in annual sales and a self-insured workers' comp plan, it could resist on a massive scale.

The Lockheed dispute triggered some reform of the state's resolution system. Starting in 1990, a year after the Lockheed claims hit the system, California began allowing parties in workers' comp disputes to submit their cases to binding arbitration before state-approved arbitrators. In some cases the state made arbitration mandatory — especially cases dealing with basic questions of insurance coverage. These developments relieved some of the pressure on the system. Employers in California now tend to say they prefer arbitrators (usually attorneys with labor experience) for their relative consistency, if nothing else.

Resisting on a massive scale

A Severe Problem

This is not to argue that California has solved its workers' comp problem. Indeed, the state stands just behind Maine, Florida and maybe Texas as regards the severity of the problem. And the reform touched only the claims *process;* it did nothing to stem the flood of claims.

Pennsylvania and California don't stand alone here; the systems in other states work badly, too. Injured workers don't receive full benefits, employers face unresolved and potentially growing financial exposures, and insurers can't close their files. Only lawyers and the other cogs in the resolution system profit from the delay.

Clearly, the state systems have eroded significantly. Workers' comp was designed to bypass lawyers and the convolutions of the court system. Exactly the reverse has come about.

Your Best Bet

The employer's best bet under these circumstances? If possible, avoid the state-run workers' comp resolution system altogether — which is to say, don't let your workers' comp claims fester to the point that you and your employee have no other way of settling things.

If you do find yourself in the embrace of the dispute resolution process, don't delay. Don't play to the system's weakness, in other words, because you can't make it into a strength.

You accomplish nothing by delaying a claim, for a variety of reasons. First, you don't make the exposure disappear. Second, the injured worker who doesn't get a fair and prompt settlement is a bomb with a trick fuse waiting for some workers' comp lawyer to set it off. There is no statute of limitations for workers' comp claims. And the longer a claim drags on, the more likely it will attract a lawyer. In fact, delay plays to the lawyer's hand by making the employer seem insensitive and callous.

Third, insurers don't like delay; they want a quick resolution. Fourth, the employer who delays settlement does nothing to hold premiums down.

There's more. Delay betrays the basic purpose of workers' comp — to assure quick and predictable results.

Chapter 13: The Myth of Reform

Laws against fraud miss the target

Public servants don't need the corrupting influence of lawyer lobbies to do the wrong thing about workers' comp. They do it quite ably on their own — as you see in the reform efforts of state after state.

Why? Workers' comp defies easy analysis. It doesn't make for good sound bites. So pols shy away from serious engagement. They portray workers' comp as an uneven battle between hapless injured workers and greedy insurers. The scenario plays better in 30 seconds on the evening news.

Like many employers, these legislators make the mistake of seeking to strengthen the law against fraud — and calling the result "reform."

But this kind of reform doesn't go far enough. It doesn't speak to abuse, which causes far more trouble than fraud, and it doesn't insulate the system against the intrusion of lawyers.

Meanwhile, the damage mounts.

Deep in the Process

Workers' comp burrows deep into the political process and festers there, like a porcupine quill in a dog's soft nose. Legislators meet, argue and tinker with reform for days, weeks, months, years — and come away with nothing much.

When legislators talk about workers' comp reform, they commonly start by making fraud a felony. They commonly end there, too. And it doesn't make much difference.

The experience of the state workers' comp pool in Wyoming makes the point. Long considered a basket case, Wyoming's state pool ran *monthly* deficits of $200,000 to $300,000 throughout 1992. These sums may look inconsequential next to the problems of bigger states, but the difference is one of pro-

Veering toward disaster

portion, not kind. Each month the Wyoming pool paid benefits totalling about $6 million, so the deficit varied between 3.3 and 5 percent of benefits — enough to send a private business down the tubes.

It was a lot of money in a small state. In 1992, for the third time in as many years, the system veered toward disaster.

Frank Galeotos, director of the State Employment Department and the administrator in charge of workers' comp issues, dominated a summer meeting of Governor Mike Sullivan's cabinet. He cited a variety of factors for the crisis, most prominently fraud.

But he couldn't say exactly how much of the deficit resulted directly from fraud — a familiar refrain, since it's so difficult to prove fraud. In fact, Galeotos admitted that, although fraud contributed to the deficits, so did rising claims. So did an increase in serious injuries. So did employer fraud and provider fraud.

A Few Steps Behind Reality

In 1989, the pool's long-running deficit had prompted the Wyoming legislature to establish a $20 million reserve to keep the pool liquid. Regulators had also allowed workers' comp insurance premiums to increase. But despite all this, in Wyoming as in other states, the regulators ran a few steps behind the harsh realities of a system gone haywire.

Galeotos told the governor's cabinet that his staff was working on a reform proposal which would make workers' comp fraud a felony rather than a misdemeanor. Galeotos also wanted more money to police fraud.

For his part, the governor wanted to try some jawboning. He suggested that Galeotos' department spread the word that when anyone defrauded the workers' comp program, everyone suffered higher rates.

Galeotos got his reform, along with some money to police fraud. And the governor did some jawboning. But both men sang a familiar and probably pointless refrain. Wyoming's "reform" attacked workers' comp fraud but not the real problem, abuse. And it did nothing about lawyers.

No better in the Golden State

The upshot: no fundamental change. No commercial insurer openly writes workers' comp insurance in Wyoming. The state pool remains a basket case. At best the state's reform put off the day of reckoning. At worst it accomplished nothing.

Bigger State, Bigger Problem

Reform fares no better in California, the biggest workers' comp marketplace in the country. Virtually no one doubts that the workers' comp mess acts as a drag on the Golden State's economy, especially in the Los Angeles basin. As the decade began, workers' comp contributed to unemployment, forced employers to close up shop or leave for fairer climes, and hampered every effort to get California out of the recession.

In California, stress claims rose by more than 700 percent through the 1980s. In 1988, the cost of workers' comp insurance averaged $13.99 per $100 of payroll in California. This ranked third in the country (behind only Montana at $18.50 and Alaska at $18.38). Meanwhile California paid such measly benefits that it ranked thirtieth among the states.

In April 1992, a blue-ribbon panel led by Peter Ueberroth, the former baseball commissioner and organizer of the 1984 Los Angeles Olympics, recommended an ambitious redesign of state government — including its regulatory, education and legal systems — in an effort to reestablish California as the mightiest economic engine in the Union.

"We're frightened about this state's future," Ueberroth said. "We started out being worried, and we ended up with the conclusion that things are much worse than we expected. [The state is] on a precipice and about ready to drop off."

The Council on California Competitiveness, created by Governor Pete Wilson as the centerpiece of his economic program, acknowledged that the state's troubles resulted in part from the recession and from the standdown in defense and aerospace

Making fraud the straw man

work — and in part from self-inflicted wounds. "Through our indifference to the need for job creation in this state, we are crippling ourselves," the report read. "The perception is becoming widely shared that California is a bad place to do business."

Among the report's first suggestions: that the state restrict workers' comp benefits and foster a greater competition among insurers.

The system, the report said, drove employers away or, worse, out of business altogether. The report cited rampant and lucrative fraud. It called workers' comp "a national disgrace because of its tolerance of fraud and abuse."

Governor Wilson had been trying to reform workers' comp since winning office in 1990. His efforts coupled with the Ueberroth report to produce a heated debate among insurers, employers, labor, doctors and lawyers.

Insurers and employers argued for limiting stress-related disabilities. At the time state law allowed a worker to collect benefits if stress contributed only ten percent to the worker's condition — one of the lowest threshholds in the country.

A Smart Move

But labor teamed up with physicians and the workers' comp bar to insist that stress claims were one thing and fraud quite another. It was a smart move. It made fraud the straw man.

"Everybody wants to stop fraud," intoned one Southern California workers' comp lawyer. "But you can [limit stress claims] and that won't do a thing to stop fraud. You just punish legitimately injured workers by making it more difficult for them to gain access to the system."

In 1989, Republicans — led by outgoing Governor George Deukmejian — had made a concerted run at workers' comp reform. Realizing that reform always sounds good to the voters, Willie Brown, the powerful speaker of the state Assembly, and the Sacramento Democrats agreed to pass Deukmejian's bill but neutered most of its impact.

The sleight-of-hand included a "reform" of California's notorious willingness to recognize stress as a contributing factor in workers' comp cases. Until 1989, a worker qualified for benefits if job-related stress contributed a mere 1 percent to the worker's condition. The 1989 "reform" increased the threshold to 10 percent.

Low threshold for stress

The package promised a potful of savings that never materialized. Worse, it passed on half of these putative savings to claimants in the form of bigger benefits — and didn't wait for the savings to show up first. The bill's proponents presented this little deal as a "no-net-change" proposition, but of course it was anything but. The savings went a-glimmering. Costs went up.

An Irresistible Lure

The hoopla over "reform" served only to advertise the lucre to be found in stress claims, and the lawyers came out of the woodwork. In 1990, stress claims mushroomed by more than 40 percent.

Pete Wilson succeeded Deukmejian as governor in the same year and promptly vowed to make workers' comp reform a reality. He attacked stress claims first, presenting a plan to increase the threshold for stress-related claims to 50 percent. He also wanted to require "clear and convincing evidence" in claims alleging mental disorder. The existing standard required only that a worker show a "preponderance of the evidence."

Wilson's plan added one more element: that stress result from a specific, sudden or extraordinary incident.

In all it was an ambitious plan. Employers hoped to save $200 million to $300 million annually in workers' comp insurance premiums.

Wilson lost this first round in the fight over stress, in 1990. He did persuade the legislature to make a crime of workers' comp fraud — again, a pointless exercise. But the idea became law because those who might otherwise oppose it knew that they would look silly if they made too much noise about a question that didn't matter anyway.

Joe Sixpack doesn't complain

The proof came when the law enforcement community weighed in. The state Department of Insurance (headed by John Garamendi, a Wilson rival) issued an artful report showing that workers' comp accounted for a tiny fraction of the fraud cases brought to department investigators. From 1979 to 1991, the department received 380 allegations of workers' comp fraud — and more than 23,000 allegations of auto insurance fraud.

Garamendi's report dodged a few realities. Auto insurance fraud actually hurts drivers — i.e., nearly everybody in California. Workers' comp fraud, in contrast, hurts insurance companies — or so Joe Sixpack thinks. So Joe Sixpack doesn't complain.

A more serious refrain came from Los Angeles District Attorney Ira Reiner, whose office had *never* prosecuted a single workers' comp fraud case. A spokeswoman called such cases "extremely difficult to investigate and extremely difficult to prosecute . . . because everything is very subjective."

Indeed.

Holding the Budget Hostage

Practicalities aside, Wilson continued his efforts to reform workers' comp in 1991, when the legislature met again. In fact, he went to extraordinary lengths: In an aggressive move, Wilson tied workers' comp reform to the state budget. He held the budget hostage to workers' comp reform. He wanted both, and he wouldn't take one without the other.

Republicans in the legislature signed on to this strategy. The Democrats couldn't muster a two-thirds majority to pass a budget on their own, so the Republicans threatened to hold up the budget if the Democrats didn't back workers' comp reform.

Employers thought they saw some leverage here, too — a chance to force Willie Brown and the Democrats to accede to reforms opposed by lawyers and labor unions, and in the meantime save themselves a lot of money on workers' comp insurance premiums.

But the reformers faced fierce opposition. Too many people gained from a system that made it easy to allege, and very difficult to disprove, job-related stress. Labor argued that stress claims weren't inherently fraudulent, notwithstanding the difficulty of diagnosing the condition. The California Psychological Association denounced the plan as ignoring conventional psychiatric wisdom.

The plaintiff's bar screamed bloody murder.

The lawyers scream murder

Willie Brown offered a proposal to allow employers to transfer workers' comp health costs over to their regular health insurance plans. The rationale, disputed by employers and insurers, was that employers would save money because health insurers showed lower administrative costs and negotiated lower medical fees than workers' comp insurers.

For a time Pete Wilson stuck to his guns in the fight over the budget. He faced a $14.3 billion budget deficit, but he refused to approve any tax package to close the gap without workers' comp reform.

'Political Terrorism'

Wilson's reform package bogged down in committee. Its fate, and that of the entire budget, rested on the inclination of Willie Brown to persuade his Democrats to go along with it in order to get a budget.

The rhetoric heated up. Brown called Wilson a "political terrorist" for linking the budget and workers' comp reform. Brown's allies drafted a tit-for-tat bill linking the budget to a pet project of the governor — Wilson's plan to establish a state-level environmental protection agency.

Brown played the media in masterly fashion, painting Wilson as the bad guy. He also called for help from his friends in labor and at the plaintiff's bar.

They responded and Brown won, by and large. With intense pressure on, Wilson's support among Republicans in the legislature faded. The governor traded away most of his demands for workers' comp reform in exchange for a budget package that socked the state's taxpayers with the biggest tax increase in history.

Lost in the shuffle was Wilson's proposal for a 50-percent threshhold for stress claims, probably the

Money and inertia block reform

single most important element of his plan. The legislature stiffened the penalties for workers' comp fraud and beefed up enforcement with $3 million, but that was it. Wilson became a very unpopular guy.

What got in his way?

Money, mainly. Money and inertia. The failure to reform the workers' comp mess in California reflects the triumph of big campaign donations and the pull of the status quo — a siren's call to the politician.

In 1988 the campaign committee of Willie Brown collected almost $2.5 million from groups interested in the doings of Sacramento's pols. Brown transferred $1 million of this princely sum into the Assembly Democrats' joint campaign fund, which went on to raise an additional $1.5 million for the year.

Fueling the Resistance

Since 1985, the California Trial Lawyers Association had donated about $260,000 to Brown and $487,500 to his counterpart in the state Senate, President Pro Tem David Roberti. The California Society of Industrial Medicine had donated more than $600,000 over the same period. The California Applicants' Attorneys Association, whose members handle workers' comp cases, spent $170,886 lobbying Brown and others from January to June of 1992 alone.

This money fueled the resistance to workers' comp reform. When Brown needed help in fighting Wilson over reform, he knew where to turn.

Wilson came back for another round the next year, in 1992, only to fail even more miserably. In his State of the State address he reemphasized his commitment to workers' comp reform. The legislature met, argued, and dithered — and came away with nothing during its regular session. Wilson recalled it into special session later in the year, and once again it argued and dithered and did nothing. In all, the legislature considered 88 pieces of legislation dealing with workers' comp, and it managed to pass only one: a monstrosity that tried to stick employers with steep premium increases, tax hikes and extended liability. Wilson vetoed it.

The smart employer doesn't wait

But hope springs eternal. As 1992 ended and 1993 came on, the press wrote about employers who relocated or expanded outside California because of workers' comp. Willie Brown formed an Assembly Democratic Economic Prosperity Team to meet with employers to talk about reform. The television show "60 Minutes" ran a story critical of California for doing little about the tide of phony claims.

Willie Brown and his allies among medical groups, attorneys and unions wrote Insurance Commissioner John Garamendi urging immediate action to enforce the law and put an end to the most outrageous fraud.

Soon after, Ueberroth's Council on Competitiveness urged tighter standards for stress claims. It also proposed limiting vocational rehabilitation benefits, which had ballooned 23 percent per year since the late 1970s, on average.

All in all, pressure built for state government to do something serious. And it may. But the smart employer in California knows better than to wait. You can't control what other people do, especially politicians. If they act, they may act wrongly. If they act rightly, they may do so too late.

The Florida Swamp

At least employers in California don't have to contend with a dead marketplace for workers' comp insurance. They can get the coverage, in other words, even if it's costly. Employers in other states should be so lucky. Their legislatures wrestle with reform again and again and accomplish little. In some states the voluntary market survives in such sorry state that it functions only in name. In the worst states this leaves employers with no choice but to buy their coverage from the state pool.

Florida's problems are legion. The legislature attempted reform almost annually in the late 1980s, very nearly to no avail.

In January 1990, Insurance Commissioner Tom Gallagher raised workers' comp premiums by 36.7

percent, on average, the biggest increase ever granted in the state. Premiums had gone up 28.8 percent the previous year, and the double whammy forced some employers to close their doors and others to go without coverage.

For a high-risk construction worker earning only $20,000 a year, a Florida employer paid more than $14,000 for workers' comp insurance. Premiums reached nearly $18,000 for employers in the state pool. Insurers in the Florida market showed the nation's third-highest workers' comp loss ratios. They paid $1.58 in claims for every $1 they collected in premiums in 1989 and 1990.

Rates had risen annually since 1982. No one disputed that rates must go up again. "Based upon the numbers I've seen, [the increase is] probably unavoidable," said the executive director of central Florida's Associated Builders and Contractors, Inc., at the time. He blamed the state's workers' comp bar for skewing the exposure.

Lawyers as Root Cause

The NCCI linked the problems to increased costs for medical care and rehabilitation, abuse among employees and — more than anything else — lawyers.

Not coincidentally, Florida had led the country in deregulating the legal profession. Like lawyers in other states, those who hung their shingles in Florida saw an opportunity in workers' comp. They made the most of the relatively lax procedural standards in workers' comp cases, and of the fact that the employer bore the effective burden of proof. Workers' comp was easy and lucrative. Stories circulated about workers' comp lawyers in Miami whose clients collected permanent partial disability settlements from five or six different employers.

But the big rate hikes in 1990 did nothing to solve Florida's problem. The NCCI argued that the hikes weren't big enough. It blamed Commissioner Gallagher for "effectively asking the insurance industry and the employers of the state to equally share the burden of a workers' compensation system that's out of control."

The state's oversight board came up with a laundry list of cost-cutting measures. The legislature legalized drug testing in certain circumstances and instituted "reforms" seeking to encourage workers to return to work as quickly as possible. In speech after speech, legislators denounced medical professionals for subjecting injured workers to unnecessary treatment, and lawyers for inundating employers in a flood of litigation.

A laundry list of 'reforms'

Insurers talked about fleeing the state. The NCCI sympathized. It debated whether to appeal Gallagher's rate proposal.

The National Federation of Independent Business, which opposed the plaintiff's bar around the country, maintained that any solution would have to entail reducing benefits.

A Significant Showdown

Gallagher agreed, privately. He admitted that nothing short of a radical redesign of the system — aimed specifically at taking lawyers out of the equation — would turn things around. Publicly, he warned that premiums would increase every year for the rest of the decade.

It looked as if Florida would be the site for the first significant workers' comp showdown.

Alarmed, workers' comp lawyers roared their disapproval. The legislature passed an ambitious bill guaranteed to fail. Among other things, the bill required small contractors to buy workers' comp insurance. They wasted no time challenging this requirement. Small contractors argued that they couldn't afford the coverage. Two Putnam County contractors filed a class action suit, arguing that the reforms — passed "in the hectic, waning hours of its 1990 [legislative] session" — violated the Florida and U.S. constitutions. Other suits followed.

None of this did much to improve things. Rates kept climbing. Roofers, for example, paid more than $1 for workers' comp insurance for every $2 in salary. For plasterers, painters and paperhangers, the rate hit $1 for every $3 in salary. For insulators and wallboard installers, it approached $1 for every $4.

Bleeding the system dry

One South Florida builder summed it up best: "The trial lawyers' group did this to us. They're bleeding dry a system that we pay into because it's supposed to be fair and honest. They're chasing work underground. And out of the state."

In the end "reform" failed in Florida for the same reason it has failed elsewhere. It didn't attack the problem at its core. It did nothing about abuse and nothing about lawyers. Instead it made people angry, and the turmoil scuttled even the best of intentions.

The Main Obstacle: Money

This brief chapter explores the obstacles that crop up when politicians try to reform the workers' comp system. These obstacles reduce to a single one: money. Money distorts the system at every step, and most of all when politicians try to do something about the mess of workers' comp.

The system strains under the weight of money.

Employees see the system as a source of easy money. They see it as an entitlement program — not a safety net but a means of income. To more and more employees, it becomes not a workers' compensation program but a program for compensating workers who'd rather do something else. It becomes an alternative to work.

Lawyers aid and abet them at every step. They intrude themselves into a system designed to function without them, and they give voice to workers who demand ever bigger, ever expanding benefits.

Their demands push up costs all around, and health professionals respond happily by providing more and more services, whether needed or not and irrespective of the cost.

Insurers find themselves in the middle, caught by the harsh fact that premium income doesn't keep up — indeed, *can't* keep up — with benefits. Insurers seek to pass the strain on to employers, and only the regulatory system stands in their way. By its very nature regulation distorts the relationship between buyer and seller in any marketplace. In the marketplace for workers' comp insurance, regulation limits supply and does nothing to limit demand. Employers *must* cover their workers' comp exposure, and insurers can't supply it at a premium acceptable to regulators.

Or else they don't supply it at all. At its worst this distortion forces insurers to abandon the voluntary market altogether, leaving employers to the mercy of the state pools.

Even where the insurance market functions relatively unfettered, however, employers find the cost burdensome and the system unworkable. To avoid it they leave one state for another, or they go without coverage, or worst of all, they abandon business.

Or they join the chorus demanding that government do something.

Money subverts real reform

The Deliberative Resources

But reform goes nowhere in the statehouses because it fails to address the root cause of the crisis, abuse, and because, once again, money comes into the picture. Money corrupts the system and its deliberative resources. Money attracts lawyers, and money enables them to subvert real reform again and again. As long as lawyers rule the streets in the world of workers' comp, no one is safe — not workers and certainly not employers. They have penetrated and corrupted a system designed to function without them: a system that cannot function *with* them.

For the employer, all this reduces to a simple point: Don't wait for your legislature to fix things. It can't or won't — or won't soon enough, in any case.

Fix things yourself. It's the only way.

Chapter 14: The Bottom Line

The numbers are terrifying.

A giant tax on all employers

In 1991, the workers' comp system cost employers $70 billion — almost twice what they paid in 1985. The cost of the average workers' comp claim more than tripled in ten years, passing the $20,000 mark.

Workers' comp insurers now lose more than $2 billion a year. A number of the largest, including Liberty Mutual and USF&G, don't write in certain states under any circumstances. Many more refuse to cover certain industries as a whole, no matter what the state.

This, of course, leaves many employers to the tender mercies of their state pools — but the insurers can't escape the clutches of the pools even so. The pools routinely post frightening deficits, and the states routinely finance these deficits by forcing commercial insurers to cough up the difference. According to one estimate, if you added up all the deficits of all the state pools, the total would equal 16 percent of all the premiums commercial insurers collect in the workers' comp insurance marketplace. What this really means is that the pools act as a giant drag on everything these insurers do. An insurer posting $1 in sales really posts only 84 cents, because the difference disappears into the great maw of the state pools.

And if you think insurers absorb these losses, think again. For the most part they pass them along to employers.

Pervasive Waste

For their part, large employers regularly post workers' comp claims exceeding $10 million a year. Small companies suffer even more. Their insurance premiums took double-digit jumps through much of

Only employers have the will

the 1980s and look certain to maintain the pace for the foreseeable future.

And this only begins to tell the story. The system creates enormous waste: physicians who spend as much as 20 cents of every dollar they make satisfying the paperwork demands of the insurance industry, and lawyers who sap the workers' comp system of uncounted sums, and workers who fall into a kind of stupor and lose all thought of engaging in productive work.

Employers know these costs all too well.

In a 1992 survey, the National Federation of Independent Business found that one in four of its members had laid off workers or postponed new hiring specifically because of the staggering costs of workers' comp.

But workers' comp is like the weather. Everybody complains about it, and nobody does much about it. Employers expect their insurers to do something. Insurers expect the medical profession to do something. Everybody expects the legislatures to do something. Nobody expects the lawyers to do anything.

Among these parties, only one has any real interest in taking control, and only one has the means of doing so: employers. *All the others are unreliable; they don't need to solve the problem.* Employers must look for their own solutions, because only employers can.

This book seeks to give employers the wherewithal to solve their workers' comp problem without regard for those who have other fish to fry. Follow the advice we offer and you lower your costs on your own, without relying on anybody else and without running afoul of the law.

A Distorted Bargain

After reading this book, you should be angry. You should understand that neither you nor your employees benefit from a system spinning out of control. Workers' comp is a bargain between employer and employees. As employer, you agree to stand liable for the costs of workplace injury, and your employees agree not to sue you for negligence. But others intrude on this bargain — lawyers, doctors, politicians, even insurers. They distort it beyond recognition. That should make you angry indeed.

Your employee's interests

The next step is to channel that anger into constructive action. Real reform must start at your level. You must take control of the system for yourself and your employees.

Here's how:

First, become a student—and then a teacher. Learn the system and teach it to your workers. Too many employers wander in the dark when it comes to workers' comp. So do too many employees. The consequence is that a workplace injury immediately plunges both employer and employee into the frightening unknown — making it a pretty good bet that, if something goes wrong, the worker's claim becomes a big one.

The Wrong Assumption

Make sure that you understand what happens when workers' comp comes into play. Make sure your employees know, too. It isn't enough to post some faded, state-required poster on your lunchroom bulletin board detailing employer responsibilities and employee rights under workers' comp in the dreary, bloated language of the bureaucrat. *You* don't read those posters, and your employees don't either.

Until they need someone to explain them.

Upon which they find a lawyer willing and able to do so.

Upon which your costs explode.

Second, play an active role in setting up your insurance. Check the details of your workers' comp insurance policy, especially your classification and the method by which your insurer calculates your premium. If you can, change your operations to get into a cheaper category. Be aggressive about this; don't let your broker or, worse, your insurer make

Manage the entire process

decisions for you. If feasible, consider self-insuring. Think about a big deductible or perhaps a risk pool.

Third, *manage* every claim. Keep track of every employee who suffers a workplace injury and files a claim. Show concern for the employee and his or her family during and after an emergency—every day, if necessary. And keep tabs on the medical professionals who treat the injury. Never assume that they have your employee's interests at heart. Or yours.

If you can afford it, employ an onsite professional, perhaps a nurse, to give injured employees immediate attention and shepherd the employee through treatment and rehabilitation. If you can't afford a fulltime onsite professional, make sure that everybody who works for you knows what to do in an emergency. Make sure that aid gets to your injured employee fast, and stay in touch with the injured employee for the duration. Encourage your supervisors to visit hospitalized employees and phone them regularly. Do it yourself.

Fourth, get your employee back to work fast. People don't like to be sick or hurt; they want to get better, and in the first two or three weeks following an injury, they can't wait to get back. They also feel anxious. If you leave them to their worries for two or three months, you guarantee yourself a mess. Your employee's self-esteem deteriorates, and work becomes the cause of the employee's troubles, not the solution.

Don't let this happen. A dropout can leave you on the hook for lifetime disability benefits.

Fifth, find out what's causing injuries in the workplace. Surprisingly, many employers don't track injuries at all. They turn away from the fact that their employees face real dangers on the job, and they don't keep records and look for signs of trouble. But you really do hold responsibility for the safety of the people who work for you—as a matter law and of equity.

Danger Spots

Study your claims history to identify your worst and most frequent injuries. Organize your safety programming to address what you find. If necessary, reorganize the workplace to do the same. If you can, eliminate the hazards altogether.

The only one who can act

Sixth, emphasize safety, and not just during training. Make it an everyday practice. Write a brief, *useful* safety manual that addresses what your employees really do in the course of their work. Cover the rudiments of emergency response and accident reporting. Make sure that your safety procedures address the dangers and that they make sense to the people who must follow them.

Review the manual with each new hire. Look into supplementing your manual with training videos and ongoing classes. Insist that your supervisors stress safety; you get nowhere if they don't buy the idea.

Seventh, get to know your local doctor. You gain several advantages if you can direct all injured workers to the same medical facility. For starters, you can negotiate a discount — easily 15 percent, even for small companies. You can also demand — and get — providers who understand the exposures and needs of your business. This knowledge guides the provider in giving appropriate treatment.

The Real Source of Reform

In all of this — learning the system, mastering your insurance coverage, keeping tabs on the injured employee, analyzing workplace hazards, emphasizing safety, and controlling medical costs — you act on the idea that the only real reform in the world of workers' comp comes from the only one who can bring it about: the employer.

But you don't undertake the impossible.

Aetna Life & Casualty, the insurance giant, started paying attention to repetitive motion injuries in the early 1980s. It started a safety program for its own employees in 1990, when the number of cases began rising among VDT users.

Aetna employs more than 45,000 people, of whom 90 percent work on VDTs. The company understood that if it sat on its hands, serious trouble could emerge in a few years.

Cost avoidance, not cost benefit

Risk managers reviewed every job for relevant factors: the number of hours employees spent in front of VDTs every day, the nature of their work, its variety, the employees' latitude in controlling work pace.

At the same time, Aetna wrote a safety handbook and began replacing badly designed chairs and desks.

How much money did these efforts save? Aetna has no idea — and that's not the point.

The company believes its program will avoid thousands of injuries and save millions of dollars in medical expenses and lost wages. The company isn't sure whether the program hurts productivity, but its risk managers consider its impact marginal at worst.

The upshot: Aetna advises its own clients to regard ergonomics in terms of cost avoidance, not cost benefit. That's a much more generous standard — and more difficult to assess.

Identifying the Problem

A.T. Cross, the Rhode Island-based pen maker, began a systematic analysis of its workers' comp costs in 1988. The company employs 1,300 people, and its workers' comp premiums had tripled in one year. Cross decided to identify which parts of its operations caused which injuries.

The analysis turned up a trail of frequent back strain among people doing bench work such as assembling pen cartridges. The problem: too much sitting. So the company raised chairs and benches, enabling workers to sit or stand.

The impact in the first year was dramatic: a 43 percent reduction in injuries involving lost time and a 71 percent drop in total lost workdays. With that kind of control over safety, Cross could afford to self-insure beginning in 1990 at a savings of close to $1 million so far.

At the *Los Angeles Times*, new employees see a 20-minute video on ergonomics, and the newspaper conducts regular ergonomic audits of individual worksites. A management-employee committee meets regularly to keep an eye out for repetitive motion trouble. Some VDT terminals flash "TAKE A

BREAK" signals every hour or so. The newspaper runs a highly publicized "RSI Room" (for repetitive stress injury) outfitted with mini-barbells and weight machines to develop strength in the hand, elbow and shoulder. The room also sports a freezer filled with ice packs. Wet-heat pads wait on a shelf nearby. All employees may use the room.

The problem submits

Solutions That Work

These stories show that employers can analyze their own problems and come up with their own solutions. Sometimes the solution costs money, and sometimes it requires reorganizing the workplace. But the solution works. And it doesn't matter whether you employ 25 people or 25,000. The workers' comp problem submits to the employer who determines to master it.

Our final case study illustrates this point well.

Workers' comp costs at Frontier Enterprises, a Texas-based restaurant chain with annual revenues of just under $30 million, jumped 75 percent between 1984 and 1989. Frontier's insurance carrier didn't monitor injured workers or manage costs closely enough to suit Frontier. And Frontier wound up paying for that mismanagement.

As a restaurant chain, Frontier faced the danger of a workers' comp claim every day. Anybody in the restaurant business knows it to be labor-intensive and hazard-filled. Frontier's 600 fulltime and 500 part-time employees worked with knives, slicers, grills, broilers, ovens and hot fats. They lifted heavy trays and walked slippery floors.

By 1990, workers' comp costs had crept up to more than 5 percent of total payroll. That was too much.

The company decided on the most radical course of action available: to drop out of the Texas workers' comp system altogether. Among other things, this left the company vulnerable to employee lawsuits.

But Frontier took a fresh look at managing worker safety and medical care. It determined to reduce both the risks and the costs of job-related injuries. It analyzed the exposures and it devised specific,

A foundation for an effective solution

practical ways of avoiding them. And it got everyone to buy the idea.

In essence, Frontier now runs its own workers' comp benefits program from beginning to end. By design, the plan is more generous than Texas law requires. Frontier pays 75 percent of an injured worker's wages after only three days of missed work. The state mandates 70 to 75 percent of wages, starting after seven days. Frontier pays all medical expenses for work-related injuries, as required by state law.

But the company requires that its workers agree to certain conditions, three of which produce most of the savings. Employees must report accidents immediately. They must seek treatment from a physician or at a hospital specified by Frontier. They must submit a written accident report within 48 hours.

These conditions enable Frontier to keep track of and communicate with injured employees and to maintain good relations with the medical folk.

Frontier's employees understand that the company pays no benefits to workers who injure themselves while intoxicated, who willfully hurt others, or who engage in horseplay. These conditions conform to state law nationwide, so any employer may impose similar requirements — though the burden of proof falls on the employer.

To prevent workplace injuries from coming back to haunt the company down the road, Frontier requires workers to sign a release of further liability once they receive treatment, recover, and get back to work. New employees sign a statement saying that they have received a copy of Frontier's program and have had a chance to ask about it.

Magnificent Results

As simple as these things sound, they form the foundation of an effective cost-conscious approach to workers' comp for Frontier. And the plan produced magnificently, right from the start. A Frontier exec told *Inc.* magazine that claims totalled $522,500 during Frontier's last year as an insured company, and its insurer threatened to increase its premium from $470,000 to a whopping $798,800.

In 1991, the first year of the new program, Frontier's claims dropped to $156,300 — a cut of 70 percent. The company paid another $24,500 for claims administration, plus $89,900 for excess insurance covering claims beyond $250,000. But that was it. The company's costs totalled $270,700, about one-third of what the company's old insurer wanted to charge.

Savings go to the bottom line

The savings flowed straight to the bottom line.

The key to Frontier's program: It wrested control of the problem from those who had no interest in solving it — insurers, hospitals, doctors and even the company's employees themselves.

Two things happen when an employer takes charge in this way. First, a deeper level of accountability pervades everything that happens in the workplace. The employee takes responsibility for reporting the accident immediately and for submitting the written report within 48 hours. Thereafter, someone becomes responsible for every step along the way, from the treatment the employee receives to the employee's recovery and return to work. Someone makes sure that the health care provider doesn't call for three X-rays when one will do. Someone makes sure that the injured employee gets a benefits check on time, and that the employee gets the appropriate rehabilitation treatment, and so on.

Nothing happens unless someone stands accountable for it.

Second, employees react differently when they know that their own employer, not some faceless insurer, acts in their behalf — more specifically, when they know that the open wallet is their employer's. Fraudulent claims, which wreak havoc on many employers, tend to fall. People know that their employer takes responsibility.

The Action That Counts

We can't emphasize this too much; indeed, it's the bottom line of this book — because it's the employer's end of the bargain with his or her employees. In the end it doesn't matter what your insurer does, or what doctors do, or lawyers, or politicians, or regulators, or

The simple elegance of the bargain

anybody else. It matters what *you* do. The bargain exists between you and your employees, and if you want to take control of your workers' comp problem, you strike a new bargain with your employees — or rather, you strike the old bargain anew. You take responsibility for the cost of workplace injury, in exchange for which your employees forego the right to clean you out. The simple elegance of this bargain brings justice to the troubled relationship between employer and employee — and that is all either needs.

Every employer who takes control in this way advances the only true reform the system will ever see: the reform of individual responsibility.

FORMS, LETTERS AND CHECKLISTS

The following 25 appendices give you primary source material, forms and checklists for dealing with the various aspects of workers' compensation. Some forms may seem to conflict — there are sample letters to send your insurance carrier and guidelines for self-insurance — but they all support various strategies discussed in the course of this book.

A caveat: Workers' comp laws and standards vary from state to state. While these materials will help you analyze exposures and manage claims, they're not a substitute for specific legal or financial advice. If you think a claim will be troublesome, talk to your insurance carrier or administrator. If you suspect problems with your insurance, talk to your state board. If you're running into trouble with the state, talk to a lawyer.

With that understood, you should find these forms helpful in keeping on top of your workers' comp situation. Feel free to use them verbatim or modify them as you see fit.

QUESTIONNAIRE FOR WORKERS' COMPENSATION INSURANCE CARRIERS

Ask the following questions when you're shopping for a workers' compensation carrier.

Name of Insurer ______________________________

Address ______________________________

City, State, ZIP ______________________________

Phone (______) ______________________________

FAX (______) ______________________________

What sort of endorsements and schedules are available that might benefit my type of business? ______________________________

____

____

In what states can you provide coverage? ______________________________

What are the limits of employers' liability?

- ☐ bodily injury by accident ______________________________
- ☐ bodily disease ______________________________
- ☐ bodily disease by aggregate ______________________________

What are the exclusions? ______________________________

____

What deductibles do you offer? ______________________________

____

Please list other companies with whom you have medical provider or management service relationships which might benefit me (i.e., PPOs, HMOs, vocational rehabilitation groups, third-party administrators, etc.). ______________________________

____

____

What can you provide in terms of services to help me minimize the chance of potential injury to my employees?

____

____

What return-to-work programs do you offer? ______________________________

____

Do you have nationwide capability? ______________________________

____

What costs and miscellaneous payments does the employer have to make in the course of an ordinary claim? ______________________________

____

What is the case load of your claims case examiners? ______________________________

____

How do you receive notice of injury? ______________________________

____

Describe the payment authority limitation for the claims staff and describe the criteria for internal audits. ______________________________

____

How quickly will you pay benefits? ______________________________

____

How do you respond if an employer believes a claim is fraudulent? __________________

____

Describe your procedures for medical claims review. ______________________________

____

____

____

Describe your procedures for auditing provider bills. ______________________________

____

____

____

Describe your current procedures for handling client or insured complaints with state insurance departments. ______________________________

____

____

Can you provide claims data electronically? ______________________________

____

Do you track employers' costs? ______________________________

Do you track regulatory issues? ______________________________

SAMPLE WORKPLACE INFORMATION POSTERS FROM VARIOUS STATES

NOTICE TO EMPLOYEES

You are required by law to post this notice. This is your official industrial insurance poster.

If a job injury occurs...

Your employer is insured with the Washington State Fund. If you become injured on the job or suffer from an occupational disease, you are entitled to workers' compensation benefits.

Benefits include:

Medical care. Medical expenses arising from your workplace injury or disease will be fully paid by the State Fund.

Disability income. If you can't work for more than three days because of your injury or illness, you may be eligible for wage-replacement benefits.

Pensions. Injuries that permanently keep you from returning to work may qualify you for a disability pension.

Partial disability benefits. You'll get a monetary award to compensate for the loss of certain bodily functions.

Death benefits for survivors. If a worker dies, the surviving spouse and children may receive a pension.

Vocational assistance. Under certain conditions, you may be eligible for help in returning to work.

In case of injury...

Report your injury. If you are injured, no matter how minor the injury seems, contact the person listed to the right.

Get medical care. You have the right to go to the doctor of your choice. All medical bills that arise from a workplace injury or occupational disease will be paid by the Washington State Fund.

Tell your doctor the injury is work-related. Your doctor will complete a Report of Industrial Injury or Occupational Disease form and send it to us. This is the first step in filing your industrial insurance claim.

Report your injury to:

____

(Employer fills in this space)

Helpful phone numbers:

____

Ambulance

____

Police

____

Fire

IMPORTANT:

Every worker is entitled to workers' compensation benefits. You cannot be penalized nor discriminated against for filing a claim. For more information, call the department's toll-free hotline at **1-800-547-8367**. Hearing-impaired, TDD customers may phone **(206) 956-5797.**

State of Washington

Department of Labor and Industries

Missouri Department of Labor and Industrial Relations
DIVISION OF WORKERS' COMPENSATION

This employer is operating under and subject to the provisions of the Missouri Workers' Compensation Law.

If A Work Injury Occurs . . .

Missouri law guarantees certain benefits to employees who are injured or become ill because of their jobs.

Any job related injury is covered, even first-aid type injuries and work-related illnesses. The key is whether it was caused by the job. (Some injuries from off-duty company, social or athletic activities — for example, the company picnic or the department bowling team — may not be covered.) Check with your supervisor if you have questions.

Workers' Compensation Benefits Include . . .

★ **Medical Care.** All medical treatment — without a deductible to the employee or dollar limit. Costs are paid directly by your employer's insurance company, so you should never see a bill. If you do receive a bill, give it to the employer's designated representative or contact the insurer listed below.

Your employer will arrange for medical treatment. If you want to change doctors you must get authorization from the employer. If you go to a doctor without authorization it is at your expense.

★ **Payment for Lost Wages.** If you're temporarily disabled by a job injury or illness, you'll receive tax-free income until the doctor says you are able to return to work. Payments are two-thirds of your average weekly pay, up to a maximum set by state law. Payments aren't made for the first three days unless you're hospitalized or unable to work more than 14 days. If you do not receive a check, contact the insurer listed below. If the injury or illness results in a permanent handicap, permanent disability payments will be made after maximum recovery. If the injury results in death, benefits will be paid to surviving dependents.

In The Event Of A Work Injury . . .

Employer Must:
1. Be sure first aid is given.
2. See that the injured employee is directed to a doctor or hospital, if necessary.

Employee Must:
1. Report the injury **IMMEDIATELY** to your supervisor or

   ______________________________ (Employee Representative)

   at ____________________ (Phone Number)
   Any delay in reporting an accident may result in loss of right to compensation benefits.
2. If you have questions about Workers' Compensation, your employer will supply you with additional information or you may contact an Information Specialist at the Division of Workers' Compensation 1-800-775-COMP.

Insurer/Adjusting or Service Company or Designated Individual If Self-Insured

Name ______________________________

Address ______________________________

Phone Number ______________________________

Fraudulent action on the part of an employer, employee, or any other person is unlawful and subject to a fine up to $10,000.

If you have questions or need more information about Workers' Compensation benefits, contact an Information Specialist at:

Missouri Division of Workers' Compensation
3315 West Truman Blvd.
Jefferson City, MO 65102-0058
1-800-775-COMP

The Division of Workers' Compensation does not discriminate against individuals with disabilities as mandated by P.L. 101-336, The American's With Disabilities Act. Alternative format available upon request.

MO. Division of Workers' Compensation 1992

SECTION 1: INFORMATION FOR EMPLOYEES

What is workers' compensation insurance?

If your employer has workers' compensation insurance and if your claim is accepted by the insurance company, this insurance:

- pays reasonable medical costs if you are injured on the job;
- may pay income benefits to replace part of wages you lose because of an on-the-job injury;
- pays income benefits if you have permanent impairment from an on-the-job injury; and
- pays death benefits to your legal beneficiaries if you are killed on the job.

How to get information from TWCC

Free help and information is available from the **Texas Workers' Compensation Commission** (TWCC) if you are injured on the job, if you have an occupational disease, or if you are the beneficiary of a worker killed on the job.

To get help and information, please call the TWCC Customer Assistance staff at the local Field Office or at **1-800-252-7031**. The TWCC staff can answer questions about:

WHAT BENEFITS MAY BE PAID

- The Customer Assistance staff can find out whether or not your employer provides workers' compensation insurance coverage.
- The Customer Assistance staff can explain how much you may receive in benefit payments and for how long. If income benefits are due, checks will be sent to you by the insurance company (or by the claims administrator if your employer is self-insured).

GETTING MEDICAL CARE

- The Customer Assistance staff can explain how to get medical care paid for by workers' compensation insurance.

REPORTING YOUR INJURY

- The Customer Assistance staff can explain how to report your injury or occupational disease to your employer on time.

FILING YOUR CLAIM

- The Customer Assistance staff can give you a TWCC claim form and explain where to mail it. They can help you if you need help filling out the claim form.
- The Customer Assistance staff can explain how to file your claim on time. If you don't file on time, all benefits can be stopped, unless you have good cause for filing late.

HOW YOUR CLAIM IS HANDLED

- The Customer Assistance staff can help if you have a question about your claim.

SAMPLE LETTER OUTLINING NOTIFICATION PROCEDURE IN THE EVENT OF INJURY OR ILLNESS

TO: All Employees

FROM: Company President

SUBJ: Workers' Compensation Injury Notification

This memo is just to clarify our procedure for anyone who is injured on the job.

If you are injured, get proper medical attention immediately. As soon as possible after that, let me know you have been injured so that you get the benefits that you are entitled to by law. We pay over $20,000 a year for this coverage, so if someone is injured, I want it to be used.

Please fill out a form to document the injury. Copies of these forms are available in the Company Forms File, in the top drawer, in the first file folder.

If you are injured, and take time off from work, we may require a release for you to come back to work.

Attached to this memo is a booklet describing the workers' comp benefits to which you are entitled. Please sign the form at the back of the booklet to show you have read it and understand it, and return it to me. We also have copies in Spanish. Please come see me if you have any questions on this subject or need a Spanish version. There are also posters up around the company to tell you what to do in case of injury.

Please sign this memo in the space provided below and return to me.

______________________________ ______________________________

Signature of employee Date

QUESTIONNAIRE FOR OCCUPATIONAL MEDICAL FACILITIES AND SERVICE PROVIDERS

Date ________________________________

Name of facility ________________________

Ask facilities and medical providers these questions to check where applicable:

I. Staffing

A. Board-certified occupational medicine physician available ☐

B. Other physicians involved in the field of:

☐ Dermatology ☐ Epidemiology ☐ General Surgery
☐ Hand Surgery ☐ Internal Medicine ☐ Orthopedics
☐ Ophthalmology ☐ Psychology ☐ Radiology
☐ Toxicology

C. Other health practitioners:

☐ Dentists ☐ Occupational health nurses ☐ Optometrists
☐ Pharmacists ☐ Physical therapists

Other: ____

D. Physicians are available for worksite consultations. ☐

E. Personnel are experienced and knowledgeable in state and federal regulations (i.e., OSHA, workers' compensation). ☐

II. Facilities

A. Distance from the plant location to the medical facility is:______________

Facilities are modern and well-equipped ☐

Hours of service are:________________

24-hour backup coverage is provided ☐

A physician is on duty at all times ☐

B. Other services available include:

☐ X-ray ☐ Physical therapy ☐ Audiometric testing
☐ Spirometry testing ☐ Vision testing
☐ Laboratory analysis ☐ An on-site pharmacy

Other ____

All equipment is maintained and calibrated according to state and federal regulations. ☐

III. Occupational Medicine

A. Specially tailored examinations are available and include:

1. Job placement examinations (preplacement) ☐
2. Health surveillance examinations ☐
3. Executive examinations ☐
4. Periodic examinations ☐

Job descriptions are requested in the screening process. ☐

B. Special examinations can be obtained for:
   1. Work evaluations ☐
   2. Return-to-work evaluation ☐
   3. Disability evaluation ☐
   4. Disabled worker ☐
   5. Other ______________________________

IV. Services provided include:

A. Prompt, personalized expert attention. (Wait for treatment is no longer than 10 minutes. Emergency cases are taken immediately.) ☐

B. Responsible workers' comp reporting plus same-day notification of results to employer. ☐

C. A full report, including employee's diagnosis, treatment and return-to-work status, is relayed via telephone to employer the day of injury and after each visit thereafter. ☐

D. Within five days of treating any employee, occupational medical facility will forward copies of doctor's first report and any narrative letter to employer. ☐

E. Facility files with appropriate agency/commission any special reports or documents as required by the jurisdiction. ☐

F. Physician evaluates availability of modified duty to facilitate returning employee to work the same day or as soon as he/she is ready. ☐

G. Treatment is not extended beyond what is needed. ☐

H. Costs of treatment follows standardized billing codes. ☐

I. A policy is in place for referral to private physicians and specialists. ☐

J. A referral is made as soon as it is necessary. ☐

K. Commonly prescribed medications and orthopedic supplies are available. ☐

L. Assistance is available for complying with state and federal regulations. ☐

M. Education and training programs are available and include:
   1. CPR and first aid training ☐
   2. Back injury prevention ☐
   3. Substance abuse ☐
   4. Stress management ☐
   5. Fitness ☐
   6. Weight control ☐
   7. Other ______________________________

V. Testimony

A member of the facility in occupational medicine is available to be called upon (or subpoenaed) to give a deposition, or to serve as either an expert or percipient witness in deposition, in a hearing, or in court. ☐

Comments:

____

____

____

____

APPENDIX FIVE

SAMPLE WORKERS' COMP POLICY

WORKERS COMPENSATION AND EMPLOYERS LIABILITY INSURANCE POLICY **WC 00 00 01 A**

Standard

INFORMATION PAGE

Insurer:

POLICY NO.

1. The Insured: ___ Individual ___ Partnership
   Mailing address: ___ Corporation or ___
   Other workplaces not shown above:

2. The policy period is from ______ to ______ at the insured's mailing address.

3. A. Workers Compensation Insurance: Part One of the policy applies to the Workers Compensation Law of the states listed here:

   B. Employers Liability Insurance: Part two of the policy applies to work in each state listed in item 3.A. The limits of our liability under Part Two are:

   Bodily Injury by Accident $ ___ each accident
   Bodily Injury by Disease $ ___ policy limit
   Bodily Injury by Disease $ ___ each employee

   C. Other States Insurance: Part three of the policy applies to the states, if any, listed here:

   D. This policy includes these endorsements and schedules:

4. The premium for this policy will be determined by our Manuals of Rules, Classifications, Rates and Rating Plans. All information required below is subject to verification and change by audit.

Classifications	Code No.	Premium Basis Total Estimated Annual Remuneration	Rate Per $100 of Remuneration	Estimated Annual Premium

Total Estimated Annual Premium $

Minimum Premium $ Expense Constant $

Countersigned by: ______

WORKERS COMPENSATION AND EMPLOYERS LIABILITY INSURANCE POLICY

In return for the payment of the premium and subject to all terms of this policy, we agree with you as follows:

GENERAL SECTION

A. **The Policy**

This policy includes at its effective date the Information Page and all endorsements and schedules listed there. It is a contract of insurance between you (the employer named in Item 1 of the Information Page) and us (the insurer named on the Information Page). The only agreements relating to this insurance are stated in this policy. The terms of this policy may not be changed or waived except by endorsement issued by us to be part of this policy.

B. **Who Is Insured**

You are insured if you are an employer named in Item 1 of the Information Page. If that employer is a partnership, and if you are one of its partners, you are insured, but only in your capacity as an employer of the partnership's employees.

C. **Workers Compensation Law**

Workers Compensation Law means the workers or workmen's compensation law and occupational disease law of each state or territory named in Item 3.A. of the Information Page. It includes any amendments to that law which are in effect during the policy period. It does not include any federal workers or workmen's compensation law, any federal occupational disease law or the provisions of any law that provide nonoccupational disability benefits.

D. **State**

State means any state of the United States of America, and the District of Columbia.

E. **Locations**

This policy covers all of your workplaces listed in Items 1 or 4 of the Information Page; and it covers all other workplaces in Item 3.A. states unless you have other insurance or are self-insured for such workplaces.

PART ONE
WORKERS COMPENSATION INSURANCE

A. **How This Insurance Applies**

This workers compensation insurance applies to bodily injury by accident or bodily injury by disease. Bodily injury includes resulting death.

1. Bodily injury by accident must occur during the policy period.
2. Bodily injury by disease must be caused or aggravated by the conditions of your employment. The employee's last day of last exposure to the conditions causing or aggravating such bodily injury by disease must occur during the policy period.

B. **We Will Pay**

We will pay promptly when due the benefits required of you by the workers compensation law.

C. **We Will Defend**

We have the right and duty to defend at our expense any claim, proceeding or suit against you for benefits payable by this insurance. We have the right to investigate and settle these claims, proceedings or suits.

We have no duty to defend a claim, proceeding or suit that is not covered by this insurance.

D. **We Will Also Pay**

We will also pay these costs, in addition to other amounts payable under this insurance, as part of any claim, proceeding or suit we defend:

1. reasonable expenses incurred at our request, but not loss of earnings;
2. premiums for bonds to release attachments and for appeal bonds in bond amounts up to the amount payable under this insurance;
3. litigation costs taxed against you;
4. interest on a judgment as required by law until we offer the amount due under this insurance; and
5. expenses we incur.

E. **Other Insurance**

We will not pay more than our share of benefits and costs covered by this insurance and other insurance or self-insurance. Subject to any limits of liability that may apply, all shares will be equal until the loss is paid. If any insurance or self-insurance is exhausted, the shares of all remaining insurance will be equal until the loss is paid.

F. **Payments You Must Make**

You are responsible for any payments in excess of the benefits regularly provided by the workers compensation law including those required because:

1. of your serious and willful misconduct;
2. you knowingly employ an employee in violation of law;
3. you fail to comply with a health or safety law or regulation; or
4. you discharge, coerce or otherwise discriminate against any employee in violation of the workers compensation law.

If we make any payments in excess of the benefits regularly provided by the workers compensation law on your behalf, you will reimburse us promptly.

G. **Recovery From Others**

We have your rights, and the rights of persons entitled to the benefits of this insurance, to recover our payments from anyone liable for the injury. You will do everything necessary to protect those rights for us and to help us enforce them.

H. **Statutory Provisions**

These statements apply where they are required by law.

1. As between an injured worker and us, we have notice of the injury when you have notice.
2. Your default or the bankruptcy or insolvency of you or your estate will not relieve us of our duties under this insurance after an injury occurs.
3. We are directly and primarily liable to any person entitled to the benefits payable by this insurance. Those persons may enforce our duties; so may an agency authorized by law. Enforcement may be against us or against you and us.
4. Jurisdiction over you is jurisdiction over us for purposes of the workers compensation law. We are bound by decisions against you under that law, subject to the provisions of this policy that are not in conflict with that law.
5. This insurance conforms to the parts of the workers compensation law that apply to:
   a. benefits payable by this insurance; or
   b. special taxes, payments into security or other special funds, and assessments payable by us under that law.
6. Terms of this insurance that conflict with the workers compensation law are changed by this statement to conform to that law.

Nothing in these paragraphs relieves you of your duties under this policy.

PART TWO
EMPLOYERS LIABILITY INSURANCE

A. **How This Insurance Applies**

This employers liability insurance applies to bodily injury by accident or bodily injury by disease. Bodily injury includes resulting death.

1. The bodily injury must arise out of and in the course of the injured employee's employment by you.
2. The employment must be necessary or incidental to your work in a state or territory listed in Item 3.A. of the Information Page.
3. Bodily injury by accident must occur during the policy period.
4. Bodily injury by disease must be caused or aggravated by the conditions of your employment. The employee's last day of last exposure to the conditions causing or aggravating such bodily injury by disease must occur during the policy period.
5. If you are sued, the original suit and any related legal actions for damages for bodily injury by accident or by disease must be brought in the United States of America, its territories or possessions, or Canada.

B. **We Will Pay**

We will pay all sums you legally must pay as damages because of bodily injury to your employees, provided the bodily injury is covered by this Employers Liability Insurance.

The damages we will pay, where recovery is permitted by law, include damages:

1. for which you are liable to a third party by reason of a claim or suit against you by that third party to recover the damages claimed

against such third party as a result of injury to your employee;

2. for care and loss of services; and
3. for consequential bodily injury to a spouse, child, parent, brother or sister of the injured employee;

provided that these damages are the direct consequence of bodily injury that arises out of and in the course of the injured employee's employment by you; and

4. because of bodily injury to your employee that arises out of and in the course of employment, claimed against you in a capacity other than as employer.

C. **Exclusions**

This insurance does not cover:

1. liability assumed under a contract. This exclusion does not apply to a warranty that your work will be done in a workmanlike manner;
2. punitive or exemplary damages because of bodily injury to an employee employed in violation of law;
3. bodily injury to an employee while employed in violation of law with your actual knowledge or the actual knowledge of any of your executive officers;
4. any obligation imposed by a workers compensation, occupational disease, unemployment compensation, or disability benefits law, or any similar law;
5. bodily injury intentionally caused or aggravated by you;
6. bodily injury occurring outside the United States of America, its territories or possessions, and Canada. This exclusion does not apply to bodily injury to a citizen or resident of the United States of America or Canada who is temporarily outside these countries;
7. damages arising out of coercion, criticism, demotion, evaluation, reassignment, discipline, defamation, harassment, humiliation, discrimination against or termination of any employee, or any personnel practices, policies, acts or omissions;
8. bodily injury to any person in work subject to the Longshore and Harbor Workers' Compensation Act (33 USC Sections 901–950), the Nonappropriated Fund Instrumentalities Act (5 USC Sections 8171–8173), the Outer Continental Shelf Lands Act (43 USC Sections 1331–1356), the Defense Base Act (42 USC Sections 1651–1654), the Federal Coal Mine Health and Safety Act of 1969 (30 USC Sections 901–942), any other federal workers or workmen's compensation law or other federal occupational disease law, or any amendments to these laws;
9. bodily injury to any person in work subject to the Federal Employers' Liability Act (45 USC Sections 51–60), any other federal laws obligating an employer to pay damages to an employee due to bodily injury arising out of or in the course of employment, or any amendments to those laws;
10. bodily injury to a master or member of the crew of any vessel;
11. fines or penalties imposed for violation of federal or state law; and
12. damages payable under the Migrant and Seasonal Agricultural Worker Protection Act (29 USC Sections 1801–1872) and under any other federal law awarding damages for violation of those laws or regulations issued thereunder, and any amendments to those laws.

D. **We Will Defend**

We have the right and duty to defend, at our expense, any claim, proceeding or suit against you for damages payable by this insurance. We have the right to investigate and settle these claims, proceedings and suits.

We have no duty to defend a claim, proceeding or suit that is not covered by this insurance. We have no duty to defend or continue defending after we have paid our applicable limit of liability under this insurance.

E. **We Will Also Pay**

We will also pay these costs, in addition to other amounts payable under this insurance, as part of any claim, proceeding, or suit we defend:

1. reasonable expenses incurred at our request, but not loss of earnings;
2. premiums for bonds to release attachments and for appeal bonds in bond amounts up to the limit of our liability under this insurance;
3. litigation costs taxed against you;
4. interest on a judgment as required by law until we offer the amount due under this insurance; and
5. expenses we incur.

F. **Other Insurance**

We will not pay more than our share of damages and costs covered by this insurance and other insurance or self-insurance. Subject to any limits of liability that apply, all shares will be equal until the loss is paid. If any insurance or self-insurance is exhausted, the shares of all remaining insurance and self-insurance will be equal until the loss is paid.

G. **Limits of Liability**

Our liability to pay for damages is limited. Our limits of liability are shown in Item 3.B. of the Information Page. They apply as explained below.

1. Bodily Injury by Accident. The limit shown for "bodily injury by accident—each accident" is the most we will pay for all damages covered by this insurance because of bodily injury to one or more employees in any one accident.

   A disease is not bodily injury by accident unless it results directly from bodily injury by accident.

2. Bodily Injury by Disease. The limit shown for "bodily injury by disease—policy limit" is the most we will pay for all damages covered by this insurance and arising out of bodily injury by disease, regardless of the number of employees who sustain bodily injury by disease. The limit shown for "bodily injury by disease—each employee" is the most we will pay for all damages because of bodily injury by disease to any one employee.

   Bodily injury by disease does not include disease that results directly from a bodily injury by accident.

3. We will not pay any claims for damages after we have paid the applicable limit of our liability under this insurance.

H. **Recovery From Others**

We have your rights to recover our payment from anyone liable for an injury covered by this insurance. You will do everything necessary to protect those rights for us and to help us enforce them.

I. **Actions Against Us**

There will be no right of action against us under this insurance unless:

1. You have complied with all the terms of this policy; and
2. The amount you owe has been determined with our consent or by actual trial and final judgment.

This insurance does not give anyone the right to add us as a defendant in an action against you to determine your liability. The bankruptcy or insolvency of you or your estate will not relieve us of our obligations under this Part.

PART THREE
OTHER STATES INSURANCE

A. **How This Insurance Applies**

1. This other states insurance applies only if one or more states are shown in Item 3.C. of the Information Page.
2. If you begin work in any one of those states after the effective date of this policy and are not insured or are not self-insured for such work, all provisions of the policy will apply as though that state were listed in Item 3.A. of the Information Page.
3. We will reimburse you for the benefits required by the workers compensation law of that state if we are not permitted to pay the benefits directly to persons entitled to them.
4. If you have work on the effective date of this policy in any state not listed in Item 3.A. of the Information Page, coverage will not be afforded for that state unless we are notified within thirty days.

B. **Notice**

Tell us at once if you begin work in any state listed in Item 3.C. of the Information Page.

PART FOUR
YOUR DUTIES IF INJURY OCCURS

Tell us at once if injury occurs that may be covered by this policy. Your other duties are listed here.

1. Provide for immediate medical and other services required by the workers compensation law.
2. Give us or our agent the names and addresses of the injured persons and of witnesses, and other information we may need.
3. Promptly give us all notices, demands and legal

papers related to the injury, claim, proceeding or suit.

4. Cooperate with us and assist us, as we may request, in the investigation, settlement or defense of any claim, proceeding or suit.
5. Do nothing after an injury occurs that would interfere with our right to recover from others.
6. Do not voluntarily make payments, assume obligations or incur expenses, except at your own cost.

PART FIVE—PREMIUM

A. **Our Manuals**

All premium for this policy will be determined by our manuals of rules, rates, rating plans and classifications. We may change our manuals and apply the changes to this policy if authorized by law or a governmental agency regulating this insurance.

B. **Classifications**

Item 4 of the Information Page shows the rate and premium basis for certain business or work classifications. These classifications were assigned based on an estimate of the exposures you would have during the policy period. If your actual exposures are not properly described by those classifications, we will assign proper classifications, rates and premium basis by endorsement to this policy.

C. **Remuneration**

Premium for each work classification is determined by multiplying a rate times a premium basis. Remuneration is the most common premium basis. This premium basis includes payroll and all other remuneration paid or payable during the policy period for the services of:

1. all your officers and employees engaged in work covered by this policy; and
2. all other persons engaged in work that could make us liable under Part One (Workers Compensation Insurance) of this policy. If you do not have payroll records for these persons, the contract price for their services and materials may be used as the premium basis. This paragraph 2 will not apply if you give us proof that the employers of these persons lawfully secured their workers compensation obligations.

D. **Premium Payments**

You will pay all premium when due. You will pay the premium even if part or all of a workers compensation law is not valid.

E. **Final Premium**

The premium shown on the Information Page, schedules, and endorsements is an estimate. The final premium will be determined after this policy ends by using the actual, not the estimated, premium basis and the proper classifications and rates that lawfully apply to the business and work covered by this policy. If the final premium is more than the premium you paid to us, you must pay us the balance. If it is less, we will refund the balance to you. The final premium will not be less than the highest minimum premium for the classifications covered by this policy.

If this policy is canceled, final premium will be determined in the following way unless our manuals provide otherwise:

1. If we cancel, final premium will be calculated pro rata based on the time this policy was in force. Final premium will not be less than the pro rata share of the minimum premium.
2. If you cancel, final premium will be more than pro rata; it will be based on the time this policy was in force, and increased by our short-rate cancelation table and procedure. Final premium will not be less than the minimum premium.

F. **Records**

You will keep records of information needed to compute premium. You will provide us with copies of those records when we ask for them.

G. **Audit**

You will let us examine and audit all your records that relate to this policy. These records include ledgers, journals, registers, vouchers, contracts, tax reports, payroll and disbursement records, and programs for storing and retrieving data. We may conduct the audits during regular business hours during the policy period and within three years after the policy period ends. Information developed by audit will be used to determine final premium. Insurance rate service organizations have the same rights we have under this provision.

PART SIX—CONDITIONS

A. **Inspection**

We have the right, but are not obliged to inspect your workplaces at any time. Our inspections are not safety inspections. They relate only to the insurability of the workplaces and the premiums to be charged. We may give you reports on the conditions we find. We may also recommend changes. While they may help reduce losses, we do not undertake to perform the duty of any person to provide for the health or safety of your employees or the public. We do not warrant that your workplaces are safe or healthful or that they comply with laws, regulations, codes or standards. Insurance rate service organizations have the same rights we have under this provision.

B. **Long Term Policy**

If the policy period is longer than one year and sixteen days, all provisions of this policy will apply as though a new policy were issued on each annual anniversary that this policy is in force.

C. **Transfer of Your Rights and Duties**

Your rights or duties under this policy may not be transferred without our written consent.

If you die and we receive notice within thirty days after your death, we will cover your legal representative as insured.

D. **Cancelation**

1. You may cancel this policy. You must mail or deliver advance written notice to us stating when the cancelation is to take effect.
2. We may cancel this policy. We must mail or deliver to you not less than ten days advance written notice stating when the cancelation is to take effect. Mailing that notice to you at your mailing address shown in Item 1 of the Information Page will be sufficient to prove notice.
3. The policy period will end on the day and hour stated in the cancelation notice.
4. Any of these provisions that conflict with a law that controls the cancelation of the insurance in this policy is changed by this statement to comply with the law.

E. **Sole Representative**

The insured first named in Item 1 of the Information Page will act on behalf of all insureds to change this policy, receive return premium, and give or receive notice of cancelation.

This endorsement changes the policy to which it is attached and is effective on the date issued unless otherwise stated.

(The information below is required only when this endorsement is issued subsequent to preparation of the policy.)

Endorsement Effective Policy No. Endorsement No.
Insured Premium $

Insurance Company Countersigned by ______________________

ACORD WORKERS' COMPENSATION APPLICATION

SET TABSTOPS AT ARROWS

MAIL TO: (INSURER/UNDERWRITER)

DATE (MM/DD/YY)

PRODUCER

CODE | SUB-CODE

APPLICANT INFORMATION

NAME

MAILING ADDRESS (Include Zip Code)

☐ INDIVIDUAL ☐ PARTNERSHIP ☐ CORPORATION ☐ OTHER

Years in Business

EMPLOYER I.D. NUMBER | RATING BUREAU I.D. NO. | ☐ QUOTE ☐ ISSUE | ☐ BOUND (Give Date Attach Copy)

LOCATIONS

#	STREET, CITY, COUNTY, STATE, ZIP CODE
1	
2	
3	

POLICY INFORMATION

INSURER	POLICY NUMBER	Proposed Eff. Date (MM/DD/YY)	Proposed Exp. Date (MM/DD/YY)	Normal Anniversary Rating Date
PREVIOUS INSURER	PREVIOUS POLICY NO.	☐ PARTICIPATING ☐ NON-PARTICIPATING	Dividend Plan/Safety Group	RETRO PLAN
COVERAGE A (STATES)	COVERAGE B (If Not $100,000) $	☐ AGENCY BILL ☐ DIRECT BILL	PAYMENT PLAN ☐ ANNUAL ☐ SEMI-ANNUAL ☐ QUARTERLY ☐	AUDIT PERIOD ☐ AT EXPIRATION ☐ SEMI-ANNUAL ☐ QUARTERLY ☐ MONTHLY

SPECIAL COMPANY AND STATE INFORMATION

RATING INFORMATION

STATE	LOC.	CLASS CODE	COMPANY USE	CATEGORIES, DUTIES, CLASSIFICATIONS	NO. OF EM-PLOYEES	ESTIMATED ANNUAL REMUNERATION	RATE	ESTIMATED ANNUAL PREMIUM

SPECIFY ADDITIONAL COVERAGES/ENDORSEMENTS

☐ BROAD FORM ALL STATES
☐ U.S.L. & H.
☐ VOLUNTARY COMPENSATION
☐ OTHER

TOTAL	$
EXPERIENCE MODIFICATION	
MODIFIED PREMIUM	$
	$
	$
PREMIUM DISCOUNT	$
	$
	$
TOTAL ESTIMATED ANNUAL PREMIUM	$
MINIMUM $ / DEPOSIT PREMIUM	$

ACORD 130 (11/81)

PLEASE COMPLETE REVERSE SIDE

SET TAB STOPS AT ARROWS

INDIVIDUALS INCLUDED/EXCLUDED

PARTNERS, OFFICERS, RELATIVES TO BE INCLUDED OR EXCLUDED. Remuneration To Be Included Must Be Part Of Rating Information Section.

#	NAME	AGE	TITLE/ RELATIONSHIP	OWNER-SHIP %	DUTIES	INC./EXC.	CLASS CODE	RE-MUNERATION
1								
2								
3								
4								
5								

PRIOR EXPERIENCE

PROVIDE INFORMATION FOR THE PAST 5 YEARS AND USE THE REMARKS SECTION FOR LOSS DETAILS

YEAR	INSURER & POLICY NUMBER	ANNUAL PREMIUM	MOD.	#CLAIMS	AMOUNT PAID	RESERVE

NATURE OF BUSINESS/DESCRIPTION OF OPERATIONS

Give comments and descriptions of business, operations and products: Manufacturing—raw materials, processes, product, equipment. Contractor—type of work, sub-contracts. Mercantile—merchandise, customers, deliveries. Service—type, location. Farm—acreage, animals, machinery, sub-contracts.

GENERAL INFORMATION

PLEASE PROVIDE ALL THE REQUIRED DETAILS FOR "YES" RESPONSES BY USING THE REMARKS AREA BELOW

	YES	NO		YES	NO
(1) Does Applicant Own, Operate Or Lease Aircraft/Watercraft?			(11) Any Employees Under 16 Or Over 50 Years Of Age?		
(2) Any Exposure To Flammables, Explosives, Caustics, Fumes?			(12) Any Employees Over 60 Years Of Age?		
(3) Any Exposure To Radioactive Materials?			(13) Any Part Time Or Seasonal Employees?		
(4) Any Work Performed Underground Or Above 15 Feet?			(14) Is There Any Volunteer Or Donated Labor?		
(5) Any Work Performed On Barges, Vessels, Docks?			(15) Any Employees With Physical Handicaps?		
(6) Is Applicant Engaged In Any Other Type Of Business?			(16) Do Employees Travel Out Of State?		
(7) Are Sub-Contractors Used?			(17) Are Athletic Teams Sponsored?		
(8) Any Work Sublet Without Certificates Of Ins.?			(18) Are Pre-Employment Physicals Required?		
(9) Is A Formal Safety Program In Operation?			(19) Any Other Insurance With This Insurer?		
(10) Any Group Transportation Provided?			(20) Any Prior Covg. Declined/Cancelled/Non-Renewed (Last 3 Yrs.)?		

INSPECTION (CONTACT/PHONE)

ACCOUNTING RECORDS (CONTACT/PHONE)

REMARKS

APPLICABLE IN NEW YORK STATE

Any person who knowingly and with intent to defraud any insurance company or other person files an application for insurance containing any false information, or conceals for the purpose of misleading, information concerning any fact material thereto, commits a fraudulent insurance act, which is a crime.

APPLICANT'S SIGNATURE		PRODUCER'S SIGNATURE	

ACORD 130 (11/81)

APPENDIX SIX

REPORT OF INJURY

This report is based on the Missouri Department of Labor and Industrial Relations' Division of Workers' Compensation's injury report.

EMPLOYER INFORMATION

Name ____

Address ______________________________________

City, State, ZIP __________________________________

Phone (______ **)** ________________________________

Nature of business and specific product ________________________

Insurance carrier and address ______________________________

____

Days per year business operates, Number of employees ________________

Date of accident or incident or disease diagnosis __________________

Time of accident ______________ ☐ a.m. ☐ p.m.

Place of accident ______________________________________

INJURED EMPLOYEE INFORMATION

Name ____

Home address ___________________________________

City, state, ZIP __________________________________

Phone: Home ___________________________________

Office ___________________________________

Social Security number, Age ______________________________

Years employed ______________________________________

Regular occupation ___________________________________

Regular department ___________________________________

Occupation when injured ________________________________

How long at current occupation? ___________________________

Work days per week, Weekly wage ___________________________

INJURY EVENT INFORMATION

Was accident or exposure on employer's premises? ☐ Yes ☐ No

Time work began for employee on injury date _____________________

How did the accident occur? (Describe fully.) _____________________

____

____

What was employee doing when injured (be specific). ________________

____

____

Name the object or subject which directly injured the employee. __________

____

Were there any witnesses? List them. ______________________________

____

____

What actions, events or conditions contributed most directly to this accident? ______

____

____

Could anything be done to prevent accidents of this type? ☐ Yes ☐ No

If so, what? ______________________________

____

NATURE OF INJURY

Describe the injury or illness in detail and indicate the part of the body affected. ____

____

____

Did injury result in death? ☐ Yes ☐ No

If so, date of death. ______________________________

Employee's dependents:

Name of dependent	Relation to employee	Address of dependent

Was there any dismemberment or other permanent disability? ☐ Yes ☐ No

State nature. ______________________________

Has employee returned to work? ______________ Date ______________

At what weekly wage? ______________________________

When did temporary disability begin? ______________ End? ______________

OTHER INFORMATION

Name and address of attending physician. ______________________________

____

Name and address of hospital. ______________________________

Actual or estimated cost of medical aid. ______________________________

Is further medical aid required? ______________________________

Name and address of individuals to whom communication should be addressed. ____

____

Date of report. ______________________________

Report completed by [signature] ______________________________

Title ______________________________

NOTICE AND ACKNOWLEDGEMENT OF RIGHT TO WORKERS' COMPENSATION BENEFITS

This form is required by Missouri's Division of Workers' Compensation for accidents involving less than $500 in total medical costs and no lost time from employment. The employee must sign the form.

I, [print/type name of employee]_______________________, understand that on the ________ day of ______________, 19_____, while engaged in employment at [location of accident]___________________________, I suffered an injury or illness for which compensation is payable under state Workers' Compensation law. As an injured employee I am entitled to workers' compensation benefits. These benefits include:

(1) MEDICAL CARE TO CURE THE INJURY. The employer/insurer must provide all reasonable and necessary medical care to cure the injury/illness. There is no deductible, and all costs are paid directly by the employer/insurer (i.e. doctor bills, medicines, hospital costs, lab test fees, X-rays, crutches, etc. plus mileage). The employer/insurer, however, has the right to choose the doctor, medical facilities, etc., and is not required to pay for the cost of any treatment not authorized by them. [Note: *This does not apply in every state.*]

(2) CASH PAYMENT FOR LOST WAGES. If an employee is unable to work more than three regularly scheduled work days because of a work-related injury/illness, the employer/insurer must provide the employee with temporary disability payments until the doctor says the employee is able to return to work. (*Note: This benefit does not apply to employees who have not missed any time from work.*)

(3) ADDITIONAL CASH PAYMENTS. Once medical treatment is completed and a determination has been made that the injury has resulted in permanent disability, the employer/insurer is responsible for permanent disability payments, with the amount of compensation being computed according to the disability schedule, as provided by law.

Also, I understand that if I do not act to secure the benefits in a timely manner, I may forfeit my right to such benefits. An employee must file a claim for compensation within two years of the date of the injury or the date of the last payment for medical treatment provided on account of the injury. (However, the two-year period is extended to three years if the employer/insurer does not file the Report of Injury with the Division of Workers' Compensation in a timely manner.)

I solemnly swear or affirm under the penalty of perjury that I have read and understand the Notice and Acknowledgement of Right to Workers' Compensation Benefits; or, through an alternative format, I have been advised of and understand the Notice and Acknowledgement of Right to Workers' Compensation Benefits.

Employee Signature: ____

Date: ____

Signature: ____

CERTIFICATE

The undersigned employer representative, without admitting liability or the compensability of the alleged injury, certifies that a true and accurate copy of this notice has been hand-delivered to the above-referenced employee on this _____ day of ___________, 19____, and is being mailed to the Division of Workers' Compensation accompanied by or affixed to the Report of Injury.

Employer Representative:____

CLAIM FOR COMPENSATION

Employees in Missouri may submit a compensation claim with the state agency regulating workers' comp if a dispute arises with their employer over compensation.

1. Claim is hereby made as follows for compensation as provided by state workers' compensation law, for personal injury (or death) of the employee by accident or occupational disease arising out of and in the court of employment. Both employer and employee have elected to accept said law at the time of the accident.
2. Name of claimant ____________________
   Address ____________________
   City, State, ZIP ____________________
3. Name of employer ____________________
   Address ____________________
   City, State, ZIP ____________________
4. Name of insurer ____________________
   Address ____________________
   City, State, ZIP ____________________
5. Injured employee's name ____________________
   Social Security Number ____________________
6. Average weekly wages ____________________
7. Date of accident/incidence of occupational disease ____________________
8. Hour ____________________ ☐ a.m. ☐ p.m.
9. Place ____________________
   Address ____________________
   City, County, State, ZIP ____________________
10. Did injury result in death? ☐ Yes ☐ No
    If so, list dependents, age, relationship, extent of dependency, address, city, state, ZIP on separate sheet.
11. Parts of body injured ____________________
12. Weeks of temporary disability to date ____________________
13. Weeks of probable future temporary disability ____________________
14. Exact nature of any permanent injury ____________________
    ____
15. How injury occurred, cause, and work employee was doing for employer at the time
    ____
16. Total compensation paid to date ____________________
17. Total value of compensation claimed ____________________

Date: ____________________

Claimant's signature ____________________

Claimant's attorney ____________________

Bar ID number ____________________

Address ____________________

ANSWER TO CLAIM FOR COMPENSATION

Missouri employers answer claims for compensation with this form.

STATE FACTS AND NOT CONCLUSIONS

1. Claimants ______________________________
____

2. Name of employer ______________________________
Address ______________________________
City, state, ZIP ______________________________

3. Name of insurer ______________________________
Address ______________________________
City, state, ZIP ______________________________

4. Injured employee ______________________________

5. Date of accident ______________________________

6. Place (city, state, ZIP) ______________________________

7. ALL OF THE STATEMENTS IN THE CLAIM FOR COMPENSATION ARE ADMITTED EXCEPT THE FOLLOWING:
(Here should be separately set forth the question number of each disputed statement in the claim for compensation, the reason why disputed, and the facts in regard thereto. Add any other facts tending to defeat the claim.)
____
____
____

Date: ______________________________
Employer's signature ______________________________
Insurer's signature ______________________________
Employer and/or insurer's attorney ______________________________
Address ______________________________
Telephone (______) ______________________________

PROTEST OF CLAIM ALLOWANCE

If an insurance carrier pays a workers' comp claim and the employer wishes to protest, the employer should send a letter to the carrier. Here is a sample protest form developed by the state of Washington's Department of Labor and Industries:

Date: ______________________________

To: Claims Manager

Re: Claimant's [employee's] name
Claim number

Dear (Claims Manager):

We protest the allowance of the above-referenced claim for the following reason(s):

- ☐ Claim was not filed within one year of injury or diagnosis of an occupational disease.
- ☐ Injury was not within the course of the worker's employment.
- ☐ The injury was self-inflicted.
- ☐ The incident as reported by injured worker is not consistent with other reports and/or witnesses.
- ☐ The injured worker's condition is not the result of the alleged injury/exposure.
- ☐ The injured worker was an out-of-state [name state] employee at the time of the injury and is not covered under workers' comp insurance.
- ☐ The injury is an aggravation of an industrial injury claim filed with the claimant's former employer. We request investigation of this fact, disallowance of a new claim and re-opening of the previous claim.

Documentation is attached.

AUTHORIZATION TO INSPECT AND/OR COPY MEDICAL RECORDS

Employers may request the medical records of injured employees. This Missouri Division of Workers' Compensation form is sent to medical care providers of injured workers and requires them to furnish their records to employers and others.

To: [medical care provider]

Employee: ____

Employer: ____

Insurer: ____

Date of accident: ____

Place and county of accident: ________________________________

You are hereby authorized to permit ________________[name] on behalf of ___________ [party], to inspect and/or copy any and all medical records you have in your possession in regard to the above captioned case, which is now pending before the Division of Workers' Compensation.

This authorization is made in accordance with [state law] which reads as follows:

> "Every hospital or other person furnishing the employee with medical aid shall permit its record to be copied by and shall furnish full information to the commission, the employer, the employee or his dependents and any other party to any proceedings for compensation under this act, and certified copies of such records shall be admissible in evidence in any such proceedings."

Date: ____

NOTICE OF COMMENCEMENT OF COMPENSATION PAYMENTS

As soon as an employer/insurance company begins compensation payments for an injured employee, detailed records are important for the state division of worker's compensation.

1. Injury number ______
2. Insurer's or employer's number ______
3. Employer's name ______
   Address ______
   City, state, ZIP ______
4. Employee's name ______
   Address ______
   City, State, ZIP ______
5. Employer's insurer ______
   Address ______
   City, State, ZIP ______
6. Date of ☐ Accident ☐ Incidence of occupational disease ______

NOTICE IS HEREBY GIVEN THE DIVISION OF WORKERS' COMPENSATION OF THE COMMENCEMENT OF COMPENSATION PAYMENTS IN THIS CASE, AS INDICATED BELOW:

7. Date first payment was made to employee ______
8. Amount of weekly payment ______
9. First day of period covered by payment ______
10. Estimated number of weeks disability will last; nature of disability ______

    ______

    ______

DEATH BENEFIT PAYMENT

11. To whom paid ______
12. Total amount of weekly payment ______
13. First day of period covered by payment ______
14. Employer's or insurer's signature ______

EMPLOYER AND INSURER ARE REQUIRED BY LAW TO NOTIFY THE DIVISION AT ONCE WHEN COMPENSATION IN THIS CASE TERMINATES.

NOTICE REJECTING CLAIM

Employees should be notified in writing if their claim is rejected. The state of Washington's Department of Labor and Industries informs employees if their claim has been rejected with the following form:

NOTICE OF DECISION

Any protest or request for reconsideration of this order must be made in writing to the Department of Labor and Industries within 60 days, or the same shall become final. A further appealable order will follow such a request.

This claim for benefits is hereby rejected for the following reason(s):

☐ That there is no proof of a specific injury at a definite time and place in the course of employment.

☐ That claimant's condition is not the result of injury alleged.

☐ That claimant's condition is not the result of an industrial injury as defined by the industrial insurance laws.

☐ That the claimant's condition pre-existed the alleged injury and is not related thereto.

☐ That the claimant's condition is not an occupational disease.

Any and all bills for services or treatment concerning this claim are rejected, except those authorized by the Department for diagnosis.

NOTICE OF TERMINATION OF COMPENSATION

The employer/insurer should advise the state when workers' compensation ends.

TO EMPLOYER AND INSURER: Be sure to give the cost of medical aid and furnish all other data items.

TO EMPLOYEE: This receipt is required by the Division of Workers' Compensation, and you are requested to sign it if it covers the payments made to you. Your signature is simply an acknowledgement of money paid and does not constitute a release.

THIS FORM MUST BE FILED WITHIN 10 DAYS OF TERMINATION OF COMPENSATION

1. Employee ____________________

   Social Security number ____________________
2. Date of accident ____________________
3. Cost of medical aid $ ____________________
4. Disability began ____________________
5. Ended ____________________
6. Total weeks of compensation ____________________
7. Average weekly wage $ ____________________
8. Present daily wage $ ____________________
9. Rate of compensation ____________________
10. Nature of disability ____________________

RECEIPT OF COMPENSATION

11. Received of ____________________

    The sum of $ ____________________
12. Dated ____________________
13. Employee's signature ____________________
14. Employee's address ____________________
15. Witness ____________________

NOTICE OF TERMINATION OF COMPENSATION

16. This is to notify the Division of Workers' Compensation and the employee that compensation payments in the above matter have terminated, the last payment having been made on ____________________,19____, for the following reasons:

    ____

    ____

Employer's or insurer's signature ____________________

PHYSICIAN'S REPORT MUST BE FILED WITH THIS FORM

APPENDIX FIFTEEN

REQUEST FOR ASSISTANCE FROM DEPARTMENT OF INSURANCE

In most states, employers may register complaints about their insurance carrier with the state department of insurance. The form below is used in California, where complaints can be registered with the Claims Services Bureau, the Rating Services Bureau or the Underwriting Services Bureau.

For use in:

- ☐ Improper denial of claim or offer of amount less than indicated by the policy
- ☐ Delay in claim settlement
- ☐ Alleged illegal cancellation or termination of insurance policy
- ☐ Alleged misrepresentation by agent, broker or solicitor
- ☐ Alleged theft of premium paid to agent, broker or solicitor
- ☐ Problems concerning insurance premiums and rates

1. Name ______________________________
   Company ______________________________
   Address ______________________________
   City, State, ZIP ______________________________
   Phone (______) ______________________________
2. Complete name of insurance company involved ______________________________
3. a) Name of policyholder ______________________________
   b) If a group policy, provide group name ______________________________
4. Policy identification or certificate number ______________________________
5. Claim number ______________________________
6. Date loss occurred or began ______________________________
7. Agent/broker ______________________________
   Address ______________________________
   City, State, ZIP ______________________________
8. File number with the Department of Insurance ______________________________
9. Name of any other governmental agency you've reported the incident to, as well as file number if known ______________________________
10. Name of attorney representing you ______________________________
11. Any court action pending ______________________________
12. Briefly describe problem ______________________________
    ____
    ____
13. What you consider a fair resolution to your problem ______________________________
    ____
    ____

Signature ______________________________

Date ______________________________

APPENDIX SIXTEEN

SUSPECTED FRADULENT CLAIM REPORT

Employers should report any suspected workers' comp fraud to the proper authorities. This is the information needed in California.

EMPLOYER

Contact name ______________________________________

Address ______________________________________

City, State, ZIP ______________________________________

Phone (______) ______________________________________

CARRIER

Contact name ______________________________________

Address ______________________________________

City, State, ZIP ______________________________________

Phone (______) ______________________________________

Claim No.: ______________________________________

1. Describe nature of suspected fraudulent activity. ______________________________________

   ____

2. What brought this activity to your attention? ______________________________________

   ____

   ____

3. What information has been developed to date to confirm suspicion of this fraudulent activity? ______________________________________

   ____

   ____

4. Do you have any reason to believe that this incident is related to any other fraudulent activity? If yes, please detail any specific information and attach documentation, if any. ______________________________________

   ____

   ____

   ____

   ____

5. List name and address of any agency, government or private, to whom you have reported this matter. ______________________________________

   ____

Date of loss: ______________________________________

Location of loss: ______________________________________

ALL PARTIES TO THE LOSS

(Indicate claimant, witness, medical clinic, medical doctor, chiropractor, attorney, body shop, other)

Name (last, first, middle) ______________________
Street/Apt. # ______________________
City, State, ZIP______________________
Date of birth ______________________
Age ______________________
Social Security no. ______________________
Driver's license no. ______________________
License plate no. ______________________
Phone (______) ______________________

Name (last, first, middle) ______________________
Street/Apt. # ______________________
City, State, ZIP______________________
Date of birth ______________________
Age ______________________
Social Security no. ______________________
Driver's license no. ______________________
License plate no. ______________________
Phone (______) ______________________

Name (last, first, middle) ______________________
Street/Apt. # ______________________
City, state, ZIP ______________________
Date of birth ______________________
Age ______________________
Social Security no. ______________________
Driver's license no. ______________________
License plate no. ______________________
Phone (______) ______________________

Name (last, first, middle) ______________________
Street/Apt. # ______________________
City, State, ZIP______________________
Date of birth ______________________
Age ______________________
Social Security no. ______________________
Driver's license no. ______________________
License plate no. ______________________
Phone (______) ______________________

Name (last, first, middle) ______________________
Street/Apt. # ______________________
City, State, ZIP______________________
Date of birth ______________________
Age ______________________
Social Security no. ______________________
Driver's license no. ______________________
License plate no. ______________________
Phone (______) ______________________

APPENDIX SEVENTEEN

LETTER TO INSURANCE CARRIER CONTESTING WORKERS' COMP CLAIM FOR SUSPECTED FRAUD

Employers contesting a workers' comp claim should send a letter to their carrier. This letter was sent by an Arizona employer.

Date ______________________________

Carrier name ______________________________

Address ______________________________

City, State, ZIP______________________________

Dear Sir / Madam:

This letter accompanies the submission of a claim form for an employee no longer with our company. The reason for the letter is to provide you information to help you fight this claim, which I believe to be fraudulent.

The ex-employee worked with us from [month, day, year] until [month, day, year], when she was laid off. She received [number] weeks' severence pay, as is our policy, on the day she left. Although she is claiming she was injured on [month, day, year], she never informed me nor her supervisor of this until after she left. She herself was a supervisor and had handled injury reports from her staff before, so she knew our injury procedure very well. This procedure includes sending someone to a doctor immediately, and not allowing them to come back to work until they receive a signed release.

She also did not lose any work time around this alleged injury. In fact, after the alleged injury, she worked overtime the next day (see attached time sheet).

I am including a detailed wage statement by pay period for a year prior to the alleged date of injury, and the claimant's personnel file.

I would like to help you fight this claim in any way I can. Please let me know if there is more I can do.

Sincerely,

Employer

APPENDIX EIGHTEEN

LETTER TO VOCATIONAL REHABILITATION FACILITY REQUESTING MODIFIED WORK PLAN

The employer's best deterrent against major workers' compensation losses is to keep the injured worker gainfully employed. Otherwise, lost time is lost money. By keeping in touch with the claimant's vocational rehabilitation counselor, the employer encourages the employee's return to work, even if on a modified basis.

Date: ____

RE: Employee/patient name
Claim number

Dear _____________:

Our company offers a modified work program for physically restricted employees. The purpose of the program is to provide meaningful work during the rehabiliation and recovery period of injured workers, while avoiding further suffering or aggravation of the injury.

[Company name] encourages release to a modified assignment as soon as possible after an injury and is willing to work within the limitations you identify. A job description(s) for available work is/are enclosed. Please indicate which positions you authorize as suitable work for the employee named above.

We appreciate a response at your earliest convenience. If you have questions about our program, please feel free to call.

Sincerely,

[Name, title, telephone]

Enclosures: Modified duty job descriptions
Doctor's release form

APPENDIX NINETEEN

JOB ANALYSIS

The trick to reducing lost time is to provide light-duty jobs that injured workers can perform. A detailed job analysis helps in providing accurate job descriptions. The following job analysis form developed by the state of Washington's Department of Labor and Industries helps the employer to determine physical demands of jobs.

1. Job Title ______________________________
2. Location ______________________________
3. Work hours ______________________________
4. Days/weeks ______________________________
5. Meal break(s) ______________________________
6. Overtime ______________________________
7. General description of the job and duties ______________________________
____
____
8. Types of equipment, machinery used on the job ______________________________
____
____
9. Types of tools used on the job ______________________________
____
____
10. Vehicles or moving equipment driven as part of the job ______________________________
____
____
11. Personal protective equipment/clothing required for the job ______________________________
____
____
12. Possible chemical exposure as regular part of the job ______________________________
____
____
13. Above or below normal temperatures as part of the job ______________________________
____
____
14. Percentage of time spent each day:

    Walking__________ Sitting __________ Standing__________
    Indoors __________ Outdoors __________ Driving __________
15. The job can ____ cannot ____ be modified to accommodate an injured or handicapped worker.
    If yes, what modifications can be made? ______________________________
    ____
    ____

16. Physical movements required:	Average frequency per day	Estimated frequency per day
A. Twisting	______	______
B. Stooping/bending	______	______
C. Squatting	______	______
D. Kneeling	______	______
E. Crawling	______	______
F. Climbing stairs	______	______
G. Climbing ladders	______	______
H. Walking indoors	______	______
I. Walking outdoors	______	______
J. Working at heights	______	______
K. Repetitive hand motion	______	______
L. Sitting with vibration	______	______

17. Physical Activity Required:		
A. Lifting/carrying (up to 10 lbs.)	______	______
B. Lifting/carrying (11-24 lbs.)	______	______
C. Lifting/carrying (25-50 lbs.)	______	______
D. Lifting/carrying	______	______
E. Reaching/working above (over 50 lbs.)	______	______
F. Reaching/working at shoulder level	______	______
G. Reaching/working below waist level	______	______
H. Pushing heavy objects		

______________________________ Physician's signature

______________________________ Employer's signature

SAMPLE FUNCTIONAL JOB DESCRIPTIONS

These detailed job descriptions were created by the Schwab Rehabilitation Center of Chicago, IL,. They illustrate exact analyses of the physical demands of jobs, as well as the modifications that could be made to accommodate injured or disabled workers.

POSITION: SOFT-PIE PREPARATION — OPERATION

The soft-pie preparation operator is responsible for:

Unpacking butter
Greasing pie tins
Proportioning and weighing fudge base
Spinning graham shells
Patching and preparing pumpkin shells
Filling cream tanks
Sifting French apple crumbs
Scrapping fruit pies
Portioning and trimming praline shells
Capping strawberries
Cutting peanut butter cups
Shaving chocolate
Pulling racks
Packing pies
Stocking pallets

Rotation through a variety of job activities may occur on any shift. Parts of this job consist of assembly line production. This job may be adapted by assigning a worker to only one of the outlined tasks. A total of 65 employees perform this job per shift, three shifts per day. Only one essential function of the job is outlined.

CHOCOLATE SHAVING

Using a two-hand lift, the worker removes a 10 lb. block of chocolate from a 50 lb. box which sits on the floor to a work table 34" high. Each 10 lb. block of chocolate is then scored with a knife and broken over the edge of the work table into 1 and 1 1/2 lb. blocks. The worker holds the chocolate in one hand and, using a vegetable peeler with a padded handle, makes downward strokes against the block of chocolate. The shavings fall onto a metal tray. The trays are then placed on a rack from 7" to 71" high. Frequency was timed at 84 strokes per minute. One tray was filled approximately every 10 minutes. This was consistent observing one worker. Filled trays are placed in a tray rack at levels from 7" to 71" high.

Measurements:

Work table height — 34"
Chocolate box — 50 lbs.
Tray — 5 lbs. filled, 17.5" x 26"
Chocolate block — 71" high

Physical requirements:

Stooping — to pick up chocolate
Lifting — from floor to 34", from 34" to 7" and up to 71" (two hand lift)
Reaching — for tools, tray, chocolate
Handling — Knife, shaver, chocolate
Grasping — trays, shaving tools
Fingering — tools, trays
Carrying — trays to rack, 2-3 feet
Standing — up to 8 hours

Frequent motion:

Wrist flexion and medial deviation, extension, stooping to floor level.

Possible modifications and/or accommodations:

1. Adapt the work space so worker can perform task in sitting position.
2. Boxes may be stored at work table height.
3. An assistant can lift the blocks of chocolate.
4. An assistant can cut the 10 lb. blocks into smaller pieces.
5. Because of the number of people performing this task, a worker could be hired to do just this task.
6. An assistant can remove the filled trays from storage racks.
7. Because of the number of workers performing this part of the assembly line task, an assistant could be hired to assist all of the workers in the above referenced tasks without negatively affecting production standards.
8. Work can be performed in alternating sitting and standing positions.

May be performed by:

1. Individual in a wheelchair
2. Individual with a developmental disability
3. Individual with a leg amputation
4. Individual with a hearing impairment
5. Developmentally disabled individual
6. Individual with a back problem

Number of other employees available to perform this task: 22

Percent of time spend performing this job task:
This task is performed constantly.

This job requires the use of two hands and visual acuity.

POSITION: LABORER

The essential functions of this position were determined to be:

Course screening
Garbage collection
Cleaning tanks
Digging ditches
Sampling

The marginal activities were listed as:

Indoor cleaning
Moving furniture
Planting trees
Snow removal

GARBAGE COLLECTION

Two workers pick up 55 gallon drums which are filled with refuse. Cans are at ground level and are lifted with a two-person lift to a 42-inch high dumpster. Approximately 15 cans per day are emptied. A five-man team usually takes 45 minutes to complete this task each day.

Physical requirements

Walking - to get garbage can and to empty the can
Lifting - 55 gallon drum
Carrying - to move cans to dumpster
Handling - drums
Reaching - to tip drums
Seeing - to handle drums, lift and empty

Skill or specialization required:

A high school diploma or GED equivalent is required. Within the first 12 months of employment, a worker must successfully complete two 1-week classes in sampling procedures and toxic waste hazards control. This is a non-union position.

Number of people available to perform job:

There is one 5-person crew. The crew works an 8-hour day from 7 a.m. to 3 p.m. Some tasks are performed by a partial crew.

Psychological considerations:

Workers work in teams and independently. At times team work is important for safety. Work is routine.

Physiological considerations:

Workers are exposed to chemicals and odors which could affect respiratory function.

Environmental considerations:

Workers are expected to work inside and out in all weather. There are frequently noxious odors present.

Safety equipment includes steel toed boots, gloves, goggles, hard hats. Certain tasks require protective clothing such as disposal coveralls and raincoats.

Cognitive skill required:

Ability to read and follow written protocol or safety standards is necessary.

Ability to follow verbal communication is important.

Recommendation regarding modification or accommodation:

1. Certain tasks, e.g. sampling, require full shift attention. A person unable to complete heavier activities could be assigned to this activity.
2. An individual who is non-verbal or hearing impaired could perform the essential functions.

APPENDIX TWENTY-ONE

"GET WELL" LETTER TO INJURED WORKER

Injured workers too easily fall through the cracks when they don't hear from their employers. Away from their jobs, they feel forgotten. Isolation can turn to alienation against the employer. Prevent this isolation by writing "get well" letters like this.

Date ______________________________________

Name ______________________________________

Address ____________________________________

City, State, ZIP______________________________

Dear______________:

We are sorry that you have suffered an injury. We value you and your contributions to our team.

During your recovery, your supervisor will contact you periodically. We are interested in knowing how your recovery is progressing and what we can do to assist.

As you know, we have a Return to Work policy. In keeping with that policy, we will be in contact with your physician to determine how soon you can return to work. When your physician authorizes a transitional return, we will work closely with you, him/her, your supervisor and a claims manager to find an available assignment. This may require changes in your current job duties or possibly a temporary duty assignment. These changes will be limited in duration and are designed to prepare you for returning to your regular job.

Our workers' compensation insurance covers on-the-job injury and illness. Your claims representative will send a "Guide to Worker Benefits" booklet which will explain your benefits in detail.

As additional information, brochures are enclosed on leave and return to work. If after reviewing this information you have further questions, please call me at [insert phone number].

Wishing you a speedy recovery and looking forward to your return!

Sincerely,

APPENDIX TWENTY-TWO

EMPLOYEE JOB OFFER—TRANSITION EMPLOYMENT

This letter, composed by the Washington Department of Labor and Industries, documents the employer offering a modified duty job to the injured employee.

Date: ______________________________________

Name of Employee ___________________________

Address ___________________________________

City, State, ZIP_____________________________

Claim

Date of injury

Dear ______________:

Your physician has released you for modified duty work. We have located a position for you which Dr. ______________ feels you will be able to do until you are able to return to your regular job.

Your position will be as follows:
[describe position, duties, hours to be worked, limitations]

You will be receiving $_________. [If paying regular wages, so state.]

We ask that you report to work on [describe day, time, location, and supervisor name, if necessary].

We look forward to seeing you and wish you a speedy recovery!

____

[Name, Title, Department]

JOB ASSIGNMENT AGREEMENT BETWEEN EMPLOYEE AND SUPERVISOR

This form documents the injured worker agreeing to modified work. It was composed by the Washington Department of Labor and Industries.

Dr. __________ has released me to return to work, provided I do not [write in the limitation from treating doctor]____

____

____

____

I agree to work within these restrictions. In the event that I am given an assignment which in my opinion is outside these restrictions, I will express this opinion immediately to my supervisor to bring about a resolution of the problem. I will not violate the restrictions as I understand them and will work cooperatively with my supervisor(s) to prevent further injury to or aggravation of my present physical condition.

____
Employee

____
Supervisor

____
Date

APPENDIX TWENTY-FOUR

NCCI EMPLOYER CLASSIFICATION STANDARDS

Each state uses its own classification system. These standard descriptions, published by the National Council of Compensation Insurance, form the basis of most systems. Use these standards for comparison, but check with your state workers' comp board before making any decisions about where your operation fits.

Abrasive wheel mfg. & drivers, 1748
Absorbent cotton mfg., 4693
Accountant, auditor or factory cost or office systematizer—traveling, 8803
Acetate textile fiber, 2305
Acetylene gas machine installation & drivers, 3724
Acetylene gas mfg. & drivers, 4635
Acetylene torch mfg., 3634
Acid mfg., 4815
Acid mfg. (MD), 4536
Acoustical ceiling installation, 5020
Acoustical material installation & drivers, 5479
Adding machine mfg., 3574
Addressing or mailing companies & clerical, 8800
Advertising co. & drivers, 9549
Advertising display service & drivers, 9501
Advertising display service—for stores & drivers, 9521
Advertising displays mfg.—wooden, 2812
Advertising material distribution—mobile & door to door, 7380
Advertising sign mfg.—celluloid, 4452
Advertising solicitors, 8742
Aerial photographer—ground laboratory employees, 4361
Aerosol products packaging, 2111
Agate or enamel wear mfg., 3224
Agricultural implement stores—not farm machinery, 8010
Agricultural machinery mfg., 3507
Agricultural tool mfg.—hand, 3126
Agronomists—research and development of new seeds, 8102
Air conditioners—portable—installation, service or repair—residential, 9519
Air conditioning filter media mfg., 2288
Air conditioning parts store, 8010
Air conditioning systems—refrigerated and evaporative air conditioning—shop and outside & drivers (AZ, CO), 5537
Air conditioning—automobile—installation, service or repair & drivers, 8380
Air conditioning—non-portable—air flow balancing & testing, 8601
Air conditioning—non-portable—machinery installation & drivers, 3724
Air conditioning—non-portable—plumbing & drivers, 5183
Air conditioning—non-portable—servicing, cleaning, oiling or adjusting—& drivers, 5190
Air conditioning—non-portable—sheet metal work & drivers, 5538
Air conditioning—portable—installation or service—& drivers, 9519
Air pressure or steam gauge mfg., 3574
Air rifle mfg.—metal parts, 3400
Aircraft engine mfg., 3826
Aircraft landing mats mfg.—by welding & driver, 3040
Aircraft operation—fixed wing NOC—& drivers. All other than flying crew, 7423
Aircraft operation—fixed wing NOC—flying crew, 7422
Aircraft operation—helicopters NOC—& drivers. All other than flying crew, 7423
Aircraft operation—helicopters NOC—flying crew, 7425
Aircraft operation—helicopters—sky crane work—flying crew, 7425
Aircraft or automobile—preparing and crating for shipment, 7360
Aircraft or helicopter operation: aerial advertising, flying crew, 7422
Aircraft or helicopter operation: aerial logging operations, flying crew, 7425
Aircraft or helicopter operation: aerial photography, flying crew, 7422
Aircraft or helicopter operation: sky crane operations, flying crew, 7425
Aircraft or helicopter operation—all other employees & drivers (AK), 7414
Aircraft or helicopter operation—ticket sellers and information clerks at airports or heliports (AK), 8003
Aircraft or helicopter: aerial application, seeding, herding or scintillometer surveying—& drivers. All employees other than flying crew, 7423
Aircraft or helicopter: aerial application, seeding, herding or scintillometer surveying—flying crew, 7409
Aircraft or helicopter: aerial forest fire fighting—flying crew, 7420
Aircraft or helicopter: air carrier—commuter—& drivers. All other than flying crew, 7423
Aircraft or helicopter: air carrier—commuter—flying crew, 7431
Aircraft or helicopter: air carrier—scheduled or supplemental—& drivers. All other than flying crew, 7403
Aircraft or helicopter: air carrier—scheduled or supplemental—flying crew, 7405
Aircraft or helicopter: flight testing by manufacturer—manufactured under an approved type certificate—flying crew, 7422
Aircraft or helicopter: patrol, photography—other than mapping or survey work—& drivers. All employees other than flying crew (ground lab. assigned to code 4361), 7423
Aircraft or helicopter: patrol, photography—other than mapping or survey work—flying crew, 7418
Aircraft or helicopter: public exhibition involving stunt flying, racing or parachute jumping—& drivers. All employees other than flying crew, 7423
Aircraft or helicopter: public exhibition involving stunt flying, racing or parachute jumping—flying crew, 7420
Aircraft or helicopter: sales or service agency & drivers. All other than flying crew, 7423
Aircraft or helicopter: sales or service agency—flying crew, 7422
Aircraft or helicopter: transportation of personnel in conduct of employer's business—flying crew, 7421
Aircraft or helicopter: transportation of personnel in conduct of employer's business—ground crew personnel, 7423
Aircraft parts and accessories store, 8010
Aircraft salvaging, 3821
Airline or helicopter—ticket sellers away from airport, 8810
Airplane mfg., 3830
Airplane propeller mfg.—wood, 2790
Airplane subassemblies mfg.—metal cowling, wing, tabs, & aileron, etc., 3076
Airplane subassemblies mfg.—wood, 2883
Airplane wheel mfg., 3303
Airplane—cam & gear mfg., 3635
Airplane—toy mfg., 2790
Airport construction—grading & drivers, 6217
Airport construction—paving & drivers, 5506
Airport or heliport operator—& drivers, 7423
Airport runway construction—concrete or cement, 5221
Airport security screening of passengers by contractor, 7720
Airport warming apron construction—concrete or cement, 5221
Alabaster novelties mfg. (AR, NH, VA, VT), 1745
Alabaster turning or carving, 1803
Alcohol dealers—bulk—including drivers, 8350
Alcohol mfg.—grain—all operations, 2130
Alcohol mfg.—potato—all operations, 2130
Alcohol mfg.—wood & drivers, 1472
Ale bottling, 2157
Ale or beer dealer—wholesale & drivers, 7390
Alfalfa dehydrating or milling, 2014
Algae farming, 0035
Alligator exhibition, 9180
Alligator farms, 0170
Aluminum coating of steel wire, 3373
Aluminum siding installation (all types except those eligible for codes 5645 or 5651), 5403

Aluminum siding installation—detached onei or two-family dwellings, 5645
Aluminum siding installation—dwellings—three stories or less in height, 5651
Aluminum storm doors or windows, 5645
Aluminum ware mfg., 3227
Aluminum windows or doors—not storm, 5102
Ambulance service companies & drivers—all other than garage employees, 7370
Ambulance service companies—garage employees, 8385
Ammonia mfg., 41312
Ammonia mfg. (KS, KY, MS), 4585
Ammonium nitrate mfg., 4811
Ammonium nitrate mfg. (FL, KS, MS, OK), 4586
Ammunition charging or loading—small arms less than .51 caliber, 4775
Amusement device operation NOC—not traveling & drivers, 9180
Amusement device operator, carnival or circus—traveling—all employees & drivers, 9186
Amusement machines—coin operated, installation, service or repair, 5192
Amusement park or exhibition operation & drivers, 9016
Amusement parks—see "Recreational"
Analytical chemist, 4511
Anhydrous ammonia—application to soil by contractors & drivers, 0050
Anhydrous ammonia—sale and distribution & drivers, 8350
Animal hair twisting—for upholstering use, 2220
Animal raising—see "Farm"
Animal show—traveling, 9186
Anodizing metal articles, 3372
Antennae mfg., 3681
Anti-aircraft gun mfg., 3548
Anti-toxin, serum or virus mfg. & drivers, 5951
Apiaries—& drivers, 0034
Aplite rock quarry, 1624
Appliance (major) store—wholesale—incidental sale of minor appliances, 8044
Appliance (minor) store—wholesale—incidental sale of major appliances, 8018
Apron mfg. from canvas material, 2576
Aquarium mfg.—glass, 4130
Archery equipment mfg., 4902
Archery range, 9016
Architect or engineer—consulting, 8601
Architectural scale model building, 2790
Arena or stadium for boxing or wrestling matches, 9016
Arena or stadium for ice shows, boat shows, automobile shows, 9016
Arena or stadium for rodeos, circuses, dolphin exhibitions, 9016
Arena or stadium for team sports events, 9182
Armor plate processing, 3620
Armored car service company, 7720
Arms mfg. NOC, 3548
Arms mfg.—small, 3574
Army or navy post exchange—all employees clerical, drivers (MO), 8049
Artesian well tool mfg., 3126
Artificial insemination of cattle—& drivers. All other than professional employees, 0083
Artificial insemination of cattle—professional employees, 8831
Artificial limb mfg., 4693
Artificial marble mfg., 4036
Artificial teeth mfg., 4692
Artificial turf installation—surface preparation only, 5506
Artificial turf—installation only, 0042
Artillery cannon mfg., 3548
Artistic metal erection work—plaques, facades, facings, 5102
Artists (refer to scope for restrictions), 8810
Asbestos cement or shingle mfg., 1852
Asbestos contractor—NOC & drivers, 5473
Asbestos contractor—pipe and boiler work exclusively & drivers, 5472
Asbestos goods mfg., 1852
Asbestos pipe covering mfg.—from sheet asbestos—no asbestos weaving, 1852
Asbestos—surface mining, 1165
Ash can mfg.—metal, 3400
Ashes, garbage or refuse collection & drivers, 9403
Asphalt laying on top of already constructed highway—& drivers, 5506
Asphalt or tar distilling or refining & drivers, 4741
Asphalt paving bricks mfg., 4021
Asphalt tile mfg., 4493
Asphalt works & drivers—operated by paving contractors at permanent location, 1463
Asphalt works & drivers—operated by road paving contractors at temporary location, 5506
Asphalt—spraying roads with liquid asphalt—& drivers, 5506
Asphalt—surface mining, 1165
Assay balance mfg., 3685
Assaying, 4511
Asylum—all other than professional employees, 9040
Asylum—professional employees 8833
Athletic team or park & drivers: all employees other than players, coaches, managers or umpires, 9182
Athletic team or park: contact sports—players, coaches, managers or umpires, 9179
Athletic team or park: noncontact sports—players, coaches, managers or umpires, 9178
Athletic team or park: players and umpires (MO), 9181
Atomic energy—project work, 9984
Atomic energy—radiation exposure NOC, 9985
Attorney—all employees & clerical, messengers, drivers, 8820
Auctioneers, 8017
Audio or intercommunication system installation—within buildings, 7605
Audio or visual recording media mfg., 4923
Audio, radio, television or video equipment installation, service or repair, 9516
Auditoriums or exhibition hall, 9016
Auditors, accountant or factory cost office systematizer—traveling, 8803
Auditors—performing audits at their employer's locations, 8810
Auto bumper mfg., 3303
Auto haulaway or driveaway—& drivers, 7219
Auto haulaway or driveaway—driving cars on or off vessels, 7317F
Auto horn mfg.—electric, 3179
Auto jack mfg.—not stamped, 3632
Auto parts mfg.—miscellaneous stamped parts such as fenders, 3400
Auto piston mfg., 3632
Auto trailer mfg.—home type, 2812
Auto window and trim molding mfg., 3146
Automatic screw machine products mfg., 3145
Automatic sprinkler head mfg., 3634
Automatic sprinkler installation & drivers, 5188
Automatic stoker or gas or oil burner installation—see "Oil burner installation"
Automobile accelerator assembly mfg., 3146
Automobile accessory store retail—NOC & drivers, 8046
Automobile body repair, 8393
Automobile brake drums—reconditioning & relining—drums removed from vehicle by others, 3632
Automobile brake repair, 8380
Automobile bumper—straightening & repair, 3303
Automobile, bus, truck or trailer body mfg.: die pressed steel, 3822
Automobile, bus, truck or trailer body mfg.: other than die pressed steel, 3824
Automobile, bus, truck or trailer body mfg.: painting, 9505
Automobile, bus, truck or trailer body mfg.: upholstering, 9522
Automobile car wash & drivers, 8380
Automobile choke mfg., 3146
Automobile clutch rebuilding—clutch removed from vehicle by others, 3632
Automobile convertible top mfg., 2576
Automobile cushions or seat mfg., 3300
Automobile dismantling & drivers, 3821
Automobile engine mfg., 3827
Automobile engine rebuilding—engine removed from vehicle by others, 3632
Automobile floor mat mfg. from felt or felt-like material, 2288
Automobile glass installation, 8380
Automobile headlight lens mfg., 4111

Automobile inspection stations, 8380
Automobile interior trim mfg. from felt or felt-like material, 2288
Automobile leasing company—long-term—sales employees, 8748
Automobile mfg. or assembly, 3808
Automobile muffler repair, 8380
Automobile parking lot & drivers, 8392
Automobile radiator mfg., 3807
Automobile radiator repair—no mfg., 8380
Automobile: radio, audio, television or video equipment installation, service or repair, 9516
Automobile rental company & drivers. All other than garage employees, 8002
Automobile rental company: garage employees, 8385
Automobile repair shop & parts department employees, drivers (LA, MO, OK, OR, RI), 8391
Automobile repair shop: parts department employees (OR), 9343
Automobile repossession operations, 7219
Automobile sales agency & drivers, 8380
Automobile sales or service agency & parts department employees, drivers, 8380
Automobile sales persons, 8748
Automobile seat cover mfg., 2501
Automobile service or repair center & drivers, 8380
Automobile service station & drivers (LA, MO, OK, OR, RI), 8387
Automobile storage garage or parking station & drivers, 8392
Automobile stunt show, 9186
Automobile sunroof installation, 8393
Automobile throttle rod mfg., 3146
Automobile towing company—no other operations & drivers, 7219
Automobile wheel mfg.—metal—not cast, 3803
Automobile window tinting, 8380
Automotive electrical apparatus repair—no removal from, installation in or repair of vehicles, 3648
Automotive lighting, ignition or starting apparatus mfg. NOC, 3648
Automotive machine shops—no work on cars—including cylinder reboring, valve grinding, turning down brake drums, etc., 3632
Automotive replacement parts distributors—wholesale, 8010
Auxiliary and reserve police—all employees & drivers (VA), 7727
Aviaries, 0034
Awning erection & drivers: canvas products, 5102
Awning erection—metal—& drivers, 5538
Awning manufacturing & erection of metal awnings—& drivers, 5538
Awning manufacturing: canvas products, 3076
Awning manufacturing—metal—no erection work, 3076
Awning or tent mfg.—shop, 2576
Awning, tent or canvas goods erection, removal or repair, 5102
Ax and sledgehammer mfg., 3126
Axle grease mfg., 4557
Axle unit assembling or mfg., 3632
Baby carriage mfg., 3865
Baby-sitting service, 8835
Bag mfg. from canvas material, 2576
Bag mfg.—paper, 4273
Bag mfg.—plastic, 4273
Bag or sack mfg.—cloth, 2578
Bag renovating, 2578
Bakeries—retail store sales, 8017
Bakery & drivers, route supervisors, 2003
Baking powder mfg. 6504
Balcony erection—iron or steel, exterior, 5040
Balcony fabrication—iron or steel, 3040
Baling press mfg.—hydraulic, 3507
Ball or roller bearing mfg., 3638
Ballast rock quarry, 1624
Balloonist—hot air, 7422
Bandage mfg.—weaving to be separately rated, 4693
Bank and trust company contractors—not employees of banks or trust companies—including contracted services such as guards, patrols, messengers, armored car crews—& drivers, 7720
Bank tellers, 8810
Banks and trust companies: armored car crews & drivers (bank employees—not contractors), 7380
Banks and trust companies: cafeteria or restaurant employees, 9079
Banks and trust companies: dispensary employees, 8833
Banks and trust companies: employees engaged in care, custody or maintenance—including night watchguards, elevator operators and starters, 9015
Banks and trust companies: office machine repair employees, 5191
Banks and trust companies: printing employees, 4299
Banks and trust companies: special officers and armed or unarmed attendants, ushers, door attendants, appraisers, field auditors, runners or messengers, 8742
Bar, lounge or tavern, 9079
Barber or beauty parlor supply houses, 8018
Barber shop, 9586
Barge building—iron or steel—State Act, 6854
Barge building—iron or steel—U.S. Act, 6843F
Bark peeling in connection with logging, 2702
Bark peeling in paper mills—chemical process, 4207
Bark peeling in paper mills—ground wood process, 4206
Bark peeling—contractors—for pulpwood, 2702
Barking mills, 2710
Barley milling, 2014
Barrel assembly, 2747
Barrel dealers including repairing—wood, 2747
Barrel mfg.—wood veneer—incl. veneer mfg., 2915
Barrel mfg.—wood veneer—no veneer mfg., 2916
Barrel or drum mfg.—steel, 3400
Barrel or drum—steel—reconditioning or repair, 3400
Barrel stock mfg., 2741
Baseball bat mfg., 2841
Baseball batting range, 9016
Baseball mask mfg., 4902
Baseball mfg., 4902
Baseball team, 9178
Baseboard mfg.—wood, 2731
Basket mfg.—willowware, 2913
Basket mfg.—wood veneer—incl. veneer mfg., 2915
Basket mfg.—wood veneer—no veneer mfg., 2916
Basketball team, 9178
Bathhouse—beach, 9015
Baths—NOC & clerical (OK), 9053
Bathtub mfg.—enameled iron, 3091
Battery charger mfg., 3643
Battery mfg.—dry, 3642
Battery mfg.—storage, 3647
Bauxite grinding, 1747
Beach cleaning—& drivers, 9402
Bean sorting or handling, 8102
Beauty parlor, 9586
Beauty school with commercial shops, 9586
Beauty supply sales—wholesale, 8018
Bed assembling—wood, 2881
Bed spring or wire mattress mfg., 3300
Bedding plant growers, 0005
Bedstead mfg. or assembly—metal, 3076
Bee raising, 0034
Beer and ale dealers—retail, 8017
Beer and soft drink dispensing equipment, cleaning & drivers, 5183
Beer bottling, 2157
Beer coil cleaning, 5183
Beer drawing equipment—cleaning and installation— & drivers, 5183
Beer or ale dealer—wholesale—& drivers, 7390
Beer vat coating with chemicals, 3726
Beet sugar mfg., 2030
Bell installation—tower—& drivers, 9534
Belt mfg.—rubber, 4410
Berry farm & drivers (FL), 0173
Berry, fruit farms or vineyards—see "Farms"
Beverage mfg.—carbonated—NOC & route supervisors drivers, 2157
Beverage powders—dry mix, blend, package, 6504
Bicycle mfg. or assembly, 3865
Bicycles—retail sale or rental—including repair, 8010
Bill posting & drivers, 9545
Billiard hall, 9089
Billiard table mfg., 2883
Binocular mfg., 4150
Bird cage mfg., 3315

Butter or cheese mfg. & route supervisors, drivers, 2070
Butter substitute mfg., 4717
Buttermilk mfg., 2070
Button mfg. NOC, 4484
Button mfg. NOC (MD, ME, VA), 4479
Button mfg.—campaign or convention, 3131
Button or fastener mfg.—metal, 3131
Buttons—covering metal or other button blanks with fabrics by machine, 4479
Cabinet dealer—kitchen, 8235
Cabinet mfg. for audio or visual device, 2883
Cabinet works—no power woodworking machinery, 2881
Cabinet works—with power machinery, 2812
Cable installation & drivers, 5190
Cable laying—by specialist contractors employing automatic equipment which, in one operation, opens the trench, lays the cable and backfills—& drivers, 6325
Cable mfg. or wire drawing—not iron or steel, 1924
Cable mfg.—insulated—electrical, 4470
Cable or wire rope mfg.—iron or steel, 3240
Cable TV—cable installation—plow-in method, 6325
Cable TV—clerical office employees, 8901
Cable TV—erection of main receiving or transmitting tower, 5040
Cable TV—extension of service into homes, 7600
Cable TV—service or repair of existing cables, 7600
Cable TV—stringing of cable on existing utility poles, 7601
Caddy—employee of country club, 9060
Caddy—employee of hotel, 9052
Caddy—independent contractor, 9060
Cage mfg.—wire, 3257
Caisson work—all operations to completion, 6252
Caisson work—pneumatic—all operations to completion (CO), 6257
Calcium carbide mfg. & drivers, 1438
Calculator mfg., 3574
Camera mfg., 4923
Camera or photograph supplies stores—retail, 8017
Camera repair, 3385
Camouflage work—decorating & drivers, 5102
Camouflage work—painting—& drivers, 5474
Camp operation NOC, 9015
Can mfg., 3220
Can recycling—beverage—& drivers, 8264
Candle mfg., 4557
Candle mfg. (FL), 4710
Candy mfg., 2041
Cannery NOC, 2111
Cannery: maintenance & security employees (OR), 9305
Cannery—crabmeat—all operations (LA), 2118
Cannery—sardines (ME), 2113
Canning or bottling carbonated beverages—see "Carborhated beverage mfg. NOC" or "Bottling NOC"
Canning—motor oil, 2111
Canning—turpentine, 2111
Canoe building, 6834
Canvas goods, awning or tent erection, removal or repair, 5102
Canvas goods mfg. NOC—shop, 2576
Canvas sidewalls—erection—at ballparks, etc., 5102
Car mfg.—railroad—& drivers, 3881
Car wheel mfg.—railroad, 3082
Carbon dioxide mfg., 4635
Carbon mfg., (LA, OK), 4565
Carbon paper or typewriter ribbon mfg., 4251
Carbonated beverage mfg. NOC & route supervisors, drivers, 2157
Carbonic acid gas mfg. & drivers, 4635
Carbonizing textile materials, 2211
Carburetor mfg., 3581
Cardboard bristol board and paperboard mfg., 4239
Cardboard mailing tube mfg., 4279
Carnival, circus or amusement device operator—traveling—all employees & drivers, 9186
Carpentry NOC, 5403
Carpentry—detached one- or two-family dwellings, 5645
Carpentry—dwellings—three stories or less, 5651
Carpentry—installation of cabinet work or interior trim, 5437
Carpentry—installation of finished wooden flooring, 5437
Carpentry—shop only—& drivers, 2802
Carpet installation, 9521
Carpet lining mfg. from woven fibers, 2220
Carpet or rug mfg. NOC, 2402
Carpet or rug mfg.—jute or hemp, 2220
Carpet pad mfg.—rubber, 4410
Carpet, rug, linoleum store—retail, 8017
Carpet, rug, linoleum store—wholesale, 8018
Carpet, rug or upholstery cleaning—shop or outside & drivers, 2585
Carriage or wagon mfg. or assembly, 3808
Carrier system—pneumatic—installation or repair & drivers, 5183
Cartridge mfg. or assembly—small arms—& drivers (CT), 4767
Cartridge mfg. or loading—see "Explosives"
Cash register mfg., 3574
Cash register—installation, service or repair, 5191
Casino gambling hall & hotel—all employees & clerical, salespersons, drivers (CT), 9044
Cask assembling, 2747
Casket or coffin mfg. or assembly—metal, 3076
Casket or coffin mfg. or assembly—wood, 2881
Casket or coffin mfg. or assembly—wood (AL, MS, OK), 2804
Casket or coffin upholstering and burial garment mfg., 9522
Cassettes—magnetic media, manufacture or assembly, 4431
Casting mfg. for others—using non-ferrous metal, 3085
Castings mfg.—metal—by lost wax process, 3336
Cat food mfg.—canning operation, 2111
Caterer, 9079
Cathedral or art glass window mfg., 4133
Cathode-ray tube mfg., 4112
Catsup mfg., 6504
Cattle dealer & salespersons, drivers, 8288
Cattle or livestock farms or ranches—see "Farms"
Caulking compound mfg., 4558
Caulking—with pressure gun, 5213
Cave expansion, 1164
Cave or cavern exhibition, 9016
Caves or caverns—operation for exhibition purposes—including guides, ticket sellers, gate attendants, maintenance employees, 9016
Caves—excavation of new areas for exhibition purposes—& drivers, 1164
Cedar chest mfg., 2883
Ceiling installation—suspended acoustical grid type, 5020
Cement block erection, 5022
Cement compound mfg.—rubber, 4410
Cement (dry) storage warehouse, 8292
Cement mfg., 1701
Cement rock quarry, 1624
Cemetery operation & drivers, 9220
Cemetery removal—opening graves, removing and reinterring remains, & drivers, 9220
Ceramic goods mfg.—spark plug cores, spools, pulleys, 4062
Ceramics mfg., 4061
Cereal mfg., 2016
Cesspool cleaning—specialist contractors—& drivers, 9402
Chain mfg.—forged, 3110
Chain mfg.—formed or welded from wire, 3257
Chain mfg.—roll or drive type 3146
Chair assembling—wood, 2881
Chalk—surface mining, 1165
Chandelier mfg., 3180
Charcoal dealers—wholesale—packaged, 8018
Charcoal mfg. & drivers, 1472
Charitable or welfare organization—all operations & drivers, 8837
Chartered fishing boat—less than 15 tons—Program I, 7038
Chartered fishing boat—less than 15 tons—Program II—State Act, 7090
Chartered fishing boat—less than 15 tons—Program II—USL Act, 7050
Chat milling—all employees & drivers, sales persons (OK), 1457
Chauffeurs & helpers NOC—commercial, 7380
Cheese or butter mfg. & route supervisors, drivers, 2070
Chemical mfg. NOC: refer to Code 4800
Chemical milling, 3372
Chemical waste disposal, 9403

Chenille carpet manufacturing, 2402
Chenille cloth manufacturing, 2220
Chenille products mfg. from chenille cloth—no carpet or cloth mfg., 2501
Chewing gum mfg., 2041
Chimney cleaning—industrial smoke stacks, 5222
Chimney cleaning—residence—by vacuum suction, 9014
Chimney construction—not metal, 5222
China decorating—by hand, 4352
Chinchilla raising, 0170
Chip harvester operation—portable or permanent, 2710
Chip or particle board mfg., 4239
Chocolate or cocoa mfg., 2041
Christmas or holiday decorations—street or outside, 5190
Christmas tree farm & drivers (MT), 0131
Christmas tree harvesting exclusively—& drivers, 0106
Christmas tree mfg.—aluminum, 2534
Christmas tree planting, cultivating and harvesting, 0005
Church: professional employees & clerical (OK), 8840
Cider bottling, 2156
Cider mfg., 2143
Cigar and cigarette lighter mfg. or assembling, 3315
Cigar mfg., 2177
Cigarette filter mfg., 2172
Cigarette mfg., 2172
Cinder dealers—& drivers, 8232
Circuit board mfg., 3681
Circus, carnival or amusement device operator—traveling—all employees & drivers, 9186
Citrus products processing (FL), 2119
City: over 100,000 population—composite rate (OR), 9425
Claim adjusters or special agents—insurance co., 8742
Clam digging, 2114
Clay flower pot mfg.—hand molded or cast, 4061
Clay flower pot mfg.—press formed, 4062
Clay milling—& drivers, 1747
Clay mining—underground, 1164
Clay or shale digging & drivers, 4000
Clay products or brick mfg. NOC & drivers, 4021
Clay target mfg.—for skeet shooting, 4902
Clean air rooms—sheet metal—shop and installation, 5538
Cleaner—debris removal, 5610
Cleaning building interiors, machinery & equipment using spray apparatus, 5474
Cleaning or dyeing & route supervisors, drivers, 2586
Cleaning or renovating building exteriors & drivers, 5213
Cleaning railroad freight cars—not tank, 5610
Cleaning tanks or tank cars, 3726
Clearing of right-of-ways for power lines, etc.—see "Electric light, power, etc."
Clerical office employees NOC, 8810
Clerical office employees NOC—Program I, 8814
Clerical office employees NOC—Program II—State Act, 8805
Clerical office employees NOC—Program II—USL Act, 8815
Clippings dealer & drivers, 8103
Clock assembly to wood base, 2881
Clock mfg., 3385
Clock repair—not jewelry store, 3385
Cloth printing, 2417
Cloth printing—silk screen—see "Silk screen process"
Cloth sponging, shrinking, inspection or mending, 8032
Clothes driers—metal—erection on roofs, 5057
Clothes driers—wood—installation in apartments, 9521
Clothes pole erection—wood, 5403
Clothing mfg., 2501
Clothing—mail order sales, wholesale or retail, 8032
Club hunting—no shooting, 8279
Club—country, golf, fishing or yacht—& clerical, 9060
Club—officers & enlisted personnel—military base, 9077F
Club—shooting (AZ), 9177
Club—social, fraternal or business—operating on own premises or facilities & clerical, 9061
Clubs—beach & clerical, 9061
Clubs—health & clerical, 9063
Clubs—NOC & clerical, 9061
Clubs—riding & drivers, 8279
Clubs—shooting, 9180
Clubs—ski & clerical, 9060
Clubs—social & clerical, 9061
Clubs—tennis, racquetball or handball—indoor, 9063
Clubs—tennis, racquetball or handball—outdoor, 9060
Coal billet or briquet mfg. & drivers, 1463
Coal dock operation & stevedoring, 7313F
Coal merchant & local managers, drivers, 8233
Coal mining—NOC, 1016
Coal mining—surface—& drivers, 1005
Coat hanger mfg.—metal, 3257
Coat hanger mfg.—wood, 2841
Cocktail lounge, 9079
Cocoa or chocolate mfg., 2041
Coconut shredding or drying, 6504
Cod liver oil mfg., 4665
Coffee brewing machine—installation, service or repair, 5192
Coffee cleaning, roasting or grinding, 6504
Coffee storage warehouse, 8292
Coffee, tea or grocery dealer—retail—& drivers, 8006
Cofferdam work—not pneumatic—all operations to completion, 6252
Coffin and casket mfg.—concrete—& drivers, 4034
Coffin mfg. or assembly—wood, 2881
Coffin or casket mfg. or assembly—metal, 3076
Coffin or casket mfg. or assembly—wood, 2881
Coffin or casket upholstering and burial garment mfg., 9522
Coil mfg.—electrical, 3681
Coin dealer, 8013
Coin wrappers and currency strap mfg., 4251
Coke mfg. & drivers, 1470
Cold storage locker—frozen foods, 8031
Collapsible white metal tube and cap mfg., 3334
Collar mfg., 2501
Collection of containerized garbage, ashes or refuse, 9403
Collectors, messengers or salespersons—outside, 8742
College or school: school bus driver (FL, GA), 7383
College—all employees other than professional or clerical, 9101
College—professional employees & clerical, 8868
Color grinding, blending or testing, 4558
Commissary work (AK, ID, LA), 9078
Commissary work—all employees other than restaurant workers, 9052
Commissary work—restaurant employees, 9058
Compressor repair or service—away from shop, 3724
Computer chip mfg., 4150
Computer device installation, inspection, service or repair, 5191
Computer system designers or programmers—exclusively office, 8810
Computer system designers or programmers—traveling, 8803
Computer—installation, service or repair, 5191
Computing, recording or office machine mfg. NOC, 3574
Concessions—beach chairs and umbrellas, 8017
Concessions—boats in parks—& drivers, 9016
Concessions—cigarette or cigar, 8017
Concessions—door attendants, 8017
Concessions—hat or coat checkrooms, 8008
Concessions—parcel or luggage checkrooms, 8017
Concessions—parking lots & drivers, 8392
Concessions—rolling chairs, 8017
Concessions—washroom attendants, 8017
Concrete block mfg., 4034
Concrete brick mfg., 4034
Concrete construction in connection with bridges or culverts, 5222
Concrete construction NOC, 5213
Concrete construction NOC—fabricating, setting up or taking down forms, 5213
Concrete construction—construction of private residences, fabricating, setting up or taking down forms, 5215
Concrete construction—monolithic, 5213
Concrete culverts installation—see Interpretation section
Concrete igloo construction—floors, 5221
Concrete igloo construction—for explosives, 5213
Concrete or cement distributing towers—installation, repair or removal & drivers, 9529

Concrete or cement work—floors, driveways, yards or sidewalks—& drivers, 5221
Concrete pre-cast slab installation—roofs and floors, 5213
Concrete pre-cast structural beams or girders—erection by concrete construction contractor casting the beams—assign appropriate "Concrete construction" class
Concrete pre-cast structural beams or girders—erection by specialty contractor not casting the beams or girders—assign appropriate "Iron or steel erection" class
Concrete pre-cast wall panel installation, 5213
Concrete private residences construction—monolithic, 5213
Concrete private residences construction—not monolithic, 5215
Concrete products mfg. & drivers, 4034
Concrete pumping operations—whether performed by a general contractor, specialist contractor or concrete ready mix dealer—assign appropriate "Concrete construction" class
Concrete ready mix operations—materials not owned by the insured, 7219
Concrete work—incidental to the construction of private residence, 5215
Concrete—dry mixing & bagging—no mfg., 8232
Concrete—ready mix dealers—see Interpretation section—classifications
Condensed milk mfg., 2065
Condenser mfg.—electrical, 3681
Condominiums or cooperatives—all employees engaged in care, custody and maintenance of premises or facilities, 9015
Conduit construction—for cables or wires—& drivers, 6325
Conduit mfg.—clay, 4021
Confection machine mfg., 3559
Confection mfg., 2041
Construction elevator or hod hoist installation, repair or removal & drivers, 9529
Construction machinery, dredge or steam shovel mfg. NOC, 3507
Construction or erection permanent yard, 8227
Construction tool mfg., 3126
Contact lens mfg., 4150
Container recycling—beverage—bottle or can & drivers, 8264
Containerized refuse collection, 9403
Contractors equipment rental—with operator—assign classification that would apply if work were performed by lessee's own employees
Contractors equipment rental—without operator, 8107
Contractors' machinery dealer & drivers, 8107
Contractor—executive supervisor, 5606
Convalescent or nursing home—all employees, 8829
Conveyor belt mfg.—wire, 3257
Conveyor mfg., 3507
Cookie mfg., 2001
Cooking utensils mfg.—steel, 3227
Cooling tower erection—prefabricated wood or metal—& drivers, 3724
Cooperage assembly, 2747
Cooperage stock mfg., 2741
Cop tube mfg. 4279
Copper or brass goods mfg., 3315
Copper plate, sheet, strip or coil stock mfg., 3027
Coppersmith shop (AL, IN, KS, MD), 3075
Coppersmith—shop, 3066
Copy machine—installation, service or repair, 5191
Copying or duplicating service—all employees clerical, salespersons (AZ), 8015
Coral rock quarry, 1624
Cord or twine mfg.—cotton, 2220
Cordage, rope or twine mfg. NOC, 2220
Cordage, rope or twine mfg.—NOC (MO, OK), 2352
Core sample drilling, 6204
Cork board mfg. and cork products mfg., 2841
Cork cutting works, 2841
Cork paper mfg.—no paper mfg., 4250
Corn detasselling, 0037
Corn flakes mfg., 2016
Corn milling, 2014
Corn products mfg., 4703
Corn shelling—portable, 0050
Cornice mfg.—concrete, 4034
Coronet mfg., 3383
Correction department employees, 7720
Correspondence schools, 8868
Corrugated or fiber board container mfg., 4244
Cosmetics mfg.—not manufacturing ingredients, 4611
Cotton batting wadding or waste mfg., 2211
Cotton classifiers, 8742
Cotton compressing & drivers, 0400
Cotton gin machine mfg., 3507
Cotton gin operation & local managers, drivers, 0401
Cotton merchant, 8103
Cotton merchant (AL, AR, GA, LA, MS, TN), 8295
Cotton picking, 0037
Cotton spinning and weaving, 2220
Cotton storage, 8103
Cottonseed feed mfg., 4670
Cottonseed oil mfg.—mechanical—& drivers, 4670
Cottonseed oil mfg.—solvent & drivers (OK), 4673
Cottonseed oil mfg.—solvent—& drivers, 4670
Cottonseed oil refining, 4683
Couches (folding) mfg., 3300
Cough drop mfg., 4611
Cough syrup compounding or preparation—no mfg. of ingredients, 4611
County employees (UT), 9416
County employees NOC, 9410
County jail—inmates only (IA), 7730
County—over 150,000 population—composite rate (OR), 9470
County—over 300,000 population—composite rate (OR), 9451
Court reporters, 8820
Crab pot mfg., 3040
Cracker mfg., 2001
Cranberry growers, 0079
Crane dealer, 8107
Crane or derrick installation, 5057
Crane rental with operator, 9534
Crane rental without operator, 8107
Crayon, pencil or pen holder mfg., 2942
Cream of wheat mfg., 2016
Creamery & route supervisors, drivers, 2070
Cream—aerated under pressure, 2157
Crematory operation & drivers, 9620
Creosote mfg. & drivers, 1472
Cricket raising, 0034
Crop inspection for farms, 8102
Crutch mfg.—wood, 2841
Cryogenic device mfg.—refrigeration unit, 3179
Cryogenic device mfg.—sheet metal work, 3076
Crystal mfg.—radio or electronic, 4150
Culm recovery—& drivers, 4000
Culvert mfg.—plate metal 3620
Culvert mfg.—sheet metal, 3066
Curator—see "Public library or museum"
Cushion mfg.—rubber, 4410
Cushion, pillow or quilt mfg., 2501
Cushion, pillow, or quilt mfg. (OK), 2571
Cutlery mfg. NOC, 3122
Cutlery parts store, 8010
Dairy farm operation, 0036
Dairy products mfg.—imitation, 6504
Dam or lock construction—concrete work—all operations, 6017
Dam or lock construction—earth moving or placing—all operations & drivers, 6018
Dam or lock construction—timber or brush cutting and removal & drivers, 2702
Dance hall—all operations, 9079
Dance hall—all operations (LA, OK, VA), 9080
Day nurseries—all other than professional employees, teachers or clerical, 9101
Day nurseries—professional employees, teachers or clerical, 5868
Daybed mfg., 3300
Deburring—metal, 3372
Decalcomania transfer mfg.—not silk screen process, 4299
Decking—sheet metal, fabrication and installation, 5538
Decorating, 5102

Decorating ceramic or glass by hand, 4352
Decorative metal erection work—plaques, facades, facings, 5102
Decortication—fibrous plants, 0401
Dehydrating coffee or tea, 6504
Dehydrating eggs, 6504
Dehydrating meats, 2095
Dehydrating milk, 2065
Dehydrating soup, 2112
Dehydrating vegetables, 2112
Delivery of goods using bicycles, 7380
Demolition operations—underwater—Program I, 7394
Demolition operations—underwater—Program II—State Act, 7395
Demolition operations—underwater—Program II—USL Act, 7398
Demonstrators in retail stores, 8017
Dental equipment installation, 5146
Dental instrument mfg., 3685
Dental laboratory, 4692
Dental supply dealers, 8017
Dentist & clerical, 8832
Derrick or oil rig erecting or dismantling—all operations—metal, 5057
Derrick or oil rig erecting or dismantling—all operations—wood, 5403
Detective or patrol agency & drivers, 7720
Detective or patrol agency—private & drivers (CT, ME, VA), 7723
Detergent mfg., 4720
Detinning, 3372
Detinning (KY), 3374
Dextrine mfg., 4703
Diamond cutting or polishing, 8013
Diaper service & route supervisors, drivers, 2585
Diatomite—digging and stripping, 4000
Die casting mfg., 1925
Diesel engines used as generators—repair, 3632
Dike or revetment construction & drivers, 6005
Dinitrotoluol explosives mfg., 4773
Dinner theater—all other employees—theater payroll greater than 50%, 9154
Dinner theater—players, entertainers—theater payroll greater than 50%, 9156
Dinner theater—theater payroll 50% or less, 9079
Directional signal mfg., 3648
Disc mfg.—magnetic, 4923
Discotheques, 9079
Dishwasher—installation, service or repair—commercial, 5190
Dismantling of pre-fabricated dwellings—see "Wrecking "
Display mfg.—cardboard, 4279
Display mfg.—paper mache, 4038
Display—window—installation, 9521
Distillation—wood—& drivers, 1472
Distillation—wood—destructive process & drivers (AL, GA, LA), 1474
Distillery—spirituous liquor, 2130
Distributing companies—if employees transported to location in cars or trucks (samples, advertising circulars, telephone directories, etc.), 7380
Distributing companies—if no transportation, assign to governing classification
Distributing companies—if no transportation or governing classification, 8017
Distributor (automobile) parts mfg., 3648
Ditch cleaning—irrigation, 0251
Diving—marine—Program I, 7394
Diving—marine—Program II—State Act, 7395
Diving—marine—Program II—USL Act, 7398
Diving—State Act (OR), 6876
Diving—U.S. Act (OR), 6873F
Dog food mfg.—butchering, 2081
Dog food mfg.—canning operation, 2111
Dog food mfg.—packaged—dry pelleted, 6504
Dog racing—see "Racetracks"
Dog show—kennel employees, 8279
Dog show—operation by owner or lessee & drivers, 9016
Doll clothing or cloth dolls or cloth parts mfg., 2501
Doll or doll parts mfg. or assembly, 4484
Dolphin training, feeding and care, 9180
Domestic service contractor—inside, 0917
Domestic workers—inside, 0913
Domestic workers—inside—occasional, 0908
Domestic workers—outside—including private chauffeurs, 0912
Domestic workers—outside—occasional—including occasional private chauffeurs, 0909
Domestic workers—residences (OR), 8989
Donut mfg.—consumption on premises, 9079
Donut mfg.—no consumption on premises, 2003
Door, door frame or sash mfg.—wood—metal covered, 3066
Door, door frame or sash mfg.—wood—metal covered (ID), 3060
Door, door frame or sash mfg.—wood—metal covered (MD), 3075
Door, door frame or sash erection—metal or metal covered, 5102
Door installation—metal or metal covered—in garages—not overhead, 5102
Door installation—overhead—& drivers, 3724
Door mfg.—metal, 3076
Door, sash or assembled millwork mfg.—wood & drivers, 2802
Doorknob mfg., 3146
Dormitory operation—by school, 9101
Doughnut mfg. & drivers, 2003
Doughnut shop—retail, 9079
Dowel mfg.—wood, 2731
Drafting employees, 8810
Drag strip operation, 9016
Drainage or irrigation system construction & drivers, 6229
Draperies or curtain mfg.—from cloth, paper or plastic—cutting and sewing, 2501
Draperies or curtains—installation in public buildings NOC, 5102
Draperies or curtains—installation in public buildings from floor or step ladders, 9521
Dredge, steam shovel or construction machinery mfg. NOC, 3507
Dredging of materials on non-navigable waters with incidental shore operations, 4000
Dredging—all types—Program I, 7333
Dredging—all types—Program II—State Act, 7335
Dredging—all types—Program II—USL Act, 7337
Dress form mfg., 4038
Dress pattern mfg.—paper, 4282
Dressed lumber mill, 2731
Dressing or polish mfg., 4557
Dressmaker forms mfg.—plastic, 4038
Dressmaking or tailoring—custom exclusively, 2503
Drift fishing boat—less than 15 tons—Program I, 7038
Drift fishing boat—less than 15 tons—Program II—State Act, 7090
Drift fishing boat—less than 15 tons—Program II—USL Act, 7050
Drilling NOC & drivers, 6204
Drilling or redrilling of oil or gas wells & installation of casing, drivers, 6235
Drilling—lead or zinc prospect—& drinkers (OK), 6215
Drivers, chauffeurs and their helpers NOC—commercial, 7380
Drug, medicine or pharmaceutical preparation mfg. & incidental mfg. of ingredients, 4825
Drug, medicine or pharmaceutical preparation—no mfg. of ingredients, 4611
Drug—packaging or repackaging, 4611
Dry cleaning and laundry store—retail—& route supervisors, drivers, 2589
Dry dock building—floating—iron or steel—State Act, 6854
Dry dock building—floating—iron or steel—U.S. Act, 6843F
Dry ice dealers—wholesale, 8018
Dry ice mfg., 4635
Drydock construction—floating—& drivers, 6801
Drydock operation—see "Ship repair or conversion"
Duct mfg.—air conditioning, 3066
Duct work—shop and installation, 5538
Ducts—for heating and air conditioning systems—fiberglass or sheet metal, fabrication & installation, 5538
Dude ranches—cattle ranches & drivers, 0083
Dude ranches—not cattle ranches—& sales persons, drivers, 9052
Dust collector systems mfg., 3507
Dye mfg.,—natural, 4825
Dye or dye intermediate mfg.: refer to the home office for individual treatment under the Chemical and Dyestuff Rating Plan
Dyeing or cleaning & route supervisors, drivers, 2586

Dyrnamite explosives mfg., 4773
Earthenware or tile mfg. NOC & drivers, 4021
Egg breaking—including canning & freezing, 8018
Egg dealers—including grading, candling, packing—wholesale, 8018
Egg or poultry producer, 0034
Electric blankets—service or repair, 9519
Electric light or power co. NOC—all employees & drivers, 7539
Electric light or power cooperative—REA project only—all employees & drivers, 7540
Electric light or power line clearing of new right-of-ways by line contractor (clearing of right-of-way performed by contractors also engaged in telephone, telegraph or alarm line construction—shall be assigned to code 7601), 7538
Electric light or power line construction & drivers, 7538
Electric or gas lighting fixtures mfg., 3180
Electric oven—installation, service or repair—commercial, 5190
Electric power or transmission equipment mfg., 3643
Electric razor mfg. or repair, 3179
Electric, telephone or alarm line—brush or weed control by spraying—existing right-of-way, 0050
Electric, telephone or alarm line—clearing brush or stumps from existing right-of-way, 6217
Electric, telephone or alarm line—clearing of new right-of-way—standing timber, 2702
Electric, telephone or alarm line—tree pruning, spraying or removal—existing right-of-way, 0106
Electrical apparatus installation or repair & drivers, 3724
Electrical apparatus mfg. NOC, 3179
Electrical cable connector mfg., 3179
Electrical cord set, radio or ignition harness assembly, 3681
Electrical hardware stores—wholesale or retail, 8010
Electrical power equipment repair or service—away from shop, 3724
Electrical wiring—within buildings & drivers, 5190
Electro-physical therapy equipment mfg., 3685
Electronic chip mfg., 4150
Electronic timers, 3631
Electroplating, 3372
Electrotyping, 4350
Elevator door bucks—installation, 5102
Elevator door fabrication—iron or steel, 3040
Elevator entrance & door installation, 5102
Elevator erection or repair, 5160
Elevator inspecting, 8720
Elevator or escalator mfg., 3042
Elevator servicing—oiling, adjusting and maintenance, 5160
Embroidery mfg., 2388
Emery cloth mfg., 1860
Emery works & drivers, 1747
Enamel or agate ware mfg., 3224
Enameled iron ware mfg., 3091
Energy conservation consultants, 8601
Engine mfg. NOC, 3612
Engine mfg.—aircraft, 3826
Engine mfg.—automobile 3827
Engine mfg.—outboard motors, 3612
Engine repair—marine—away from water, 8380
Engineer or architect—consulting, 8601
Engraving, 4352
Entertainer—bar, cocktail lounge, night club, 9079
Envelope mfg., 4251
Escalator erection or repair, 5160
Escalator or elevator mfg., 3042
Essential oils mfg. & distillation, 4825
Estate—private—see Basic Manual Rule XIV—domestic workers—residences
Ether—suction machine mfg., 3685
Evaporated milk mfg., 2065
Excavation & drivers, 6217
Excavation—rock—& drivers (ID, OK, VA), 1605
Excelsior mfg., 2731
Exercise or health institute & clerical, 9063
Exhibition booth fabrication, 2812
Exhibition—see "Amusement park"
Exhibitions—trade show or conventions, setting up or taking down, 5146
Explosives or ammunition mfg.: cartridge charging or loading & drivers (AL, AZ, ID, IN), 4766
Explosives or ammunition mfg.: cartridge mfg. or assembly—small arms—& drivers (CT), 4767
Explosives or ammunition mfg.: fireworks mfg. & drivers (CO. OK, TN), 4761
Explosives or ammunition mfg.—bag loading—propellant charges—& drivers, 4770
Explosives or ammunition mfg.—black powder mfg. & drivers, 4799
Explosives or ammunition mfg.—cap, primer fuse booster or detonator assembly & drivers, 4779
Explosives or ammunition mfg.—cartridge charging or loading & drivers, 4775
Explosives or ammunition mfg.—cartridge mfg. or assembly—small arms—& drivers, 3574
Explosives or ammunition mfg.—cartridge or shell case mfg.—metal, 3315
Explosives or ammunition mfg.—explosives distributors & drivers, 4777
Explosives or ammunition mfg.—fireworks mfg. & drivers, 4779
Explosives or ammunition mfg.—high explosives mfg. & drivers, 4773
Explosives or ammunition mfg.—projectile, bomb, mine or grenade loading & drivers, 4776
Explosives or ammunition mfg.—projectile or shell mfg., 3639
Explosives or ammunition mfg.—shell case loading & drivers, 4775
Explosives or ammunition mfg.—smokeless powder mfg.—single base—& drivers, 4774
Express co.—see "Trucking"
Exterminator & drivers, 9014
Exterminator or termite control work—all operations (AZ), 5650
Exterminators—carpentry & fumigation—see code 9014 scope
Extract mfg., 4825
Eyeglass mfg., 4150
Eyelet mfg., 3270
Fabric coating or impregnating NOC, 4493
Fabric coating—rubber or plastic, 4410
Facade fabrication—metal, 3041
Factory cost or office systematizer, accountant or auditor—traveling, 8803
Fan mfg., 3179
Farina mfg., 2016
Farm—animal raising (AZ), 0006
Farm—animal raising (fur bearing) & drivers, 0170
Farm—berry or vineyard—& drivers, 0079
Farm—berry picking (OR), 0117
Farm—cattle or livestock raising NOC & drivers, 0083
Farm—dairy & drivers, 0036
Farm—egg or poultry producer & drivers, 0034
Farm—field crops & drivers, 0037
Farm—fish hatchery & drivers, 0113
Farm—florist & drivers, 0035
Farm—gardening—market or truck and vine yards—all employees (AZ), 0017
Farm—gardening—market or truck—& drivers, 0008
Farm—goat or sheep raising & drivers, 0169
Farm—livestock or cattle raising NOC & drivers, 0083
Farm—NOC & drivers, 0037
Farm—nursery employees & drivers (includes incidental landscape gardening), 0005
Farm—orchard & drivers, 0016
Farm—poultry or egg producers & drivers, 0034
Farm—sheep or goat raising & drivers, 0169
Farm—vegetable—& drivers, 0008
Farm—vineyard or berry—& drivers, 0079
Farm machinery dealer—all operations & drivers, 8116
Farm machinery operation—by contractor—& drivers, 0050
Farm machinery—leasing or renting without operators, 8116
Farm product—alfalfa, 0037
Farm product—animals—fur bearing, 0170
Farm product—apples, 0016
Farm product—apricots, 0016
Farm product—asparagus, 0008
Farm product—bananas, 0016

Fire escape installation: inside of buildings, 5102
Fire escape installation: outside of buildings, 5040
Fire extinguisher mfg., 3315
Fire extinguisher—service or recharge, 4635
Fire extinguishing systems—dry chemical—installation and service & drivers, 5188
Fire flooding—drilling in connection with oil or gas well, 6235
Fire patrol or protective corps & drivers, 7704
Fire plug—installation, repair and maintenance, 7520
Firefighters & drivers 7704
Firefighters—medical only and driver (IN), 7699
Firefighters—not volunteer & drivers (CT), 7710
Firefighters—volunteer—& drivers (CT), 7711
Fireplace construction, 5022
Fireproof equipment mfg., 3076
Fireproof shutter—erection or repair, 5040
Fireproof tile setting, 5022
Fireworks dealer, 4777
Fireworks exhibition & drivers, 9180
Fireworks mfg., 4779
Fish curing, 2101
Fish evaporating, pickling, salting, smoking, 2101
Fish hatcheries, 0113
Fish oil mfg., 4665
Fishing rod and tackle mfg., 4902
Fishing tackle repair, 4902
Fishing vessels—NOC—Program I, 7039
Fishing vessels—NOC—Program II—State Act, 7091
Fishing vessels—NOC—Program II—USL Act, 7051
Fixtures or furniture installation—portable—NOC, 5146
Flags and bunting erection—& drivers, 5102
Flashlight case mfg., 3315
Flashlight mfg. or assembling, 3179
Flax spinning and weaving, 2220
Flaxseed oil mfg.—not using solvent extraction process, 4683
Flaxseed oil mfg.—using solvent extraction process, 4686
Flea market operation, 9015
Flint or spar grinding & drivers, 1741
Floating boat dock construction, 6003
Flock coating ot textiles, 2413
Floodlights—erection of temporary floodlights—drivers, 3724
Floodlighting of stadiums, parks, etc.—drivers, 7538
Floor construction—concrete, self-bearing, 5213
Floor covering—installation of linoleum, asphalt or rubber tiling (ceramic tile installation to be separately rated), 9521
Floor coverings—retail—carpets, rugs, linoleum, 8017
Floorcoverings—wholesale—carpets, rugs, linoleum, 8018
Floor installation—floating or access, 5146
Floor laying—linoleum, asphalt, rubber or composition tiling, 9521
Floor laying—mastic floor mix—& drivers, 5221
Floor laying—parquet, 5437
Floor laying—tile—ceramic, 5348
Floor sanding or scraping—wood floors, 5437
Floor tile mfg.—rubber, 4410
Floor waxing or polishing, 9014
Flooring dealer—hardwood, 8235
Flooring mfg.—wood, 2731
Florist—farm, 0035
Florist—store—& drivers, 8001
Flour mixing and blending—no milling, 6504
Flower or feather mfg.—artificial, 2534
Fluorescent tube mfg., 4112
Fluorspar mining—& drivers, 1164
Flypaper mfg., 4250
Foam rubber mfg., 4410
Food concessionaires at sporting events, 9079
Food mixers—installation, service or repair—commercial, 5190
Food products (nonperishable) storage warehouse, 8292
Food sundries mfg. NOC & salespersons, drivers (OK), 6513
Food sundries mfg. NOC—no cereal milling, 6504
Food vendors—mobile, 7380
Foot goods mfg.—arch supports, bunion straps, 4693
Football or basketball mfg.—(bladder mfg. to be separately rated), 2688
Football team, 9179
Forest firefighting—& drivers, 7704
Forest patrollers (OR), 2697
Forest rangers—& drivers, 7720
Forging work—drop or machine, 3110
Foundry—ferrous—NOC, 3081
Foundry—non-ferrous, 3085
Foundry—soil pipe using pit method, 3081
Foundry—steel castings, 3082
Fountain pen mfg., 4432
Fox raising, 0170
Fraternal society & clerical, 9061
Fraternity or sorority houses—& clerical, 9061
Freezers—installation, service or repair—residential, 9519
Freight cars—icing, 7360
Freight handling—explosives or ammunition—under contract—coverage under Longshore Act, 7350F
Freight handling—explosives or ammunition—under contract—coverage under State Act, 7360
Freight handling NOC—coverage under Longshore Act, 7350F
Freight handling NOC—coverage under State Act, 7360
Fringe or braid mfg., 2380
Frozen bakery products mfg., 2003
Frozen fruit processing or packing, 2112
Frozen or frosted food products mfg.—see interpretation section—classifications
Frozen vegetable products mfg.—preparation similar to canning, 2111
Fruit evaporating or preserving, 2112
Fruit farm, 0016
Fruit juice mfg., 2143
Fruit or vegetable stores—wholesale (OK), 8048
Fruit packing, 2105
Fruit picking on ground (OR), 0116
Fry kettle—installation, service or repair—commercial, 5190
Fuel and material dealer NOC—no secondhand building materials or lumber—& local managers, drivers, 3232
Fuel pump mfg.—auto, 3581
Fuel storage—underground, 7515
Fulminate explosives mfg., 4773
Fumigation, 9014
Fund-raising campaigns, 8742
Funeral director & drivers, 9620
Fur clothing—cleaning, tumbling, glazing, combing and ironing, 2586
Fur clothing mfg., 2501
Fur coat and jacket mfg.—custom made, 2503
Fur dressing or dyeing, 2600
Fur mfg.—preparing skins, 2600
Fur plate mfg., 2501
Fur pointing, 2534
Furnace cleaning—suction method, 9014
Furnace installation—hot air—& drivers, 5538
Furnace installation—hot water or steam—& drivers, 5183
Furnace mfg.—all types (OR), 3168
Furnace mfg.—oil or gas fired, 3169
Furnishing goods mfg. NOC, 2501
Furniture assembly—wood—from manufactured parts, 2881
Furniture mfg.—metal, 3076
Furniture mfg.—rattan, willow or twisted fiber, 2913
Furniture mfg.—wood—NOC, 2883
Furniture mfg.—wrought iron, 3041
Furniture moving & storage, drivers, 8293
Furniture or fixtures installation—portable—NOC, 5146
Furniture rental—chairs, coat racks, dishes, etc., 8044
Furniture stock mfg., 2735
Furniture upholstering, 9522
Furniture—stripping and/or refinishing, 9501
Furriers—repairing or remodeling fur garments, 2501
Fuse mfg.—household, 3648
Galvanizing or tinning-not electrolytic, 3373
Gambling vessels—15 tons or greater, 7016, 7024, 7047
Gambling vessels—less than 15 tons, 7038, 7090, 7050
Game and fish wardens, 7720
Games—see "Recreational facilities"
Garages operated by hotels, etc., 9052
Garbage and refuse—collecting in containers, 9403

Garbage, ashes or refuse collection & drivers, 9403
Garbage or refuse collection—exclusive mechanical operation—& drivers (MT), 9405
Garbage works, 7590
Garden furniture mfg.—concrete, 4034
Gardening—see "Farm"
Garment rack mfg.—metal, 3076
Gas bench and retort installation—& drivers, 3724
Gas burner installation—see "Oil or gas burner installation"
Gas company: gas works & salespersons, drivers (AL, GA, TN), 7500
Gas company—natural—local distribution & drivers, 7502
Gas dealer—l.p.g. & drivers, 8350
Gas dealer—l.p.g. & salespersons, drivers (AL, AZ, FL, GA, LA, MS, MO, OK), 8353
Gas distributing—l.p.g.—local & drivers, 7502
Gas holder erection, 5040
Gas main or connection construction & drivers, 6319
Gas meter mfg., 3574
Gas or electric lighting fixtures mfg., 3180
Gas or oil lease operator—natural gas—all operations & drivers, 1320
Gas or oil lease work NOC—natural gas—by contractor—& drivers, 6216
Gas, steam and hot water apparatus—supplies, dealers—& drivers, 8111
Gas well or pipeline—see "Oil or gas"
Gas works & drivers, 7502
Gasket or washer mfg.—not metal, 2651
Gasoline or oil dealer & drivers, 8350
Gasoline pump installation & drivers, 3724
Gasoline recovery & drivers, 4740
Gasoline recovery and drivers (KS, LA, NM), 4743
Gasoline recovery from casing head or natural gas—absorption process, 4740
Gasoline station—retail—& drivers NOC, 8380
Gasoline station—retail—self-service, 8381
Gear mfg. or grinding, 3635
Gelatine mfg.: not food, 4653
Gelatine mfg.: refined food product, 6504
Generator mfg., 3648
Geophysical exploration NOC—all employees & drivers, 7380
Geophysical exploration NOC—all employees & drivers (AK, AZ OK), 8607
Geophysical exploration—seismic—all employees & drivers, 8606
Geophysical research or analytical laboratory, 4511
Gin distillery, 2130
Glass bottom boat—tourist attraction—Program I, 7038
Glass bottom boat—tourist attraction—Program II—State Act, 7090
Glass bottom boat—tourist attraction—Program II—USL Act, 7050
Glass—crystal engraving, 4113
Glass merchant, 4130
Glass mfg.—& drivers, 4101
Glass mfg.—blown sheet window—& drivers, 4101
Glass mfg.—cut, 4113
Glass mfg.—polished plate—& drivers, 4101
Glass mfg.—rolled—& drivers, 4101
Glass window mfg.—stained, 4133
Glass yarn weaving, 2302
Glassware mfg. NOC, 4114
Glassware mfg. using automatic blowing machines, 4114
Glassware mfg.—no automatic blowing machines, 4111
Glazier—away from shop—& drivers, 5462
Glove lining mfg., 2670
Glove mfg.—including baseball, boxing, handball and punching bag gloves, 2670
Glove mfg.—leather or textile, 2670
Glove mfg.—rubber, 4410
Glove or mitten mfg.—knit, 2362
Glucose mfg., 4703
Glue mfg. & drivers, 4653
Goggle mfg., 4150
Gold leaf mfg., 3383
Golf ball mfg., 4902
Golf cart mfg. or assembly—entire vehicle, 3808
Golf club heads or shafts mfg.—wood, 2841
Golf clubs mfg., 4902
Golf clubs—mfg. or assembling, 4902
Golf course, not miniature—public or private, 9060
Golf courses operated by hotels, etc., 9052
Golt driving range, 9016
Grading of land NOC & drivers, 6217
Grain bin mfg., 3066
Grain elevator construction—concrete, 5213
Grain elevator operation & local managers, drivers, 8304
Grain, feed or hay dealer & local managers, drivers, 8215
Grain milling, 2014
Grain sampling operation, 8709
Grandstands or bleachers erection—portable—wood or metal, 5403
Granite cutting or polishing, 1803
Granite quarry, 1624
Graphite mfg.—not artificial—& drivers, 1452
Graphite—surface mining, 1165
Grates—installing or replacing in steam boilers—by specialist contractors—& drivers, 3724
Gravel mfg., 1710
Gravel or sand digging & drivers, 4000
Grazing land maintenance, 0037
Grease or oil mixing or blending, 4557
Green chain operation—lumber, 2710
Greenhouse erection—all operations, 5402
Greyhound breeding, training and racing & driver (FL), 7204
Grill mfg.—concrete, 4034
Grindstone mfg.—no quarrying, 1803
Grist mills, 2014
Grocery, tea or coffee dealer—retail—& drivers, 8006
Grocery, tea or coffee dealer—retail—& salespersons, drivers (OK), 8753
Grouting: drilling of holes—& drivers, 6204
Grouting: placing of cement or plastic compound, 5213
Groyne construction—consisting wholly of pile driving, 6003
Gun mfg.—20mm and larger, 3548
Guniting—not chimneys—all operations & drivers, 5213
Gunstock mfg., 2841
Gutter (drainage) mfg., 3066
Gymnasium appliance mfg., 4902
Gymnasiums and health clubs, 9063
Gypsum—surface mining, 1165
Hair goods mfg., 2534
Hair—preparation for brush manufacturers (dehairing to be separately rated), 2600
Hand bill distribution—see "Distributing companies"
Hand luggage mfg., 2683
Handbag frame mfg.—metal, 3146
Handicapped rehabilitation—educational or training center, 8837
Handle mfg., 3146
Handle mfg.—wood, 2841
Harbor tour boat—less than 15 tons—Program I, 7038
Harbor tour boat—less than 15 tons—Program II—State Act, 7090
Harbor tour boat—less than 15 tons—Program II—USL Act, 7050
Hardware mfg. NOC, 3146
Harness or saddle mfg., 4902
Hat block mfg.—wood, 2841
Hat cleaning, 8017
Hat frame mfg.—ladies—from buckram, 2501
Hat mfg., 2501
Hat mfg.—straw (OK), 2531
Hatchery—bird, 0034
Hatters' fur mfg., 2623
Hauling & stringing of oil or gas pipe lines, 7222
Hay baling & drivers, 0050
Hay, grain or feed dealer & local managers, drivers, 8215
Hay loader mfg., 3507
Health or exercise institute & clerical, 9063
Health spa or steam bath NOC & clerical, 9063
Hearing aid mfg., 3681
Hearing aid stores, 8013
Heat treating—metal, 3307
Heater or radiator mfg., 3175
Heel mfg.—wood—covering to be separately rated, 2841

Heel or sole mfg.—rubber, 4410
Helmet mfg.—sports, 4902
Hemp or jute spinning and weaving, 2220
Highway guard rails—installation, 5506
Highway maintenance, 5506
Highway operations—toll roads—see Interpretation section—classifications
Highway patrol—state highway commission, 7720
Highway sign erection, 9552
Hockey team, 9179
Hod hoist or construction elevator installation, repair or removal & drivers, 9529
Hoisting systems mfg., 3507
Home for aged—all employees, 8829
Home improvement center—& drivers—all other than store employees, 8232
Home improvement center—store employees, 8058
Homeless—rehabilitation of, 8837
Homemaker service, 8835
Hone or oil stone mfg. (AR, NH, VA, VT), 1745
Honeycomb packaging products mfg., 4244
Horn goods mfg.—fabricated products mfg., 4452
Horn mfg., 3383
Horn mfg.—automobile, 3648
Horse shoe mfg., 3146
Horse shoeing, 3111
Horse show—operation by owner or lessee—& drivers, 9016
Horse show—stable employees, 8279
Hose mfg.—rubber, 4410
Hose mfg.—woven fire hose from linen thread, 2402
Hosiery dyeing and finishing, 2361
Hosiery mfg., 2361
Hospital equipment installation, 5146
Hospital: cafeteria & kitchen employees (OR), 9366
Hospital—all other than professional employees, 9040
Hospital—professional employees, 8833
Hospital—veterinary—& drivers, 8831
Hotel & salespersons, drivers—all other than restaurant employees, 9052
Hotel and restaurant kitchen equipment mfg.—sheet metal, 3066
Hotel—restaurant employees, 9058
Hothouse erection—all operations, 5402
House furnishings installation NOC & upholstering, 9521
Household appliances—electrical—installation, service or repair—& drivers, 9519
Household furnishings or wearing apparel dealer—retail—& drivers, 8006
Housing authority & clerical, salespersons, drivers, 9033
Hovercrafts—operated over water—Program I, 7019
Hovercrafts—operated over water—Program II—State Act, 7027
Hovercrafts—operated over water—Program II—USL Act, 7062
Hub and spoke mfg.—wood, 2841
Hub cap mfg., 3315
Humidity control mfg., 3574
Humus digging and bagging—& drivers, 4000
Hunting and fishing guides, 7720
Hunting guides—club, 9180
Hunting or fishing guides, including camp or lodge operations—all employees & drivers (AK), 9094
Hybrid seed plant operation, 8102
Hydraulic device mfg.—jacks, auto lifts, 3612
Hydrofoils—operated over water—Program I, 7019
Hydrofoils—operated over water—Program II—State Act, 7027
Hydrofoils—operated over water—Program II—USL Act, 7062
Hydrogen or oxygen mfg. & drivers, 4635
Hydrogen peroxide mfg., 4825
Hydrogenation of oils, 4717
Hydroponic growing of vegetables, 0035
Ice cream cabinet installation & service, drivers—by ice cream manufacturers, 2039
Ice cream cabinet installation & service, drivers—by specialist contractors, 5190
Ice cream cabinet mfg.—metal, 3076
Ice cream cone mfg., 2001
Ice cream mfg. & drivers, 2039
Ice cream vendors—mobile, 7380
Ice dealer & drivers, 8203
Ice harvesting & storing, drivers, 8203
Ice mfg., 2150
Ice mfg.—block, 2150
Ice mfg.—cube or crushed, 8203
Ice skate mfg., 3146
Ice skating rink, 9016
Ices mfg., 2039
Icing refrigerator cars, 7360
Ignition coil mfg., 3648
Incandescent lamp mfg., 4112
Incense mfg., 4825
Incubator mfg.—metal, 3076
Incubator mfg.—wood, 2812
Ink mfg. 4557
Ink (writing), mucilage or paste mfg. (GA, MO), 4597
Inked ribbon preparation, 4251
Insect control—spraying from aircraft, 7409
Insect control—spraying from ground by specialist contractor, 0050
Insect raising, 0034
Insecticide mfg.—household, 4819
Inspection of risks for insurance or valuation purposes NOC, 8720
Inspectors of merchandise on vessels or docks—coverage under Longshore Act, 8709F
Inspectors of merchandise on vessels or docks—coverage under State Act, 8719
Inspectors—municipal, township, county or state employee, 9410
Instrument mfg. NOC, 3685
Instrument mfg.—airplane, 3685
Instrument mfg.—surveyors, 3685
Insulation mfg.—mineral process, 1699
Insulation mfg.—paper, 4263
Insulation work NOC & drivers, 5479
Insulation—steam pipe or boiler & drivers, 5183
Insulin mfg., 4825
Intercommunication systems installation or repair & drivers, 7605
Interior decorators—house furnishings installation, 9521
Iodine mfg., 4825
Iron (clothing presser) mfg., 3179
Iron or steel erection NOC, 5057
Iron or steel erection—construction of dwellings not over two stories in height, 5069
Iron or steel erection—decorative, 5102
Iron or steel erection—door or sash erection—metal or metal covered, 5102
Iron or steel erection—exterior (balconies, fire escapes, staircases, etc.), 5040
Iron or steel erection—frame structures not over two stories in height, 5059
Iron or steel erection—frame structures over two stories in height, 5040
Iron or steel erection—metal bridges, 5040
Iron or steel erection—metal bridges (VA), 5067
Iron or steel erection—non-structural—interior, 5102
Iron or steel erection—radio, television or water towers, smokestacks, gas holders, 5040
Iron or steel merchant & drivers, 8106
Iron or steel mfg.: doubling process, 3018
Iron or steel mfg.—rolling mill & drivers, 3018
Iron or steel mfg.—steel making & drivers, 3004
Iron or steel scrap dealer & drivers, 8265
Iron or steel—fabrication ironworks—shop—decorative or artistic—foundries & drivers, 3041
Iron or steel—iron or steel works—shop—structural—& drivers, 3030
Iron or steel—iron works—shop—ornamental—& drivers, 3040
Irrigation or drainage system construction & drivers, 6229
Irrigation or drainage system or canal maintenance, 0251
Irrigation pipe installation—agricultural—above ground & drivers (MT), 6365
Irrigation works operation & drivers, 0251
Isinglass mfg., 4653
Ivory or bone goods mfg., 4452

Jail employees, 7720
Jalousie or jalousie screen erection—metal or glass, 5645
Jalousie or jalousie screen manufacture—metal or glass, 3076
Jam mfg., 2112
Janitorial service by contractor: includes window cleaning (FL), 9001
Janitorial service by contractor: no window cleaning (FL), 9000
Jar mfg., 4114
Jar ring mfg.—rubber, 4410
Jelly mfg., 2112
Jetty construction—consisting wholly of pile driving, 6003
Jetty or breakwater construction—all operations to completion & drivers, 6005
Jewelers findings mfg., 3131
Jewelry mfg., 3383
Jewelry repair—not jewelry store, 3383
Jewelry tray manufacture—fabric, 2501
Jewelry tray manufacture—wooden, 2841
Jockeys—horse (CO), 8277
Jockeys—horse, 8279
Juke box mfg., 3559
Juke boxes—installation, service or repair—& salespersons, drivers, 5192
Junk dealer & drivers, 8263
Jute or hemp spinning and weaving, 2220
Kaolin grinding, 1747
Kaolin milling & drivers (GA, SC), 1751
Kaolin mining—surface—& drivers (GA, SC), 1169
Keg assembling, 2747
Keg mfg.—metal, 3400
Kennels—boarding and breeding—dog and cat & drivers, 8831
Key case mfg. from leather, imitation leather or vinyl, 2688
Kitchen cabinets—installation, 5437
Kitchen cabinets—manufacture, 2812
Kitchen equipment installation—commercial, 5146
Knife mfg., 3122
Knit goods mfg. NOC, 2362
Label mfg.—paper, 4251
Label mfg.—woven labels, 2380
Labor union—all employees, 8755
Laboratory animals—breeding or care, 0170
Lace mfg., 2386
Lacquer or spirit varnish mfg., 4439
Ladder mfg.—wood, 2802
Laminated wood building beams and columns mfg., 2802
Lamp mfg.—wooden, 2883
Lamp or portable lantern mfg. NOC, 3223
Lamp shade frame mfg.—wire, 3257
Lamp shade mfg.—parchment or textile—(frame manufacturing to be separately rated), 2501
Landscape gardening & drivers, 0042
Lantern or lamp mfg. NOC, 3223
Lard refining, 4683
Lard refining (IL, IN, MO), 4716
Last block mfg., 2741
Last or shoe form mfg., 2790
Lath mfg.—wood, 2710
Lathing & drivers, 5443
Launch (ship) building—iron or steel—State Act, 6854
Launch (ship) building—iron or steel—U.S. Act, 6843F
Laundry and dry cleaning store—retail—& route supervisors, drivers, 2589
Laundry, dry cleaning or dyeing NOC & route supervisers, drivers (AK), 2592
Laundry machinery mfg.—commercial or household, 3632
Laundry NOC & route supervisors, drivers, 2585
Laundry—self-service, 8017
Law office—all employees & clerical, messengers, drivers, 8820
Lawn maintenance, 9102
Lawn mower mfg., 3507
Lawn mower repair, 3632
Lawn or shrub spraying & drivers (FL), 0153
Lawn ornament mfg.—concrete, 4034
Lawn sprinkler systems installation—underground, 5183
Lead mfg. & drivers, 1430
Lead or zinc mining & drivers (KS, MO, OK), 1154
Lead pencil mfg., 2942
Lead works & drivers, 3027
Leather belting installation or repair—& drivers, 3724
Leather belting mfg., 2688
Leather dressing, 2623
Leather embossing, 2623
Leather goods mfg. NOC, 2688
Leather mfg.—imitation, 4493
Leather mfg.—patent or enamel, 2623
Leather skiving, 2688
Lens mfg.—ground, 4150
Letter service shop & clerical, 8800
Levee construction—all operations to completion & drivers, 6045
Library—public—see "Public library"
Licorice extract mfg., 4825
Light bulb mfg., 4112
Light prisms in sidewalks—installation or repair—& drivers, 5221
Lighter (ship) building—iron or steel—State Act, 6854
Lighter (ship) building—iron or steel—U.S. Act, 6843F
Lightning rod mfg., 3315
Lime mfg., 1642
Lime mfg.—quarry—surface—& drivers, 1655
Limestone crushing, 1710
Limestone cutting or polishing, 1803
Limestone milling—powdered, 1747
Limestone quarry, 1624
Limousine company—garage employees, 8385
Limousine company—non-scheduled & drivers—all other than garage employees, 7370
Limousine company—scheduled & drivers—all other than garage employees, 7382
Linen cloth mfg., 2220
Linen thread mfg., 2220
Lingerie mfg., 2501
Lining mfg.—hat, 2501
Lining reservoirs, lagoons, ponds—rubber or plastic, 5102
Linings—sewing into coats by hand, 2501
Linoleum installation, 9521
Linoleum mfg., 4493
Linotype or hand composition, 4308
Liquefied petroleum gas—see "Gas distributing"
Liquid waste collection, 9403
Liquor bottling—not beer or wine, including warehousing, rectifying or blending, 2131
Liquor or wine store—retail, 8017
Liquor or wine store—wholesale, 8018
Lithograph mounting and finishing, 4279
Lithographing, 4299
Lithographing stone mfg.—no quarrying—& drivers, 1803
Livery co.—see "Limousine co."
Livery or boarding stable—not sales stable—& drivers, 8279
Livery or boarding stable—not sales stable—drivers (FL), 7201
Livestock dealer or commission merchant & salespersons, drivers, 8288
Livestock sales co. & salespersons, drivers, 8288
Lock or dam construction—see "Dam or lock construction"
Locker mfg.—automatic, 3559
Locker mfg.—sheet metal, 3076
Locksmith—including shop, 8010
Locks—installation in new buildings, 5437
Locomotive works, 3507
Log cabin mfg.—sawmill operation, 2710
Log hauling & drivers (MT), 2727
Log processing—posts & rails for fences, 2710
Log scaling, 8601
Logging equipment maintenance & repair (AK, MT, OR, SD), 2703
Logging or lumbering: certified loggers & drivers (ME), 2721
Logging or lumbering & drivers, 2702
Logging or lumbering: log hauling & drivers (OR), 9310
Logging or lumbering: mechanized equipment operators (ME, SD), 2709
Logging or lumbering: mechanized equipment operations & drivers (OR), 2725

Logging or lumbering—mechanized harvesting exclusively— & drivers (MS), 2719
Logging or lumbering—pulpwood only—& drivers (GA, LA, MS, TN), 2705
Logging road construction and maintenance (MT, OR), 5611
Logging tool mfg., 3126
Loom harness or reed mfg., 3515
Loom harness or reed mfg. (RI, SC, VA), 3516
Loose leaf ledger or notebook mfg., 4251
Luggage mfg., 2683
Luggage stores—retail, 8017
Lumber remanufacturing, 2731
Lumberyard—store employees, 8058
Lumberyard—warehouse & drivers—all other than store employees, 8232
Macaroni mfg., 2002
Machine gun mfg.—.50 caliber or less, 3574
Machine shop NOC, 3632
Machine tools (small) mfg.—drop or machine forged, 3114
Machine tools (small) mfg.—not drop or machine forged, 3113
Machinery dealer NOC—store or yard—& drivers, 8107
Magnaflux testing and inspection, 4511
Magnesite mfg., 1701
Magnesium metal mfg.—all operations and drivers, 1438
Magnesium metal mfg.—all operations and driver (TN), 1429
Mailing or addressing co. & clerical, 8800
Malt house & drivers, 2121
Malted milk mfg. from powdered milk, sugar, malt, cocoa, 6504
Malted milk mfg.—including dehydration of milk, 2065
Managers—local—see Interpretation section—classifications
Manicure products mfg., 3122
Manicurists, 9586
Manure dealers—& drivers, 9403
Map mfg.—relief—made of plaster, 4038
Mapping or survey work—aerial—photography—flying crew, 7422
Mapping or survey work—aerial—photography—ground laboratory, 4361
Marble cutting or polishing, 1803
Marble mfg.—artificial, 4036
Marble or stone setting—inside, 5348
Margarine mfg., 4717
Marina & drivers—coverage under Longshore Act, 6826F
Marina & drivers—coverage under State Act, 6836
Marine appraiser or surveyor, 8720
Marine railway operation & drivers, 6872F
Market research—interviewing consumers in field, 8742
Marl grinding, 1747
Marl—digging and stripping, 4000
Masonry NOC, 5022
Massage salons, 9063
Match mfg., 4279
Match mfg. (IL), 4730
Match stick mfg., 2841
Mattress or box spring mfg., 2570
Mattress pad mfg. from felt on felt-like material, 2288
Matzoth mfg., 2001
Mausoleums in cemeteries—erection only, 5022
Mayonnaise mfg., 6504
Meat products mfg. NOC, 2095
Meat slicers or grinders—service or repair, 5191
Medical apparatus—sterilization using X-ray process, 4511
Medical diagnostic lamp mfg., 3685
Medical research or analytical laboratory, 4511
Medicine, drug or pharmaceutical preparation mfg. & incidental mfg. of ingredients, 4825
Medicine, drug or pharmaceutical preparation—no mfg. of ingredients, 4611
Melba toast mfg.—no baking of bread, 6504
Memorial plaque fabrication—metal, 3041
Mental health group care homes—all employees clerical (OR), 8842
Mercerizing textile, 2413
Mercerizing yarn, 2416
Merry-go-round operation—not traveling, 9180
Messengers, collectors or salespersons—outside, 8742
Metal ceiling or wall covering installation & shop, drivers, 5538
Metal cleaning—pickling, 3372
Metal coating—rubber or plastic, 4410
Metal extraction from ores—non-ferrous, 1438
Metal finishing (deburring), 3372
Metal goods mfg. NOC, 3400
Metal partition installation, 5146
Metal sash installation, 5102
Metal scrap dealer & drivers, 8500
Metal service centers (not junk or scrap dealers)—& drivers, 8106
Metal shredding plant, 8265
Metal stamping mfg., 3400
Metal tag mfg.—stamped, 3400
Metallurgical research or analytical laboratory, 4511
Meter maids, 7720
Meter readers for utility company—assign to utility's classification (e.g., 7520)
Meter—electric—installing, repairing and testing—including shop; & drivers, 5190
Mica goods mfg. & mica preparing, 1853
Mica grinding, 1741
Mica splitting, 1853
Mica—surface mining, 1165
Microbiology research or analytical laboratory, 4511
Microfilming, 4361
Microwave oven mfg., 3179
Military reservation construction—carpentry, 5651
Military reservation construction—concrete—not monolithic, 5215
Military reservation construction—iron or steel erection not over two stories in height, 5069
Military reservation dismantling or wrecking—see "Wrecking"
Military tank hull mfg. or assembly, 3620
Milk bottle cap mfg.—paper—including printing, 4279
Milk bottle exchange—all employees & drivers, 2070
Milk depot or milk dealer & route supervisors, drivers, 2070
Milk products mfg. NOC, 2065
Mill supply dealers, 8018
Millinery mfg., 2501
Millinery mfg. (LA, OK, VA), 2532
Milling grain, 2014
Millstone mfg., 1803
Millwright work NOC & drivers, 3724
Mineral mining—underground, 1164
Mineral wool mfg., 1699
Miniature golf course, 9016
Mining NOC—not coal—surface & drivers, 1165
Mining NOC—not coal—underground—& drivers, 1164
Mining or ore milling machinery mfg., 3507
Mining tool mfg., 3126
Mining—fluorspar—& drivers (KY), 1213
Mink raising, 0170
Mirror mfg., 4131
Missile bases, 9088
Missiles firing and bunker, 9088
Missiles—construct underground launch pad, 6252
Mitten or glove mfg.—knit, 2362
Mobile crane and hoisting service contractors—NOC—all operations including yard employees and drivers, 9534
Mobile home delivery—by specialist contractor—delivery only, 7219
Mobile home delivery—by specialist contractor—including placement, hook-up of plumbing, electrical and incidental installation activities, 8380
Mobile home repair—on-site; assign to appropriate classification for dwelling repair, 8380
Mobile home repair—shop—by dealer or specialist contractor, 8380
Mobile home sales—all employees other than salespersons, 8380
Mobile home sales—salespersons, 8748
Mobile home windstorm tie-down installation—by dealer, 8380
Mobile home windstorm tie-down installation—by specialist contractor, 6400
Mobile home windstorm tie-down installation—by trailer camp operator, 9015
Mobile or trailer home mfg. & drivers (AZ, FL, GA, ID, IN, KS), 2797
Model airplane mfg.—balsa wood 4902

Model ships, railroad or aircraft kit mfg.—high grade, 2790
Modular homes (factory built)—wood, 2802
Modular or prefabricated home mfg.—not mobile—shop work & drivers (VA), 2805
Molasses or syrup refining, blending or mfg., 2021
Mold mfg.—aluminum for plastics industry, 2790
Molding mfg.—wood, 2731
Monument dealer—wholesale or retail, 1803
Monuments in cemeteries—erection only, 5221
Mop head mfg.—from cotton waste, 2220
Mop mfg.—assembly only, 2835
Mortar mfg., 4036
Mosaic, stone, terrazzo or tile work—inside, 5348
Mosquito netting—cutting, sewing, 2501
Moss gathering, 0037
Motel, motor court or cabin—restaurant employees, 9058
Motel, motor court or cabin—salesmen & drivers—all other than restaurant employees, 9052
Motion picture film exchange projection rooms, & clerical, 4362
Motion picture: development of negatives, printing & all subsequent operations, 4360
Motion picture production: all operations up to the development of negatives & clerical, drivers, 7610
Motion picture: production—in studios or outside—all operations up to the development of negatives & clerical, drivers (MT), 9610
Motor (heavy) repair or service—away from shop, 3724
Motor mfg.—fractional horsepower, 3179
Motor oil—used, reclaiming, recycling or rerefining, 4740
Motorboat—not exceeding 150 feet in length—building or repair—State Act, 6834
Motorboat—not exceeding 150 feet in length—building or repair—U.S. Act, 6824F
Motorcycle mfg. or assembly, 3851
Moulds mfg.—machined metal moulds for white metal castings, 3113
Mountain climbing instructors and guides, 9180
Mouthpiece mfg.—rubber, 4410
Mucilage, ink (writing) or paste mfg., 4557
Mud dealers—oil well drivers, 8107
Muffler installation or repair—& drivers, 8380
Municipal employees (UT), 9417
Municipal social workers—all professional staff (VA), 9411
Municipal, township, county or state employee NOC, 9410
Museum—privately owned, 9016
Museum—public—see "Public library or museum"
Mushroom raising—& drivers, 0035
Music roll mfg.—perforated paper, 4282
Musical instrument mfg.—metal—NOC, 3383
Musical instrument mfg.—metal—NOC (OK), 3686
Musical instrument mfg.—wood—NOC, 2923
Musician—bar, cocktail lounge, night club, 9079
Mustard mfg., 6504
Nail mfg., 3270
Nailhead ornamentation, 2388
Napkin mfg., 4279
National guard and other state military organizations—officers and members thereof (VA), 7724
National guard units, 7720
Necktie mfg.—knitted, 2362
Needle mfg., 3119
Neon lamp mfg., 4112
Neon sign mfg., 3064
Neon sign—manufacture and erection, 9552
Net mfg., 2380
News agent or distributor of magazines or other periodicals—not retail dealer—& salespersons, drivers, 8745
News butchers, 8017
Newspaper operation—newscarriers or route carriers (OK), 4312
Newspaper operation: publishing (OK), 4311
Newspaper publishers—employees such as designers, proofreaders and editors, 8810
Newspaper publishing, 4304
Nightclubs, 9079
Nitro starch explosives mfg., 4773
Nitroglycerine explosives mfg., 4773
Non-stick surfaces—coating of cooking utensils, 9501
Noodle mfg., 2002
Notebook or loose-leaf ledger mfg., 4251
Novelties mfg.—plaster, 4038
Nurseries—day—all other than professional employees, teachers or clerical, 9101
Nurseries—day—professional employees, teachers or clerical, 8868
Nurserypersons—see "Farm"
Nursing home: all other employees (FL), 9047
Nursing home: professional employees (FL), 8841
Nursing or convalescent home—all employees, 8829
Nursing—home health, public & traveling—all employees, 8835
Nut cleaning or shelling, 6504
Nut farm, 0016
Nut or bolt mfg., 3132
Nylon textile fiber mfg., 2305
Oat milling, 2014
Oatmeal mfg., 2016
Ochre grinding, 1747
Office machine or appliance installation, inspection, adjustment or repair, 5191
Office or factory cost systematizer, accountant or auditor—traveling, 8803
Oil analyzing at oil well site in trailers away from well, 6237
Oil burner and oil burner parts store, 8010
Oil cloth mfg., 4493
Oil drilling platform building—floating—iron or steel—State Act, 6854
Oil drilling platform building—floating—iron or steel—U.S. Act, 6843F
Oil mfg.—cottonseed—see "Cottonseed oil mfg."
Oil mfg.—vegetable—NOC, 4683
Oil mfg.—vegetable—solvent extraction process, 4686
Oil or gas burner installation & drivers—commercial type, 3724
Oil or gas burner installation & drivers—domestic, 5183
Oil or gas geologist or scout, 8601
Oil or gas geologists or scout & drivers (OK), 8605
Oil or gas lease operator—all operations & drivers, 1320
Oil or gas lease work NOC—by contractor—& drivers, 6216
Oil or gas pipeline construction & drivers, 6233
Oil or gas pipeline operation & drivers, 7515
Oil or gas well acidizing—all employees & drivers, 6206
Oil or gas well cementing & drivers, 6206
Oil or gas well cleaning or swabbing of old wells having previously produced gas or oil—by contractor—no drilling—& drivers, 1322
Oil or gas well drilling or redrilling & drivers, 6235
Oil or gas well—dirt construction operator, 6216
Oil or gas well—installation or recovery of casings & drivers, 6236
Oil or gas well—instrument logging or survey work—& drivers, 6237
Oil or gas well—oil treating service, 6216
Oil or gas well—perforating of casing—all employees & drivers, 6214
Oil or gas well—roustabout service, 6216
Oil or gas well—shooting & drivers, 6235
Oil or gas well—specialty tool operation NOC—by contractor—all employees & drivers, 6213
Oil or gas well—supplies or equipment dealer—new—store or yard only—& drivers, 8107
Oil or gas well—supplies or equipment dealer—used—& local managers, drivers, 8204
Oil or gas well—tank cleaning service, 6216
Oil or gasoline dealer & drivers, 8350
Oil or grease mixing or blending, 4557
Oil or hone stone mfg. (AR, NH, VA, VT), 1745
Oil refining—petroleum—& drivers, 4740
Oil rig building—mobile offshore jackup type—drivers (MS), 6829F
Oil rig or derrick erecting or dismantling—metal—all operations, 5057
Oil rig or derrick erecting or dismantling—wood—all operations, 5403
Oil still erection or repair, 3719
Oil still pipe insulation & drivers, 5183
Oil well drilling rigs—warehousing and sale—& drivers, 8106
Oil well tool mfg., 3126
Oiling of roads by oil distributors—& drivers, 8350
Oiling of roads in connection with spreading of sand—& drivers, 5506
Oil—reclaiming of used motor oil—& drivers, 4740
Ointment compounding or preparation—no mfg. of ingredients, 4611
Opera glasses mfg., 4150

Ophthalmologist—dispensing of optical goods, 8013
Ophthalmologist—no dispensing of optical goods, 8832
Optical goods mfg. NOC, 4150
Optical stores—(surface grinding of lens to be separately rated 4150), 8013
Optometrist, 8013
Orchard and grove owners and operators—all openations & drivers (FL), 0052
Ordinance research or analytical laboratory, 4511
Ore dock operation & stevedoring, 7313F
Ore milling & drivers, 1452
Ore milling or mining machinery mfg., 3507
Ore mining—surface, 1165
Ore mining—underground, 1164
Organ building & installation, 2923
Ornament or plaster statuary mfg., 4038
Ornamental figure mfg.—concrete, 4034
Orphanages:—see "Asylums"
Outboard motor mfg., 3612
Oven mfg.,—containing mechanical parts, 3169
Oven mfg.—metal industrial drying ovens, 3066
Oven mfg.,—no mechanical parts, 3066
Overhead doors installation & drivers, 3724
Oxygen or hydrogen mfg. & drivers, 4635
Oyster boats—Program I, 7079
Oyster boats—Program II—State Act, 7097
Oyster boats—Program II—USL Act, 7070
Oystermen, 2114
Package or parcel delivery—see "Trucking"
Packaging—contract, 8018
Packing case mfg., 2759
Packing house—all operations, 2089
Paint mfg., 4558
Paint stores—retail, 8017
Paint stores—wholesale, 8013
Painting murals on walls—artists, 5474
Painting of stripes on parking lots, 5474
Painting of stripes on streets, roads or highways, 5474
Painting or paper hanging NOC & shop operations, drivers, 5474
Painting—automobile or carriage bodies, 9505
Painting—metal bridges & shop operations, drivers, 5037
Painting—metal structures—over two stories in height—& drivers, 5037
Painting—ship hulls, 6874F
Painting—shop only & drivers, 9501
Pallet & skid mfg.—wood, 2759
Pallet manufacture and repair—wood, 2759
Panel mfg.—sheet metal, 3076
Panel mfg.—veneered, no veneer mfg., 2916
Panelling dealer, 8235
Paper corrugating or laminating, 4250
Paper crepeing, 4250
Paper goods mfg. NOC, 4279
Paper hanging & drivers, 5491
Paper mache goods mfg., 4038
Paper mfg., 4239
Paper oiling, paraffining, parchmentizing or waxing, 4250
Paper plate mfg., 4279
Paper ruling, 4299
Paper sheeting or slitting and winding, 4279
Paper stock or rag dealer—used—& drivers, 8264
Paper towel mfg., 4279
Paper twine mfg., 4279
Parachute mfg., 2501
Parachute mfg. (CT, VA), 2560
Parade float fabrication, 2812
Parcel or package delivery—see "Trucking"
Park NOC—all employees & drivers, 9102
Parking meters installation, service or repair—& salespersons, drivers, 5192
Particle board mfg., 4239
Partition installation—metal, 5146
Partition mfg.—sheet metal, 3076
Partition system installation—stud, 5445
Paste, ink (writing) or mucilage mfg., 4557
Pastry mfg., 2003
Patio block mfg.—small—concrete, 4034
Patrol or detective agency & drivers, 7720
Pattern making NOC, 2790
Paving or repaving—floors, driveways, yards or sidewalks—& drivers, 5221
Paving or road surfacing on scraping NOC & yards drivers (MO), 5505
Paving—see "Street or road"
Paving—wood block—interior—& drivers, 5221
Pawn shops, 8017
Pea de-vining at cannery, 2111
Peanut butter mfg., 6504
Peanut handling (VA), 2055
Peanut handling, 8102
Peanut oil mfg.—not using solvent extraction process, 4683
Peanut oil mfg.—using solvent extraction process, 4686
Peanut storage warehouse, 8292
Peat digging—& drivers, 4000
Peat moss mixture mfg., 4583
Peg and skewer mfg.—wood, 2841
Pen mfg.—fountain or ballpoint, 4432
Pen point mfg., 3119
Pencil mfg., 2942
Pencil mfg.—mechanical, 4432
Pencil, penholder or crayon mfg., 2942
Pencil stock mfg.—wood, 2735
Penholder, crayon or pencil mfg., 2942
Penicillin mfg., 4825
Penitentiary employees, 7720
Penny arcades, 8017
Peppermint distillation by farmers, 0037
Percolator mfg., 3179
Perfume compounding or preparation—no mfg. of ingredients, 4611
Perlite mfg., 1699
Pet cemetery, 9220
Pet grooming & drivers, 8831
Pet shops—retail, 8017
Petroleum research or analytical laboratory, 4511
Pharmaceutical, drug or medicine preparation mfg. & incidental mfg. of ingredients, 4825
Pharmaceutical, drug or medicine preparation—no mfg. of ingredients, 4611
Pharmaceutical or surgical goods mfg. NOC, 4693
Pharmaceutical or surgical supply stores—primarily serving walk-in trade, 8017
Pharmacology research or analytical laboratory, 4511
Phonograph record mfg., 4431
Phosphate mining & drivers (FL), 1218
Phosphate rock—surface mining, 1165
Phosphate works & drivers, 4581
Photo films and dry plates mfg., 4923
Photoengraving, 4351
Photoflash bulb mfg., 4112
Photoflood lamp mfg., 4112
Photographer—all employees & clerical, salespersons, drivers, 4361
Photographic composition—computerized, 8810
Photographic composition—see Interpretation section—classifications
Photographic supplies mfg., 4923
Physical therapists, 8832
Physician & clerical, 8832
Piano case mfg., 2883
Piano keys mfg., 2923
Piano mfg., 2923
Piano or organ dealer—& drivers, 8044
Piano stores—& drivers, 8044
Piano tuning—away from shop, 5191
Pickle mfg., 2110
Pickled pepper mfg., 2110
Pickled tomato mfg., 2110
Picrates explosives mfg., 4773
Picric acid explosives mfg., 4773
Picture frame assembling—from manufactured parts, 2881

Picture frame moulding mfg., 2731
Picture hook mfg., 3315
Pier construction—concrete, 5213
Pile driving & drivers, 6003
Pile driving equipment mfg., 3507
Pillow, quilt or cushion mfg., 2501
Pilot boats—Program I, 7038
Pilot boats—Program II—State Act, 7090
Pilot boats—Program II—USL Act, 7050
Pilot car service—"wide load ... etc.", 7382
Pilots who guide vessels—Program I, 7016
Pilots who guide vessels—Program II—State Act, 7024
Pilots who guide vessels—Program II—USL Act, 7047
Pin ball machines—service or repair—& salespersons, drivers, 5192
Pin mfg., 3270
Pinstriping—automobiles, 9505
Pipe bending and cutting, 3111
Pipe cleaner mfg., 2380
Pipe manufacturing NOC & drivers, 3022
Pipe mfg.—plastic, extrusion method, 4459
Pipe mfg.—sewer or drain clay, 4021
Pipe mfg.—wooden, tobacco (MD, MO, OK, VA, VT), 2791
Pipe mfg.—wooden, tobacco, 2841
Pipe or tube mfg. NOC & drivers, 3022
Pipe or tube mfg.—iron or steel & drivers, 3028
Pipe or tube mfg.—lead—& drivers, 3027
Pipe testing or inspection—destructive—including radiographic or X-ray processes, 3365
Pipe testing or inspection—non-destructive—other than radiographic or X-ray processes, 8720
Pipe testing—destructive, oil or gas pipes not under construction, 6213
Pipeline or gas well—see "Oil or gas"
Pipeline reclamation—oil or gas—& drivers, 6233
Pistol mfg.—.50 caliber or less, 3574
Piston mfg.—automobile, 3632
Piston pin mfg., 3635
Piston ring mfg., 3635
Pizza crust mfg., 2003
Planing or molding mill, 2731
Planing or molding mill: maintenance & security employees (OR), 9315
Plant protection—special employees hired for plant protection during strike periods—& drivers, 7720
Plants (fibrous) goods mfg., 2913
Plaster board or plaster block mfg. & drivers, 4036
Plaster form mfg., 4038
Plaster mill (OK) 1703
Plaster mill, 1701
Plaster novelties mfg., 4038
Plaster or staff mixing & drivers, 4036
Plaster statuary or ornament mfg., 4038
Plastering NOC & drivers, 5480
Plastering or stucco work—on outside of buildings, 5022
Plastic armor application, 5213
Plastic goods mfg. by dipping process, 4452
Plastic or vinyl sign mfg.—computerized—see 4299
Plastic scrap reclaiming—foamed or expanded plastics, 4410
Plastic thread mfg., 2305
Plastic yarn weaving, 2302
Plastics mfg.—fabrcated products NOC, 4452
Plastics mfg.—molded products NOC, 4484
Plastics mfg.—sheets, rods or tubes, 4459
Plastics—laminated molded products mfg. by laminating liquid plastic impregnated fibers, with the use of brush or spray, either in or over a mold or form NOC, 4484
Playing cards mfg., 4299
Pleating and stitching or tucking—not clothing manufacturing, 2388
Plowshare mfg., 3126
Plumber's hand tool mfg.—drop or machine forged, 3114
Plumber's hand tool mfg.—not drop or machine forged, 3113
Plumbers' supplies dealer & drivers, 8111
Plumbers' supplies mfg. NOC, 3188
Plumbing NOC & drivers, 5183
Plush or velvet mfg., 2300
Plywood dealers—& drivers, 8235
Plywood mfg.—including veneer mfg., 2915
Plywood mfg.—no veneer mfg., 2916
Pneumatic device mfg.—drills, riveters, hammers, 3612
Pneumatic unloaders mfg., 3507
Pocketbook mfg., 2688
Pocketbook mfg. from leather, imitation leather or vinyl, 2688
Pole, post or tie yard & drivers, 2960
Police officers & drivers, 7720
Police officers—medical only—& drivers (IN), 7725
Polish or dressing mfg., 4557
Polishing and buffing—small articles—shop only—no mfg., 3372
Pollution control systems mfg., 3507
Polyester textile fiber mfg., 2305
Pony rides, 9180
Pool halls, 9089
Popcorn dealers, 8102
Popcorn mfg., 6504
Porcelain frit mfg., 1438
Porcelain ware—mechanical press forming, 4062
Porcelainizing of metal products, 3224
Portable toilets—rental, installation, service, 9402
Post exchange—military base, 9077F
Potash, borax or salt producing or refining & drivers, 4568
Potash mining & drivers (NM), 1219
Potato chip mfg., 6504
Potato flour mfg., 2014
Potato storage warehouse, 8292
Pottery mfg.—china or tableware, 4053
Pottery mfg.—earthenware—glazed or porcelain—hand molded or cast, 4061
Pottery mfg.:—earthenware—glazed or porcelain—hand molded or cast: no manufacture of sinks, bathtubs and commodes (NM), 4063
Pottery mfg.—porcelain ware—mechanical press forming, 4062
Potting soil mixture mfg., 4583
Poultry dealers—wholesale—including dressing, 8021
Poultry or egg producer, 0034
Poultry processors (OR), 2086
Poultry sexers, 0034
Powder puff mfg.—from fabrics or dressed wool skins, 2501
Powdered milk mfg., 2065
Power boats—engaged in menhaden fishing only—Coverage I (VA), 7076
Power boats—engaged in menhaden fishing only—Coverage II (VA), 7094
Power plow or traction engine mfg., 3507
Pre-cast concrete—see "Concrete pre-cast"
Pre-fabricated house mfg.—wood—shop work, 2802
Precious metal dealer, 8013
Precious stone setting, 8013
Precision machined parts mfg. NOC, 3629
Premium auditors—insurance, 8803
Preserves (fruit) mfg., 2112
Prestressed concrete beam mfg., 4034
Prestressed concrete girder mfg., 4034
Printed circuit mfg., 3681
Printing, 4299
Printing or bookbinding machine mfg., 3548
Prison cell erection—steel, 5102
Private estate—see "Domestic Workers—residences"
Probation officers, 7720
Projectile or shell mfg.—see "Explosives"
Public health nursing association—all employees, 8835
Public library or museum—all other than professional employees or clerical, 9101
Public library or museum—professional employees & clerical, 8810
Puffed wheat mfg., 2016
Pulley block mfg.—wood, 2841
Pulp mfg.—chemical process, 4207
Pulp mfg.—ground wood process, 4206
Pump installation & drivers—commercial, 3724
Pump installation & drivers—domestic or residential, 5183
Pump mfg., 3612
Punch mfg.—for marking metal, 3113
Putty mfg., 4558

Pyrometer mfg., 3685
Pyroxylin mfg., 4459
Quarry NOC & drivers, 1624
Quarry—cement rock—surface—& drivers, 1654
Quarry—dimension stone & drivers (GA IN, TN, VT), 1604
Quarry—limestone—surface—& drivers, 1655
Quickprint shops, 4299
Quilt, cushion or pillow mfg., 2501
Quilted cloth mfg.—for garments and garment linings, 2501
Quonset structure construction—sheet metal—shop and installation, 5538
Race car drivers, 9180
Racetrack operation—horse or dog: all other employees—including starters & assistants—& drivers, 9016
Racetrack operation—horse or dog: pari-mutuel clerks, cashiers & clerical employees, 8810
Racetrack operation—horse or dog: racing officials other than starters or assistants, 8720
Racetrack operation—horse or dog: stable hands or kennel employees—& drivers, 8279
Radiator cabinet or shield mfg.—metal, 3076
Radiator mfg.—automobile, 3807
Radiator or heater mfg., 3175
Radio or television broadcasting station—all employees & clerical, drivers, 7610
Radio or television broadcasting station—field announcers, 7610
Radio or television parts and accessories stores, 8010
Radio or television stores, 8017
Radio set mfg., 3681
Radio transmission tower erection, 5041
Radio tube mfg., 4112
Radio, video, audio or television set installation, service or repair & drivers, 9516
Radiographers—see "Pipe testing or inspection"
Radiography research or analytical laboratory, 4511
Rag or paper stock dealer—used—& drivers, 8264
Railings fabrication—iron or steel, 3040
Railroad car cleaning, 5610
Railroad car dismantling, 8265
Railroad construction: laying of tracks or maintenance by contractors—& drivers, 7855
Railroad construction—all operations including clerical, salespersons & drivers—Program I, 6702
Railroad construction—all operations including clerical, salespersons & drivers—Program II—State Act, 6703
Railroad construction—all operations including clerical, salespersons & drivers—Program II—USL Act, 6704
Railroad operation NOC: all employees & drivers, 7133
Railroad operation—all employees including clerical—Program I, 7151
Railroad operation—all employees including clerical—Program II—State Act, 7153
Railroad operation—all employees including clerical—Program II—USL Act, 7152
Railroad operation—street—& drivers—all other than yard employees, 7382
Railroad operation—street—yard employees, 8385
Railroad switch & road crossing signals installation, 6325
Range mfg.—gas or electric, 3169
Rangers—forest—& drivers, 7720
Rattan, willow or twisted fiber products mfg., 2913
Rayon mfg., 2305
Razor blade mfg.—safety, 3270
Razor mfg. NOC (not electric), 3122
Razor mfg. or repair—electric, 3179
Razor mfg.—safety, 3270
Razor mfg.—safety (AL, CT), 3120
Ready mixed concrete dealer & drivers (NM), 8236
Real estate agency—outside employees & collectors, 8742
Reaper mfg., 3507
Rebabbitting of auto connecting rods, 3632
Recording machine mfg. (office type), 3574
Recording tape or disk mfg., 4923
Recreational center or library—military base, 9077F
Recreational or amusement devices: archery ranges & drivers, 9016
Recreational or amusement devices: ball or dart throwing at targets—& drivers, 9016
Recreational or amusement devices: baseball batting ranges—& drivers, 9016
Recreational or amusement devices: golf courses—miniature—& drivers, 9016
Recreational or amusement devices: golf driving ranges—& drivers, 9016
Recreational or amusement devices: kiddie rides at permanent locations & drivers, 9016
Recreational or amusement devices: penny arcades—operation, 8017
Recreational or amusement devices: pony rides—& drivers—excluding track maintenance, 9180
Recreational or amusement devices: pony rides—care & maintenance of track, 9016
Recreational or amusement devices: shooting galleries (air rifles) & drivers, 9016
Recreational or amusement devices: skee ball alley operation, 8017
Recreational or amusement devices: tennis courts—public—operation, 9016
Recreational vehicle campgrounds or parks—all operations & drivers, 9015
Recycling dealer—cans or bottles, 8264
Recycling operations—all employees & drivers (AK), 8812
Reed or loom harness mfg. (RI, SC, VA), 3516
Reforestation or slash piling and drivers (OR), 0124
Refractory products mfg. & drivers, 4024
Refractory products mfg.—all employees & drivers (MO), 4018
Refrigerated show case mfg.—wood, 2812
Refrigeration car loading or unloading, 7360
Refrigeration cars—icing or re-icing, 7360
Refrigeration cars—pre-cooling, 9014
Refrigeration—commercial—cleaning, oiling or adjusting—& drivers, 5190
Refrigeration—commercial or domestic—pipe fitting—including the installation of tubing; drivers, 5183
Refrigeration—commercial—installation or repair of compressors, motors & drivers, 3724
Refrigeration—domestic—cleaning, oiling or adjusting—& drivers, 9519
Refrigeration—domestic—installation, service or repair—& drivers, 9519
Refrigerator mfg.—metal—household or commercial—all other than refrigerating unit, 3076
Refrigerator mfg.—metal—household or commercial—mfg. or assembling refrigerating unit, 3179
Refrigerator parts store, 8010
Refrigerator, stove or washing machine stores—& drivers, 8044
Refrigerator, stove, washing machine, service or repair—including incidental shop operations; drivers, 9519
Refuse, ashes or garbage collection & drivers, 9403
Refuse container (dumpster) mfg., 3620
Religious organization: all other employees, 9101
Religious organization: professional employees & clerical, 8868
Religious organization: professional employees & clerical (AZ), 8840
Rendering works NOC & drivers, 4665
Rental—hand-held machinery or equipment NOC, 8010
Rental—heavy equipment, 8107
Reporters, 8742
Residence—private—see "Domestic workers—residences"
Rest home—all employees, 8829
Restaurant and hotel—kitchen equipment mfg.—sheet metal, 3066
Restaurant NOC, 9079
Restrooms—cleaning, 9014
Retirement living centers: all other employees, salespersons & drivers, 8826
Retirement living centers: food service employees, 8825
Retirement living centers: health care employees, 8824
Revetment or dike construction & drivers, 6005
Ribbon mfg.—textile fabrics, 2302
Rice milling, 2014
Rice storage warehouse, 8292
Riding academy or club & drivers, 8279
Riding academy or club & drivers (MO), 7207

Rifle mfg.—.50 caliber or less, 3574
Rigging NOC & drivers, 9534
Rigging NOC & drivers (LA), 9530
Riverboat gambling vessel—less than 15 tons—Program I, 7038
Riverboat gambling vessel—less than 15 tons—Program II—State Act, 7090
Riverboat gambling vessel—less than 15 tons—Program II—USL Act, 7050
Road or street making machinery mfg., 3507
Road or street sodding or beautification work, 0042
Roads—oiling: delivery and spreading of oil in conjunction with spreading of sand or gravel by oil distributors—& drivers, 5506
Roads—oiling: delivery and spreading of oil on roads by oil distributors—& drivers, 8350
Roasting of nuts, 6504
Rock asphalt quarry, 1624
Rock excavation & drivers, 6217
Rock wool mfg., 1699
Rocket engine ignitor mfg. & drivers (GA, UT), 4759
Rocket engine mfg.—solid propellant—& drivers (GA, UT), 4758
Rocket or missile testing or launching & drivers, 9088
Rodeos—facilities maintenance, 9016
Rodeos—traveling, 9186
Roller derbies, 9179
Roller or ball bearing mfg., 3638
Roller skate mfg., 3146
Roller skating rink, 9016
Rolling mill NOC & drivers, 3027
Rolling mill—iron or steel mfg. & drivers, 3018
Roof coating mfg.—stucco type, 4036
Roof tile mfg.—concrete, 4034
Roof truss mfg.—wood, 2802
Roofing compound mfg.—of asphalt and asbestos, 4741
Roofing granules mfg., 1741
Roofing or building paper or felt preparation—no installation, 4283
Roofing paper or roofing felt mfg., 4283
Roofing slate mfg. or slate splitting & drivers, 1624
Roofing—all kinds—& yard employees, drivers, 5551
Roof—insulation, 5551
Roof—pressure washing, 5551
Roof—waterproofing, 5551
Rooming houses or boarding houses—& salespersons, drivers, 9052
Rope, cordage or twine mfg. NOC, 2220
Rowboat—not exceeding 150 feet in length—building or repair—State Act, 6834
Rowboat—not exceeding 150 feet in length—building or repair—U.S. Act, 6824F
Rubber band mfg., 4410
Rubber goods mfg. NOC, 4410
Rubber reclaiming, 4410
Rubber stamp mfg. or assembly, 4299
Rubber stock dealer—used—& drivers, 8264
Rubber tile installation, 9521
Rubber tire dealer—retail—& drivers, 8380
Rubber tire dealer—wholesale, no installation, 8018
Rubber tire mfg., 4420
Rubber tire recapping or retreading, 8380
Rug, carpet or upholstery—cleaning—shop or outside—& drivers, 2585
Rug mfg.—braided rugs, 2402
Rug or carpet mfg. NOC, 2402
Rug or carpet mfg.—jute or hemp, 2220
Rum distillery, 2130
Rustproofing tools or other metal articles, 3373
Rye milling, 2014
Sack or bag mfg.—cloth, 2578
Saddle or harness mfg., 4902
Saddle soap mfg., 4557
Saddle tree mfg., 2841
Saddlery hardware mfg., 3146
Safe mfg. or repairing, 3507
Safety pin mfg., 3270
Sail making, 2576
Sailboat—not exceeding 150 feet in length—building or repair—State Act, 6834
Sailboat—not exceeding 150 feet in length—building or repair—U.S. Act, 6824F
Salad dressing mfg., 6504
Sales stable & salespersons, drivers, 8288
Salesperson—auto dealership, 8748
Salesperson—automobile leasing company, long- term, 8748
Salesperson—boats at inland locations, 8748
Salesperson—mobile home, 8748
Salesperson—outboard engines, 8748
Salespersons, collectors or messengers—outside, 8742
Salespersons, collectors or messengers outside—Program I, 8737
Salespersons, collectors or messengers outside—Program II—State Act, 8734
Salespersons, collectors or messengers outside—Program II—USL Act, 8738
Salespersons—trimming windows, 9521
Salt, borax or potash producing or refining & drivers, 4568
Salvage operation & incidental wrecking—see "Wrecking"
Salvage operation—no wrecking or any structural operations, 5705
Sample distributors—transported by car or truck, 7380
Sand blasting of castings, 1803
Sand or gravel digging & drivers, 4000
Sand or gravel research or analytical laboratory—for precious stones, 4511
Sand paper mfg., 1860
Sandfracturing in connection with oil well work, 6206
Sanding floors—contract, 5437
Sandwich preparation—not sold directly to consumer, 6504
Sanitarium—all other than professional employees, 9040
Sanitarium—professional employees, 8833
Sanitary landfill, 6217
Sash, door or assembled millwork dealer & drivers, 8235
Sash, door or assembled millwork mfg.—wood—& drivers, 2802
Sash mfg.—metal, 3066
Satellite dish installation (concrete work or wiring in building interiors to be separately classified), 3724
Satellite dish—electronic component mfg., 3681
Satellite dish mfg.—metal mesh, 3076
Sauerkraut mfg., 2110
Sausage casing mfg.—wholesale—including cleaning, 2095
Sausage casing mfg.—wholesale—no cleaning other than washing, 8018
Sausage or sausage casing mfg., 2095
Saw filer mfg.—drop or machine forged, 3114
Saw filer mfg.—not drop or machine forged, 3113
Saw mfg., 3118
Sawdust dealers, 8018
Sawmill, 2710
Sawmill: maintenance & security employees (OR), 9311
Saws—sharpening, 3118
Scaffolds or sidewalk bridges—installation, repair or removal & drivers, 9529
Scale mfg.—automatic, 3559
Scale mfg. (VT), 3582
Scales—installation or adjustment & salespersons, drivers—coin operated type, 5192
Scales—installation or adjustment—counter type, 5191
Scales—installation or adjustment—platform or beam type, 3724
Scanner mfg.—for pricing at cash registers, 3179
Scenic railroad at amusement park, 9180
School bus contractor—including incidental charter service: all other employees & drivers (MD, NH), 7373
School bus driver employed by independent bus company, 7382
School bus driver employed by school district, 7380
School: cafeteria & kitchen employees (OR), 9349
School—pilot training—flying instructors, 7422
Schools—all other than professional & clerical employees, 9101
Schools—professional employees & clerical, 8868
Schools—trade or vocational—all other than professional or clerical employees, 9101
Schools—trade or vocational—professional employees & clerical, 8868

Silo erection—wood, 5403
Silverware mfg., 3383
Silverware mfg. (RI), 3381
Sink mfg.—enameled iron, 3091
Siren mfg., 3648
Sisal garnetting, 2211
Skate mfg., 3146
Skating rink operation & drivers, 9016
Skee ball alley operation, 8017
Ski instructors, 9180
Ski manufacturing—other than wood—use code commensurate with principal mfg. process
Ski manufacturing—wood, 2841
Ski shop employees at winter resorts, 8017
Ski trail operation—cross-country, 9102
Skiing operations—tows, instructors, patrols, cable chair sky rides, 9180
Skin divers in navigable water—Program I, 7394
Skin divers in navigable water—Program II—State Act, 7395
Skin divers in navigable water—Program II—USL Act, 7398
Skylight mfg., 3066
Slag digging and crushing—& drivers, 1624
Slag excavation & drivers (AL), 1420
Slate grinding, 1741
Slate milling & drivers, 1803
Slate quarry, 1624
Slate splitting or roofing slate mfg. & drivers, 1624
Slaughtering, 2081
Sledgehammer mfg., 3126
Slipper mfg., 2660
Slot machine mfg.—not vending machines, 3574
Smelting, sintering or refining—lead—& drivers, 1430
Smelting, sintering or refining—metals—not iron or lead—NOC & drivers, 1438
Smelting—electric process—& drivers, 1433
Smoke alarm mfg., 3179
Smokestack or chimney lining—not metal, 5222
Snap fasteners mfg., 3270
Sneaker mfg., 4417
Snow fence mfg.: cutting lath from logs, 2710
Snow fence mfg.: wire twisting, 3257
Snow removal—clearing snow from streets or roads—& drivers, 9402
Snowmobile mfg. or assembly—entire vehicle, 3808
Snuff mfg., 2172
Soap dispenser—installation and inspection, 5191
Soap mfg.—liquid, 4720
Soap or synthetic detergent mfg., 4720
Soapstone or soapstone products mfg., 1803
Soapstone or soapstone products mfg. (AR, NH, VA, VT), 1745
Soccer team, 9178
Sod dealer—no farming, 0037
Sod farming, 0037
Soda fountain or counter installation, 5146
Soda water fountain or apparatus mfg., 3076
Soda water fountain or apparatus mfg. (IL, MO, OK) 4940
Soft drink distributors—wholesale—no bottling, 8018
Soft drink or beer dispensing unit equipment—cleaning & drivers, 5183
Soft drinks—canning—carbonated, 2157
Sott drinks—canning—not carbonated, 2156
Soil conditioner mfg., 4583
Soil inspection for farms, 8102
Soil testing research or analytical laboratory, 4511
Solvents dealers—bulk—& drivers, 8350
Sorority or fraternity houses, 9061
Sound systems installation or repair—& drivers, 7605
Soundproofing—see "Insulation work NOC"
Soybean oil mfg.—not using solvent extraction process, 4683
Soybean oil mfg.—using solvent extraction process, 4686
Spar or flint grinding & drivers, 1741
Spark plug mfg., 3648
Speaker enclosure mfg. including assembly of components, 2883
Speaker mfg., 3681
Speech therapists, 8832
Speedometer or taxi meter mfg., 3574
Speedways—automobile races, 9016
Spice growing, 0037
Spice mills, 6504
Spike mfg., 3132
Spirit varnish or lacquer mfg., 4439
Spirituous liquor bottling, 2131
Spirituous liquor distillery, 2130
Spool mfg.—wood, 2841
Sporting goods mfg. NOC, 4902
Sporting goods—retail, 8017
Spring mfg., 3303
Spring mfg.—wire, 3257
Sprinkler head mfg., 3634
Sprinkler installation—fire, 5188
Sprinkler installation—irrigation, 6229
Sprinkler installation—residential, 5183
Stable or breeding farm & drivers, 8279
Staff or plaster mixing & drivers, 4036
Stage scenery fabrication, 2812
Stair building (wooden)—erection, 5437
Staircase fabrication—iron or steel, 3040
Stamp dealer, 8013
Staple mfg., 3270
Starch mfg., 4703
State agencies, administrative (OR), 9498
State agencies, all other (OR), 9499
State agencies, higher education (OR), 9497
State employees (UT), 9415
State employees NOC, 9410
Stationery mfg., 4251
Stave mfg. (VA), 2740
Stave mfg.—wood, 2741
Steam heating or power co.—all employees & drivers, 7539
Steam heating or power co.—all employees & salespersons, drivers (AL, OK), 7570
Steam mains or connections construction & drivers, 6319
Steam or air pressure gauge mfg., 3574
Steam or air pressure gauge mfg. (IL, OK), 3571
Steam pipe or boiler insulating & drivers, 5183
Steam shovel, dredge or construction machinery mfg. NOC, 3507
Steamship line or agency—port employees: superintendents, captains, engineers, stewards or their assistants, pay clerks, 8726F
Steamship line or agency—port employees: talliers, checking clerks and repacking of damaged containers—coverage under Longshore Act, 8709F
Steamship line or agency—port employees: talliers, checking clerks and repacking of damaged containers—coverage under State Act, 8719
Steel frame erection—interior—by carpentry contractors for one- or two-family dwellings, 5645
Steel frame erection—interior—by carpentry NOC—type contractors, 5403
Steel frame erection—interior—by contractors engaged in wallboard installation, 5445
Steel frame erection—interior—by specialist contractor, 5102
Steel grit mfg., 1438
Steel locker installation, 5146
Steel mfg. fabrication or erection—see "Iron or steel"
Steel or iron merchant & drivers, 8106
Steel or iron scrap dealer & drivers, 8265
Stereotyping, 4350
Stevedoring NOC, 7309F
Stevedoring: talliers and checking clerks engaged in connection with stevedore work—coverage under State Act, 8719
Stevedoring: talliers and checking clerks engaged in connection with stevedore work—coverage under U.S. Act, 8709F
Stevedoring—by hand or hand trucks exclusively, 7317F
Stevedoring—containerized freight & drivers, 7327F
Stevedoring—explosive materials under contract, 7323F
Stevedoring—freight handling NOC—coverage under Longshore Act, 7350F
Stevedoring—freight handling NOC—coverage under State Act, 7360
Stevedoring—freight handling—explosives or ammunition—coverage under State Act, 7362

Stockyard & butchering, 2081
Stockyard & salespersons, drivers, 8288
Stoker installation—see "Oil or gas burner installation"
Stoker mfg., 3632
Stone crushing & drivers, 1710
Stone crushing—by road building contractors as part of road project—& drivers, 5508
Stone cutting or polishing NOC & drivers, 1803
Stone cutting or polishing—granite & drivers (VT), 1811
Stone digging for stone crushing plant, 4000
Stone mining—underground, 1164
Stone, mosaic, terrazzo or tile work—inside, 5348
Stone or marble setting—inside, 5348
Storage battery service station & drivers, 8380
Storage warehouse NOC, 8292
Storage warehouse—cold, 8291
Storage warehouse—furniture & drivers, 8293
Store: agricultural implement—not farm machinery, 8010
Store: automobile accessories—retail NOC & drivers, 8046
Store: automotive replacement parts distributors—wholesale, 8010
Store: bicycles—retail sale or rental—including repair, 8010
Store: clothing, wearing apparel or dry goods—retail, 8008
Store: clothing, wearing apparel or dry goods—wholesale, 8032
Store: coffee, tea or spice—retail, 8006
Store: dairy products—retail, 8006
Store: delicatessen—retail, 8006
Store: department—retail, 8039
Store: drug—retail, 8017
Store: drug—wholesale, 8047
Store: dry goods—retail, 8008
Store: dry goods—wholesale, 8032
Store: electrical hardware—wholesale or retail, 8010
Store: fish, meat or poultry dealer—retail, 8031
Store: fish, meat or poultry dealer—wholesale, 8021
Store: five and ten cent, 8050
Store: florist & drivers, 8001
Store: frozen or frosted food—retail, 8006
Store: fruit or vegetable—retail, 8006
Store: fruit or vegetable—wholesale, 8018
Store: furniture & drivers, 8044
Store: grocery convenience—retail, 8061
Store: grocery—retail, 8006
Store: grocery—wholesale, 8018
Store: grocery—wholesale (AZ, MO, OK), 8034
Store: hardware, 8010
Store: hide or leather dealer, 8105
Store: jewelry—retail or wholesale, 8013
Store: leather or hide dealer, 8105
Store: meat, fish or poultry dealer—wholesale, 8021
Store: meat, fish or poultry—retail, 8031
Store: meat, grocery and provision (combined)—retail NOC (supermarket type), 8033
Store: radio or television parts and accessories, 8010
Store: retail—NOC, 8017
Store: ship chandler, 8010
Store: shoe—retail, 8008
Store: shoe—wholesale, 8032
Store supermarket, 8033
Store: vegetable or fruit—retail, 8006
Store: vegetable or fruit—wholesale, 8018
Store: wholesale NOC, 8018
Stores—furniture—inside sales employees (LA), 8754
Storm doors or storm sash—installation—wood or metal, 5645
Stove mfg., 3169
Stove—installation, service or repair—residential, 9519
Street and road maintenance operations—public employees (MT), 9420
Street cleaning & drivers, 9402
Street or road construction & drivers (MO), 5515
Street or road construction or maintenance drivers (OK), 5611
Street or road construction or reconstruction by other than state, county or municipality & drivers (AK, UT), 5516
Street or road construction—beautification work, 0042
Street or road construction—paving or repaving & drivers, 5506
Street or road construction—rock excavation & drivers, 5508
Street or road construction—sub-surface work & drivers, 5507
Street or road maintenance, construction or reconstruction by state, county or municipality—all employees & drivers (AK, UT), 5509
Street or road maintenance or beautification & drivers (FL), 5509
Street or road maintenance—municipal, county or state department—& drivers (CT), 5509
Street or road making machinery mfg., 3507
Street or road sodding or beautification work, 0042
Street railroads, 7382
Street railroads—garage employees, 8385
Stucco or plastering work—on outside of buildings, 5022
Stump removal operations—by specialist contractors & drivers, 5507
Subway construction: assign appropriate construction or erection classifications
Sugar cane milling—all operations (LA), 2022
Sugar cane plantation & drivers (FL, LA), 0030
Sugar mfg.—beet, 2030
Sugar refining, 2021
Sulphur producing—all employees & drivers (LA), 6205
Sulphur refining: refer to home office for treatment under Chemical and Dyestuff Rating Plan Sun dial fabrication—metal, 3041
Sunflower oil mfg.—not using solvent extraction process, 4683
Sunflower oil mfg.—using solvent extraction process, 4686
Sunglasses store, 8013
Super charger mfg., 3581
Supply boats—large vessels—Program I, 7016
Supply boats—large vessels—Program II—State Act, 7024
Supply boats—large vessels—Program II—USL Act, 7047
Supply boats—Program I, 7020
Supply boats—Program II—State Act, 7028
Supply boats—Program II—USL Act, 7131
Surgical dressings mfg., 4693
Surgical instrument mfg., 3685
Surgical or pharmaceutical goods mfg. NOC, 4693
Surveyor, 8601
Suspender mfg., 2501
Swap meet operation, 9015
Sweeping—parking lots & streets, 9402
Swimming instructors—independent, 9180
Swimming pool construction—iron or steel, 5069
Swimming pool construction—not iron or steel—all operations & drivers, 5223
Swimming pool maintenance—residential, 9014
Swimming pool—public—operation, 9015
Synthetic rubber intermediate mfg., 4804
Synthetic rubber intermediate mfg. (IL, LA), 4750
Synthetic rubber mfg., 4751
Synthetic yarn mfg., 2302
Syrup mfg.—for carbonated beverages, 4825
Syrup mfg.—fruit—for soda fountains, 2112
Syrup or molasses refining, 2021
Syrup or molasses refining—blending or mfg., 2021
Table & desk top mfg.—veneered, no veneer mfg., 2916
Table assembling—wood, 2881
Table pad mfg.—from cardboard and fabric, 4307
Table tennis set mfg., 4902
Tableware mfg.—glass—no automatic blowing machines, 4111
Tack mfg. (nail type), 3270
Tailor shop, 8017
Tailoring or dressmaking—custom exclusively, 2503
Talc mill & drivers, 1747
Talc—surface mining, 1165
Tallow chandlers, 4557
Tank building—metal—shop, 3620
Tank building—wood—shop, 2802
Tank charging—gases or compressed air, 4635
Tank cleaning—oil or gas storage: inside, 3726
Tank cleaning—oil or gas storage: outside, 5474
Tank erection or repair—metal—within buildings exclusively, 3726
Tank erection—spherical steel, 5040
Tank erection—wooden, 5403
Tank gun mfg., 3548
Tank installation—gas stations—& drivers, 3724

Tank, seat or cabinet mfg.—toilet—wood, 2883
Tanning, 2623
Tanning extract mfg., 4825
Tanning parlor as a separate enterprise, 9586
Tanning parlor in conjunction with health club, 9063
Tape mfg.—magnetic, 4923
Tar—see "Asphalt or tar"
Tarpaulin mfg. from canvas material, 2576
Tattooing parlors, 9586
Taxicab company—& drivers—all other than garage employees, 7370
Taxicab company—garage employees, 8385
Taxidermist, 9600
Taximeter or speedometer mfg., 3574
Taximeters—installation or repair—& drivers, 8380
Tea, coffee or grocery dealer—retail—& drivers, 8006
Telephone answering service, 8810
Telephone book delivery—see "Distribution companies"
Telephone booth—shop and installation, 5538
Telephone installation—by specialist contractor, not telephone company, 7605
Telephone mfg., 3681
Telephone or telegraph apparatus mfg., 3681
Telephone or telegraph co.: all employees except office, exchange or clerical, 7600
Telephone or telegraph co.: office, exchange, or clerical, 8901
Telephone poles—treating, 2960
Telephone, telegraph or fire alarm line construction & drivers, 7601
Telescope mfg.—with lens grinding, 4150
Television antenna mfg., 3146
Television cable company—clerical employees, 8901
Television dinner mfg.: all other kinds—except meat, 2003
Television dinner mfg.: meat, 8021
Television or radio broadcasting station—all employees & clerical, drivers, 7610
Television or radio broadcasting station—field announcers, 7610
Television or radio stores, 8017
Television, radio, telephone or telecommunication device mfg. NOC, 3681
Television set mfg., 3681
Television transmission tower erection, 5040
Television tube mfg., 4112
Television, video, audio or radio set installation service or repair & drivers, 9516
Tennis ball mfg., 4902
Tent, awning or canvas goods erection, removal or repair, 5102
Tent or awning mfg.—shop, 2576
Termite control, 9014
Terra cotta mfg., 4053
Terrazo, mosaic, stone or tile work—inside, 5348
Tetryl explosives mfg., 4773
Textile fiber mfg.—synthetic, 2305
Textile machinery mfg., 3515
Textile mending—invisible textile weaving of wearing apparel, 2501
Textile or fiber waste reprocessing, 2211
Textile—bleaching, dyeing, mercerizing, finishing, 2413
Theater NOC—all employees other than players, entertainers or musicians, 9154
Theater NOC—players, entertainers or musicians, 9156
Theater seats installation, 5146
Theater—drive-in—all employees, 9154
Thermal flooding—drilling in connection with oil or gas well, 6235
Thermometer mfg., 3685
Thermostat installation—electric—& drivers, 5190
Thermostat installation—not electric—& drivers, 5183
Thermostat mfg., 3179
Thread or yarn dyeing or finishing, 2416
Thread or yarn mfg.—cotton, 2220
Thread or yarn mfg.—silk, 2302
Tie, post or pole yard & drivers, 2960
Tile installation—non-ceramic, 9521
Tile mfg.—decorative—non-structural, 4062
Tile or earthenware mfg. NOC & drivers, 4021
Tile, stone, mosaic or terrazzo work—inside, 5348
Timber buyers and cruisers, 8601
Timber wharf construction, 6003
Timekeepers—construction or erection, 5610
Tin foil mfg., 3334
Tinning or galvanizing—not electrolytic, 3373
Tinware mfg.—pie plates, pails, waste baskets, ash cans, dustpans, 3400
Toaster mfg., 3179
Tobacco farms, 0037
Tobacco mfg.—NOC (KY) 2173
Tobacco rehandling or warehousing, 2174
Tobacco store—retail, 8017
Tobacco store—wholesale, 8017
Toilet or towel supply co. & route supervisors, drivers, 2587
Toilet tissue mfg., 4279
Tool mfg.—agricultural, construction, logging, mining, oil or artesian well, 3126
Tool mfg.—drop or machine forged NOC—forging, 3110
Tool mfg.—drop or machine forged NOC—machining, 3114
Tool mfg.—not drop or machine forged—NOC, 3113
Tool sharpening—industrial tools, 3632
Toothpaste compounding or preparation—no mfg. of ingredients, 4611
Toothpick mfg., 2841
Torpedo mfg., 3548
Towel or toilet supply co. & route supervisors, drivers, 2587
Towing service—see "Auto towing companies"
Township employees NOC, 9410
Toxicology research or analytical laboratory, 4511
Toy mfg.—cardboard, 4279
Toy mfg.—cloth stuffed animals or toys, 2501
Toy mfg.—stamped metal, 3400
Toy mfg.—wood, 2841
Trackless trolley operators, 7382
Trackless trolley—garage employees, 8385
Tracks—stock car, jalopy races, 9016
Traction engine or power plow mfg., 3507
Tractor mfg.—caterpillar type, 3507
Traffic barricade & safety light mfg. and erection, 9552
Traffic control arm unit—installation, service or repair, 5192
Traffic signal installation, 6325
Trailer body mfg.—not "home" type—see Interpretation section—classifications
Trailer mfg.—"home" type, 2812
Trailer parks or trailer camps—all operations & drivers, 9015
Train operation—miniature at amusement park, 9180
Transformer mfg., 3681
Transistor research or analytical laboratory, 4511
Trappers—animal, 7720
Tree planting for reforestation, 0005
Tree pruning, spraying, repairing, trimming or fumigating & drivers, 0106
Tree removal operations—limited number from developed sites, 6217
Tricycle mfg., 3865
Trimmings or ribbons—hand sewing on finished garments, 2388
Trimmings—manufacturing fancy trimming or piping not manufacturing binding tape or ribbon, 2388
Trinitrotoluol explosives mfg., 4773
Trombone mfg, 3383
Trophy mfg.—wooden, 2881
Truck engine mfg., 3827
Truck leasing company—long-term—& drivers—all employees other than salespersons, 8380
Truck leasing company—long-term—sales employees, 8748
Truck mfg. or assembly—entire vehicle, 3808
Truck or trailer body repair shop—all employees & park department employees, drivers (AL, CT), 8399
Truck rental & drivers—all employees other than garage employees, 8002
Truck rental—hauling explosives or ammunition—all employees & drivers, 8385
Truck weighing station inspectors—permanent location, 7720
Trucking NOC—garage & dock employees (OR), 9328
Trucking—common carrier—all employees & drivers (OK), 7223
Trucking—common carrier—all employees drivers, includes depot employees (IA, MS), 7223

Trucking—hauling explosives or ammunition—all employees & drivers (AZ, MO), 7250
Trucking—local hauling only—& drivers (MO), 7228
Trucking—long distance hauling—& drivers (MO), 7229
Trucking—mail, parcel or package delivery—all employees & drivers, 7231
Trucking—mail, parcel or package delivery—under contract with the U.S. Postal Service—all employees & drivers, 7232
Trucking—motor truck freight operations—drivers (UT), 7223
Trucking—NOC—all employees & drivers, 7219
Trucking—oil field equipment—all employees & drivers, 7222
Trucking—parcel or package delivery—all employees & drivers, 7230
Trunk mfg.—metal frames or fittings to be separately rated, 2883
Tub assembling—cooperage, 2747
Tube mfg.—metal—collapsible, 3334
Tube mfg.—see "Pipe or tube"
Tubing mfg.—iron or steel—for automobile exhaust systems, 3028
Tubing mfg.—non-ferrous—for automobile exhaust systems, 3022
Tuck pointing, 5022
Tugboat building—iron or steel—State Act, 6854
Tugboat building—iron or steel—U.S. Act, 6843F
Tugboats—Program I, 7020
Tugboats—Program II—State Act, 7028
Tugboats—Program II—USL Act 7131
Tunnel (vehicular) or bridge operations & drivers, 9019
Tunnel—spray cleaning of interior, 9402
Tunneling—not pneumatic—all operations, 6251
Tunneling—pneumatic—all operations, 6260
Turbo supercharger mfg. or repair, 3581
Turpentine farm & drivers, 0016
Turpentine farm & drivers (VA), 0301
Turpentine or resin mfg.—steam or non-destructive process—& drivers (AL, FL, GA, LA, MS), 1473
Tweezers mfg., 3122
Twine, cordage or rope mfg. NOC, 2220
Twine or cord mfg.—cotton, 2220
Twist drills mfg.—drop or machine forged, 3114
Twist drills mfg.—not drop or machine forged, 3113
Type foundry, 3336
Typewriter mfg., 3565
Typewriter ribbon or carbon paper mfg., 4251
Typewriter—installation, service or repair, 5191
U.S.O. activities performed by Travelers' Aid Society, 8742
U.S.O. activities—mobile units, 7380
U.S.O. activities—permanent location, 9063
U.S.O. activities—refer to 9063 for classification treatment
Umbrella mfg., 2501
Umbrella mfg. (CT, VA), 2560
Undercoating—automobiles, 9505
Underpinning buildings or structures & drivers, 5703
Undertaker & drivers, 9620
United States armed service risk—all employees & drivers, 9077
Upholstering, 9522
Upholstering—away from shop, 9521
Upholstery, carpet or rug cleaning & drivers, 2585
Vacuum cleaner service and repair, 9519
Vacuum mfg., 3179
Valve mfg., 3634
Van conversion operation, 8393
Varnish mfg.—oleo-resinous, 4561
Varnish mfg.—spirit, 4439
Vault construction or installation, 5057
Vegetable growing, 0008
Vegetable oil mfg.—see "Oil mfg.—vegetable"
Vegetable packing & drivers, 8209
Velvet or plush mfg., 2300
Vending machine mfg., 3559
Vending or coin operated machines—installation, service or repair & salespersons, drivers, 5192
Veneer mfg., 2714
Veneer products mfg.—including veneer mfg., 2915
Veneer products mfg.—no veneer mfg., 2916
Venetian blind assembly, 2881
Venetian blind installation, 9521
Venetian blind laundries—& drivers, 2585
Ventilating system installation—see "Air conditioning"
Vermiculite mfg., 1699
Vessels—NOC—Program I, 7016
Vessels—NOC—Program II—State Act, 7024
Vessels—NOC—Program II—USL Act, 7047
Vessels—not self-propelled—Program I, 7046
Vessels—not self-propelled—Program II—State Act, 7098
Vessels—not self-propelled—Program II—USL Act, 7099
Vessels—sail—Program I, 7036
Vessels—sail—Program II—State Act, 7088
Vessels—sail—Program II—USL Act, 7048
Vibroflotation process—building foundations, 6204
Video, audio, radio and television equipment installation, service or repair & drivers, 9516
Video games—coin operated, installation, service or repair, 5192
Vinegar bottling, 2156
Vinegar mfg., 2143
Vinyl siding installation—all other than 5645 or 5651 type dwellings, 5403
Vinyl siding installation—detached one- or two-family dwellings, 5645
Vinyl siding installation—dwellings—three stories or less, 5651
Virus, anti-toxin or serum mfg. & drivers, 5951
Vitamin mfg., 4825
Vitriol mfg., 4815
Vocational rehabilitation trainees (AZ), 9921
Vodka distillery, 2130
Voluntary personnel (AZ), 8411
Volunteer firefighters, rescue squad and life saving crews—all employees & drivers (VA), 7711
Volunteer municipal personnel & drivers (OR), 8411
Volunteer rescue team or group & drivers (CO), 7719
Voting machine mfg., 3574
Wagon or carriage mfg. or assembly, 3808
Wall coating mfg.—stucco type, 4036
Wall covering or metal ceiling installation & shop, drivers, 5538
Wall switches mfg.—electrical, 3179
Wallboard installation—within buildings—& drivers, 5445
Wallet mfg. from leather, imitation leather or vinyl, 2688
Wallpaper mfg., 4301
Wallpaper or paint stores—retail, 8017
Wallpaper or paint stores—wholesale, 8018
Warehouse space rental—no storing of goods for others, 9015
Warehousing NOC, 8292
Warehousing—cold storage, 8291
Warehousing—furniture—& drivers, 8293
Washer or gasket mfg.—not metal, 2651
Washing machines—coin operated, installation, service or repair, 5192
Washing machines—installation, service or repair—residential, 9519
Washing or cleaning of interior walls, 9014
Watch case mfg., 3383
Watch case mfg. (RI), 3381
Watch mfg., 3385
Watchguards—construction or erection, 5610
Watchmaker tool mfg.—drop or machine forged, 3114
Watchmaker tool mfg.—not drop or machine forged, 3113
Water cooling tower erection—see Interpretation section—classifications
Water flooding—drilling in connection with oil or gas well, 6235
Water heater mfg., 3169
Water main or connection construction & drivers, 6319
Water meter mfg., 3634
Water skiing exhibitions, 9180
Water softener—installation or service—domestic—& drivers, 5183
Water towers—erection, 5040
Waterproofing: application by brush or hand caulking gun, 5474
Waterproofing: excavation work necessary or incidental thereto, 6217
Waterproofing: exterior walls or subterranean structures by apparatus inserted in ground, 9014
Waterproofing: exterior—with trowel, 5022
Waterproofing: interior—with trowel, 5480
Waterproofing: spray gun, cement gun or other pressure apparatus, 5213
Waterwell cleaning—cistern type—& drivers, 9402

Waterworks operation & drivers, 7520
Wax mfg., 4557
Wax products mfg., 4557
Waxed paper mfg., 4279
Wearing apparel or household furnishings dealer—retail—& drivers, 8006
Weather stripping installation, 5437
Weaving mills using mixed yarns, 2302
Webbing mfg., 2380
Weed clearing by vessel—Program I, 7016
Weed clearing by vessel—Program II—State Act, 7024
Weed clearing by vessel—Program II—USL Act, 7047
Weed control—spraying from aircraft, 7409
Weed control—spraying from ground by specialist contractor, 0050
Weighers, samplers or inspectors of merchandise on vessels or docks or at railway stations or warehouses—coverage under State Act, 8719
Weighers, samplers or inspectors of merchandise on vessels or docks or at railway stations or warehouses—coverage under U.S. Act, 8709F
Weight control services, 8832
Welding or cutting NOC & drivers, 3365
Welding rod mfg., 3257
Welding supply dealers, 8018
Welding torch mfg., 3634
Welding—microscopic, 3365
Welding—robotic, 3365
Welfare or charitable organization—all operations & drivers, 8837
Well drilling, 6204
Welting mfg.—leather, latex, burlap, paper, twine, etc., 2688
Wheat milling, 2014
Wheel mfg.—automobile, metal—not cast, 3803
Wheel or caster mfg.—wood, 2841
Wheelbarrow mfg.—metal, 3126
Wheelbarrow mfg.—wood, 2802
Whip mfg., 4902
Whiskey bottling—not beer or wine, including warehousing, rectifying or blending, 2131
Whiskey distillery, 2130
Whiskey still mfg., 3620
White water rafting trips—Program I, 7038
White water rafting trips—Program II—State Act, 7090
White water rafting trips—Program II—USL Act, 7050
Whiting mfg., 4558
Wig styling, 9586
Willow, rattan or twisted fiber products mfg., 2913
Willow ware mfg., 2913
Windmill erection—metal, 5057
Windmill mfg.—wood, 2802
Window frame & sash installation or repair—metal, 5102
Window sash mfg.—aluminum, 3076
Window screen mfg.—wood, 2802
Window screen or screen door installation—metal or wood separately rated, 5645
Window shade roller mfg., 2841
Window shades—installation, 9521
Window shutter installation—wooden, 9521
Window tinting—brush or spray-on method, 5474
Window tinting—plastic film exclusively, 5491
Window trimming, 9521
Windshield wiper mfg., 3648
Wine bottling, 2156
Winery, 2143
Wiping cloth dealer and laundry operations, drivers, 8103
Wire cloth mfg., 3255
Wire drawing or cable mfg.—not iron or steel, 1924
Wire drawing—iron or steel, 3241
Wire fence mfg., 3257
Wire goods mfg. NOC, 3257
Wire insulating or covering, 4470
Wire mattress or bed spring mfg., 3300
Wire rope or cable mfg.—iron or steel, 3240
Wood bridge construction—pile driving over water, 6003
Wood carving—by hand or machine, 2790
Wood chip mfg., 2710
Wood dealers—kindling and firewood & drivers, 8232
Wood flour mfg., 2014
Wood preserving & drivers, 2960
Wood shaving mfg., 2710
Wood turned products mfg. NOC, 2841
Woodenware mfg. NOC, 2841
Woodworking machine mfg., 3632
Wool combing or scouring, 2211
Wool combing or scouring (RI, SC, VA), 2260
Wool merchant, 8103
Wool pulling, 2623
Wool separating, 2211
Wool spinning and weaving, 2286
Worm raising, 0034
Wreath or blanket mfg.—evergreen, 0035
Wrecking—marine & salvage operations—Program I, 7394
Wrecking—marine & salvage operations—Program II—State Act, 7153
Wrecking—marine & salvage operations—Program II—USL Act, 7152
Wrecking—not marine—all operations-concrete or concrete encased, 5213
Wrecking—not marine—all operations—iron or steel, 5057
Wrecking—not marine—all operations—masonry, 5022
Wrecking—not marine—all operations—piers or wharfs, 6003
Wrecking—not marine—all operations—wooden—including dwellings, 5403
Wrought iron furniture mfg., 3041
X-ray apparatus mfg., 3685
X-ray equipment, installation, service & repair, 5191
X-ray tube mfg., 4112
Yachts—not exceeding 150 feet in length—building or repair—State Act, 6834
Yachts—not exceeding 150 feet in length—building or repair—U.S. Act, 6824F
Yachts—private—sail or power—Program I, 7037
Yachts—private—sail or power—Program II—State Act, 7089
Yachts—private—sail or power—Program II—USL Act, 7049
Yarn mfg.—wool, 2286
Yarn or thread dyeing or finishing, 2416
Yarn or thread mfg.—cotton, 2220
Yarn or thread mfg.—silk, 2302
Yeast mfg., 6504
YMCA, YWCA, YMHA or YWHA, institution—all employees & clerical, 9063
Zipper mfg., 3131
Zoo operated by a municipality, 9102
Zoo—private, 9016
Zoo—private, engaged in wild animal training, 9180

IRS SS-8 EMPLOYMENT FORM

Form **SS-8**
(Rev. October 1990)
Department of the Treasury
Internal Revenue Service

Determination of Employee Work Status for Purposes of Federal Employment Taxes and Income Tax Withholding

OMB No. 1545-0004
Expires 10-31-93

Paperwork Reduction Act Notice.—We ask for the information on this form to carry out the Internal Revenue laws of the United States. You are required to give us this information. We need it to ensure that you are complying with these laws and to allow us to figure and collect the right amount of tax.

The time needed to complete and file this form will vary depending on individual circumstances. The estimated average time is: **recordkeeping,** 34 hrs., 41 min., **learning about the law or the form,** 6 min. and **preparing and sending the form to IRS,** 40 min. If you have comments concerning the accuracy of these time estimates or suggestions for making this form more simple, we would be happy to hear from you. You can write to both the **Internal Revenue Service,** Washington, DC 20024, Attention: IRS Reports Clearance Officer, T:FP, and the **Office of Management and Budget,** Paperwork Reduction Project (1545-0004), Washington, DC 20503. **DO NOT** send the tax form to either of these offices. Instead, see the instructions for information on where to file.

Instructions

This form should be completed carefully. If the firm is completing the form, it should be completed for **ONE** individual who is representative of the class of workers whose status is in question.

If a written determination is desired for more than one class of workers, a separate Form SS-8 should be completed for one worker from each class whose status is typical of that class. A written determination for any worker will apply to other workers of the same class if the facts are not materially different from those of the worker whose status was ruled upon.

Please return Form SS-8 to the Internal Revenue Service office that provided the form. If the Internal Revenue Service did not ask you to complete this form but you wish a determination on whether a worker is an employee, file Form SS-8 with your District Director.

Caution: *Form SS-8 is* ***not*** *a claim for refund of social security tax or Federal income tax withholding. Also, a determination that an individual is an employee does not necessarily reduce any current or prior tax liability.*

Name of firm (or person) for whom the worker performed services		Name of worker	
Address of firm (include street address, apt. or suite no., city, state, and ZIP code)		Address of worker (include street address, apt. or suite no., city, state, and ZIP code)	
Trade name		Telephone number	Worker's social security number
Telephone number	Firm's taxpayer identification number		

Check type of firm:
☐ **Individual** ☐ **Partnership** ☐ **Corporation** ☐ **Other** (specify) ▶

This form is being completed by: ☐ FIRM ☐ WORKER

If the form is being completed by the worker, do you object to disclosing your name or the information on this form to the firm? . . . ☐ **Yes** ☐ **No**

(If your answer is "Yes," we cannot furnish you a determination on the basis of this form. You may write to your District Director for further information. **Do not complete the rest of the form, unless the IRS requests it.**)

All items must be answered or marked "Unknown" or "Not Applicable" (NA). **If you need more space, attach another sheet.** This form is designed to cover many work activities, so some of the questions may not pertain to you.

Total number of workers in this class (if more than one, please see item 19) ▶ ____________

This information is about services performed by the worker from ▶ ____________ (Month, day, year) to ____________ (Month, day, year)

What was the first date on which the worker performed services of any kind for the firm? ▶ ____________ (Month, day, year)

Is the worker still performing services for the firm? . . . ☐ **Yes** ☐ **No**

If "No," what was the date of termination? ▶ ____________ (Month, day, year)

In which IRS district are you located? ____________

1a Describe the firm's business ____________

b Describe the work done by the worker ____________

2a If the work is done under a written agreement between the firm and the worker, attach a copy.

b If the agreement is not in writing, describe the terms and conditions of the work arrangement ____________

Form **SS-8** (Rev. 10-90)

Form SS-8 (Rev. 10-90) Page 2

c If the actual working arrangement differs in any way from the agreement, explain the differences and why they occur ....

....

....

3a Is the worker given training by the firm? ☐ Yes ☐ No

If "Yes":

What kind? ....

How often? ....

b Is the worker given instructions in the way the work is to be done? ☐ Yes ☐ No

If "Yes," give specific examples. ....

c Attach samples of any written instructions or procedures.

d Does the firm have the right to change the methods used by the worker or direct that person on how to do the work? ☐ Yes ☐ No

Explain your answer ....

....

e Does the operation of the firm's business require that the worker be supervised or controlled in the performance of the service? ☐ Yes ☐ No

Explain your answer ....

....

4a The firm engages the worker:

☐ To perform and complete a particular job only

☐ To work at a job for an indefinite period of time

☐ Other (explain) ....

b Is the worker required to follow a routine or a schedule established by the firm? ☐ Yes ☐ No

If "Yes," what is the routine or schedule? ....

....

....

c Does the worker report to the firm or its representative? ☐ Yes ☐ No

If "Yes":

How often? ....

For what purpose? ....

In what manner (in person, in writing, by telephone, etc.)? ....

Attach copies of report forms used in reporting to the firm.

d Does the worker furnish a time record to the firm? ☐ Yes ☐ No

If "Yes," attach copies of time records.

5a State the kind and value of tools and equipment furnished by:

The firm ....

....

The worker ....

....

b State the kind and value of supplies and materials furnished by:

The firm ....

....

The worker ....

....

c What expenses are incurred by the worker in the performance of services for the firm?

....

d Does the firm reimburse the worker for any expenses? ☐ Yes ☐ No

If "Yes," specify the reimbursed expenses ....

....

6a Will the worker perform the services personally? ☐ Yes ☐ No

b Does the worker have helpers? ☐ Yes ☐ No

If "Yes": Are the helpers hired by: ☐ Firm ☐ Worker

If hired by the worker, is the firm's approval necessary? ☐ Yes ☐ No

Who pays the helpers? ☐ Firm ☐ Worker

Are social security taxes and Federal income tax withheld from the helpers' wages? ☐ Yes ☐ No

If "Yes": Who reports and pays these taxes? ☐ Firm ☐ Worker

Who reports the helpers' incomes to the Internal Revenue Service? ☐ Firm ☐ Worker

If the worker pays the helpers, does the firm repay the worker? ☐ Yes ☐ No

What services do the helpers perform? ....

Form SS-8 (Rev. 10-90) Page 3

7 At what location are the services performed? ☐ Firm's ☐ Worker's ☐ Other (specify) ....

8a Type of pay worker receives:
☐ Salary ☐ Commission ☐ Hourly wage ☐ Piecework ☐ Lump sum ☐ Other (specify) ....
b Does the firm guarantee a minimum amount of pay to the worker? ☐ Yes ☐ No
c Does the firm allow the worker a drawing account or advances against pay? ☐ Yes ☐ No
If "Yes": Is the worker paid such advances on a regular basis? ☐ Yes ☐ No
d How does the worker repay such advances? ....

9a Is the worker eligible for a pension, bonuses, paid vacations, sick pay, etc.? ☐ Yes ☐ No
If "Yes," specify ....
b Does the firm carry workmen's compensation insurance on the worker? ☐ Yes ☐ No
c Does the firm deduct social security tax from amounts paid the worker? ☐ Yes ☐ No
d Does the firm deduct Federal income taxes from amounts paid the worker? ☐ Yes ☐ No
e How does the firm report the worker's income to the Internal Revenue Service?
☐ Form W-2 ☐ Form 1099 ☐ Does not report ☐ Other (specify) ....
f Does the firm bond the worker? ☐ Yes ☐ No

10a Approximately how many hours a day does the worker perform services for the firm? ....
b Does the worker perform similar services for others? ☐ Yes ☐ No ☐ Unknown
If "Yes": Are these services performed on a daily basis for other firms? ☐ Yes ☐ No ☐ Unknown
Percentage of time spent in performing these services for:
This firm ....% Other firms...........% ☐ **Unknown**
Does the firm have priority on the worker's time? ☐ Yes ☐ No
If "No," explain ....
c Is the worker prohibited from competing with the firm either while performing services or during any later period? ☐ Yes ☐ No

11a Can the firm discharge the worker at any time without incurring a liability? ☐ Yes ☐ No
If "No," explain ....
b Can the worker terminate the services at any time without incurring a liability? ☐ Yes ☐ No
If "No," explain ....

12a Does the worker perform services for the firm under:
☐ The firm's business name ☐ The worker's own business name ☐ Other (specify) ....
b Does the worker advertise or maintain a business listing in the telephone directory, a trade journal, etc.? ☐ Yes ☐ No ☐ Unknown
If "Yes," specify ....
c Does the worker represent himself or herself to the public as being in business to perform the same or similar services? ☐ Yes ☐ No ☐ Unknown
If "Yes," how? ....
d Does the worker have his or her own shop or office? ☐ Yes ☐ No ☐ Unknown
If "Yes," where? ....
e Does the firm represent the worker as an employee of the firm to its customers? ☐ Yes ☐ No
If "No," how is the worker represented? ....
f How did the firm learn of the worker's services? ....

13 Is a license necessary for the work? ☐ Yes ☐ No ☐ Unknown
If "Yes," what kind of license is required? ....
By whom is it issued? ....
By whom is the license fee paid? ....

14 Does the worker have a financial investment in a business related to the services performed? ☐ Yes ☐ No ☐ Unknown
If "Yes," specify and give amounts of the investment ....

15 Can the worker incur a loss in the performance of the service for the firm? ☐ Yes ☐ No
If "Yes," how? ....

16a Has any other government agency ruled on the status of the firm's workers? ☐ Yes ☐ No
If "Yes," attach a copy of the ruling.
b Is the same issue being considered by any IRS office in connection with the audit of the worker's tax return or the firm's tax return, or has it recently been considered? ☐ Yes ☐ No
If "Yes," for which year(s)? ....

17 Does the worker assemble or process a product at home or away from the firm's place of business? ☐ Yes ☐ No
If "Yes":
Who furnishes materials or goods used by the worker? ☐ Firm ☐ Worker
Is the worker furnished a pattern or given instructions to follow in making the product? ☐ Yes ☐ No
Is the worker required to return the finished product to the firm or to someone designated by the firm? ☐ Yes ☐ No

Form SS-8 (Rev. 10-90) Page **4**

Answer items 18a through n if the worker is a salesperson or provides a service directly to customers.

18a Are leads to prospective customers furnished by the firm? . . . ☐ Yes ☐ No ☐ Does not apply
b Is the worker required to pursue or report on leads? . . . ☐ Yes ☐ No ☐ Does not apply
c Is the worker required to adhere to prices, terms, and conditions of sale established by the firm? . . . ☐ Yes ☐ No
d Are orders submitted to and subject to approval by the firm? . . . ☐ Yes ☐ No
e Is the worker expected to attend sales meetings? . . . ☐ Yes ☐ No
If "Yes": Is the worker subject to any kind of penalty for failing to attend? . . . ☐ Yes ☐ No
f Does the firm assign a specific territory to the worker? . . . ☐ Yes ☐ No ☐ Does not apply
g Who does the customer pay? ☐ Firm ☐ Worker
If worker, does the worker remit the total amount to the firm?. . . ☐ Yes ☐ No
h Does the worker sell a consumer product in a home or establishment other than a permanent retail establishment? . ☐ Yes ☐ No
i List the products and/or services distributed by the worker, such as meat, vegetables, fruit, bakery products, beverages (other than milk), or laundry or dry cleaning services. If more than one type of product and/or service is distributed, specify the principal one. ----------
j Did the firm or another person assign the route or territory and a list of customers to the worker? . . . ☐ Yes ☐ No
If "Yes," please identify the person who made the assignment. ----------
k Did the worker pay the firm or person for the privilege of serving customers on the route or in the territory? . . . ☐ Yes ☐ No
If "Yes," how much did the worker pay (not including any amount paid for a truck or racks, etc.)? $----------
What factors were considered in determining the value of the route or territory? ----------
l How are new customers obtained by the worker? Explain fully, showing whether the new customers called the firm for service, were solicited by the worker, or both. ----------
m Does the worker sell life insurance? . . . ☐ Yes ☐ No
If "Yes":
Is the selling of life insurance or annuity contracts for the firm the worker's entire business activity? . . . ☐ Yes ☐ No
If "No," state the extent of the worker's other business activities ----------
Does the worker sell other types of insurance for the firm? . . . ☐ Yes ☐ No
If "Yes," state the percentage of the worker's total working time spent in selling such other types of insurance ----------%
At the time the contract was entered into between the firm and the worker, was it their intention that the worker sell life insurance for the firm: ☐ on a full-time basis ☐ on a part-time basis
State the manner in which such intention was expressed. ----------
n Is the worker a traveling salesperson or city salesperson? . . . ☐ Yes ☐ No
If "Yes":
Specify from whom the worker principally solicits orders on behalf of the firm. ----------
If the worker solicits orders from wholesalers, retailers, contractors, or operators of hotels, restaurants, or other similar establishments, specify the percentage of the worker's time spent in such solicitation. ----------%
Is the merchandise purchased by the customers for resale, or is it purchased for use in their business operations? If used by the customers in their business operations, describe the merchandise and state whether it is equipment installed on their premises or a consumable supply. ----------
----

19 Attach the names and addresses of the total number of workers in this class from page 1, or the names and addresses of 10 such workers if there are more than 10.
20 Attach a detailed explanation for any other reason why you believe the worker is an independent contractor or is an employee of the firm.

IMPORTANT INFORMATION NEEDED TO PROCESS YOUR REQUEST

Under section 6110 of the Internal Revenue Code, the text and related background file documents of any ruling, determination letter, or technical advice memorandum will be open to public inspection. This section provides that before the text and background file documents are made public, identifying and certain other information must be deleted.

Are the names, addresses, and taxpayer identifying numbers the only items you want deleted? . . . ☐ Yes ☐ No

If you checked "No," and believe additional deletions should be made, we cannot process your request unless you submit a copy of this form and copies of all supporting documents indicating, in brackets, those parts you believe should be deleted in accordance with section 6110(c) of the Code. Attach a separate statement indicating which specific exemption provided by section 6110(c) applies to each bracketed part.

Under penalties of perjury, I declare that I have examined this request, including accompanying documents, and to the best of my knowledge and belief, the facts presented are true, correct, and complete.

Signature ▶ **Title ▶** **Date ▶**

If this form is used by the firm in requesting a written determination, the form should be signed by an officer or member of the firm.
If this form is used by the worker in requesting a written determination, the form should be signed by the worker. If the worker wants a written determination with respect to services performed for two or more firms, a separate form should be furnished for each firm.
Additional copies of this form may be obtained from any Internal Revenue Service office.

GPO : 1991 0 - 306-072

APPENDIX TWENTY-SIX

STATE-BY-STATE SELF-INSURANCE GUIDELINES

This is a guide to state self-insurance requirements. While general parameters remain consistent, each state applies its rules in its own way.

STATE	MAILING ADDRESS	FORMS REQUIRED	FILING FEE	TERM	RENEWAL	SECURITY DEPOSIT	EXCESS INSURANCE	REPORTS REQUIRED	TAXES, FEES AND ASSESSMENTS
AL	Workers' Compensation Division Department of Industrial Relations Industrial Relations Building Montgomery, AL 36131 (205) 242-2868	WC-18-Rev. 1/93 — Employer's Application for Self-Insurance. Must include an outline of claims program and a copy of any agreement with a service company. If a parent is covering subsidiaries, a Board of Directors' resolution is required or an endeminty agreement as provided by Statute	$250	Continuous, until revoked	Automatic, subject to filing annual reports	Minimum $200,000: Cash or Securities, Surety Bonds, or Letter of Credit **Note:** Primary Security for Self-Insurance purposes is statutory membership in Alabama Self-Insurance W/C Guaranty Trust Assoc.	Not always required but will be considered in determining financial ability to qualify	Annual audited financial statement due at the end of fiscal year WC Form #10 — "Assessment Report" due March 1 of each succeeding calandar year	A.S.I. W/C Guaranty Assoc. Assessment 1.5% of security amount Admin. Trust Fund Assessment — variable percentage based on claims paid for previous year
AK	Department of Labor Worker's Compensation Division P.O. Box 25512 Juneau, AK 99802-5512 (907) 465-6055	Application for a Certificate to Self-Insure, (Form 07-6129). A copy of Board of Directors' resolution to self-insure 3 yrs. audited fin. statements if Parent Guarantor Form 07-61734	None	One year, unless revoked sooner. Board can revoke on 10 days' notice	New application, Form 07-6130, and financial information must be filed annually at least 60 days before expiration of self-insurance certificate	Required for new self-insurer. Minimum security deposit $300,000, satisfied by surety bond, deposit of securities, or letter of credit	Both specific excess insurance and aggregate excess insurance required, but requirement may be waived	Audited financial reports for the 3 most recent fiscal years. A self-insurer may be required to file current claims data quarterly	None. There is a Second Injury Fund applicable to all employers, which varies between 0 & 6% of premium paid in previous year
AZ	Self-Insurance Administrator The Industrial Commission of Arizona 800 West Washington, Ste 301 Phoenix, AZ 85007 (602) 542-1836	ICA-03-0029 – Application for Authorization to Self-Insure. Corporate resolution covering any subsidiaries. Classification of employees according to insurance rate classes, with payroll ICA-02-0058 – Option Election Form	None	One year	Renew annually by anniversary date. Allow at least 1 month prior to such date for processing	Option 1: A minimum $250,000 security bond and specific excess insurance with $250,000 self-insured retention and a $10 million limit Option 2: Security bond in the amount of 125% of outstanding workers' compensation accrued losses while self-insured. Minimum bond: $100,000. This will fluctuate yearly with fluctuations in losses **Note:** Opinion 2 only available upon renewing Surety bonds, treasury bonds securities, and letters of credit from federally insured fin. institution are acceptable	Required under Option 1 above	Certified financial reports for 3 years, and claims or premium experience for 3 years. Resume of claims personnel or adjusting company. Payroll by rate classes Description of safety program Arrangements to provide benefits, either self-administration or a third party administrator	A 3% Administrative Fund Tax and an approximative 1.5% Special Fund Tax are levied once each year, based on a hypothetical premium if employer were insured by Arizona State Compensation Fund

STATE	MAILING ADDRESS	FORMS REQUIRED	FILING FEE	TERM	RENEWAL	SECURITY DEPOSIT	EXCESS INSURANCE	REPORTS REQUIRED	TAXES, FEES AND ASSESSMENTS
AR	Arkansas Workers' Compensation Commission Self-Insurer Division 4th and Spring Street P.O.Box 950 Little Rock, AR 72203 – 0950 (501) 682-2781	1. A-1-SID – "Employer's Application for the Privilege of Paying Compensation Provided in the Arkansas Workers' Compensation Act as Self–Insurer." Payroll, loss data and 3 yrs. Audited finicial reports	$1,000 paid to Arkansas Self-Insurer Guaranty Trust Fund	Annual	May 1 of each year	Amount determined upon review of application. Minimum $100,000. Actual amount dependent upon employer's workers' compenstion experience and financial status. A surety bond by a qualified company or a certificate of deposit from an Arkansas bank or a letter of credit from Arkansas fin. institution is acceptible	Aggregate and specific excess insurance with liability limits and retention amounts acceptable to the Commission may be required. The minimum excess insurance requirements will be determined by the Commission	1. Loss Summary Reports – A-25-SID and A-25B-SID 2. Payroll Report – A-28-SID 3. Current Certificate of Excess Workers' Compensation Insurance 4. Current Financial Statement – Due by April 1	Annual tax approximately 3% of manual premium
CA	Self-Insurance Plans State of California 2265 Watt Avenue, Suite 1 Sacramento, CA 95825 (916) 483-3392	A 4-1 Application for Certificate of Consent to Self-Insure (contains all required forms to apply) A 4-2 Application for public entities	Single $500 each add'l $100	Continuous until revoked	Automatic – subject to payment of yearly license fee assessment (Jan – Dec for private, July — June for public), filing required reports, and payment of user funding assessment	New applicants: Amount determined upon review of application, based on sum of prior 3 years' incurred liability Existing self-insurers: minimum $220,000 or 135% of self-insurer's liability, whichever is greater. Surety bond, cash and securities, or letter of credit are acceptable	Not required, for individual companies, but required for group	Self-Insurer's Annual Report due March 1 for previous calendar year. Failure to submit report may result in a civil penalty	Assessments based on # of employees and # of locations (1500-5500.00 paid depending on # of employees; $200 fee for each location)
CO	Colorado Department of Labor and Employment, Division of W/C Attn: Self-Insurance Administrator 1120 Lincoln Street, Suite 1200 Denver, CO 80203 (303) 764-2976	Employer's Application for Self-Insurance, which includes manual payroll data, financial records, and list of the named employees handling claims	$1,600, with annual fee on renewal of $1,600	Continuous until revoked	Automatic, but sixty (60) days following anniversary date of permit, must submit a report including most recent certified financial statement; a copy of payroll statement to Division of Labor for Premium Tax purposes; total number of workers' compensation claims for current year and each of preceding four (4) years; total payments and reserves on claims for the current year and each of the preceding four (4) years; certificate of required excess insurance, and if bond has been tendered for security, evidence that it is in force	Minimum amount $300,000. Executive Director may consider cash, government bonds or other forms of liquid security, surety bond, and letter of credit	Specific excess insurance with policy limits and retention amounts acceptable to the Executive Director required. Aggregate excess may be required	Premium tax reports are submitted each six months. Accident reports required annually. Certified financial statement annually	None

STATE	MAILING ADDRESS	FORMS REQUIRED	FILING FEE	TERM	RENEWAL	SECURITY DEPOSIT	EXCESS INSURANCE	REPORTS REQUIRED	TAXES, FEES AND ASSESSMENTS
CT	Workers' Compensation Comm Attn: Self-Insurance Unit 1890 Dixwell Avenue Hamden, CT 06514 (203) 230-3400	No. 18-76 – Application, which includes number of employees in Connecticut, present insurance carrier, residual claim procedures, insurance and bond information, and audited financial statements for last 3 years	None	One year	Must be requested 60 days prior to expiration of current authority	Surety bond required, amount determined at discretion of Chairman	Specific excess insurance by carrier licensed in state	Must file updated application for renewal, with prior year's loss experience and Connecticut payroll Annual audited financial report	Administrative Fund assessment is prorated, capped at 4% of paid losses for previous year Second Injury Fund – is variable based on paid losses for previous yr
DE	Administrator Industrial Accident Board 820 N. French St., 6th Floor Wilmington, DE 19801 (302) 577-2884	Employer's Application for the Privilege of Paying Compensation Without Insurance. The application includes information about number and location of employees in Delaware, three years of loss experience and recent financial statements	None	30 days prior to expiration of current authority	None since October 1, 1988	None	Specific excess insurance is permitted, but not required. Aggregate excess is permitted, but not required	Most recent financial statement with initial application Annual payroll and classification Financial reports	Administration Fund (4% of manual premium) and Second Injury Fund (1% of manual premium). Second Injury Fund may have an assessment if amount in fund falls below $250,000
WASH. D.C	Government of the District of Columbia Department of Employment Services Office of Workers' Compensation P.O. Box 56098 Washington, D.C. 20011 (202) 576-6265	Application for Self-Insurance (Form #40 DC WC) Self-Insurer's Affidavit of Financial Responsibility	None	One year	Automatic as long as continuing deposit of security and appropriate financial and other reports made yearly	$100,000 minimum indemnity bond, negotiable securities or letter of credit from financial institution The administrator may require more	A mandatory requirement	Annual Financial Statement Annual Report of 12 mos. Payroll under manual rate classes Report of Injury Experience Statement of Safety Program, Loss/Run Statement	Cost of the administration of the Act, pro-rated among the carrier and self-insurers (15% of previous years paid claims)
FL	Department of Labor & Employment Security Division of Workers' Compensation Bureau of Self-Insurance 101 East Gaines St. Fletcher Building, Rm # 562 Tallahassee, FL 32399-4103 (904) 488-8888	BSI-1 – Application for self-insurance (Florida operations, manual payroll, loss experience and 3 yrs of BSI-19 "Certificate of Serving for Self-Insurance", financial statements)	None. $500 for Florida Self-Insurers Guaranty Association	Continuous until revoked	Automatic	Amount determined upon review of application Minimum – $100,000. Surety bond, negotiable securities acceptable or letter of credit from Florida Bank	Required. Specific Excess for companies with net worth up to 2.5 million. Aggregate excess for all companies with net worth under 5 million	Annual Payroll Reports Annual Financial Statement Annual Loss Reports	1% of manual premium paid to Guaranty Trust Assoc. Annually Annual fee for administration, 1.662 and for Special Disability Assessment, 3.26%, both computed on standard premium;

STATE	MAILING ADDRESS	FORMS REQUIRED	FILING FEE	TERM	RENEWAL	SECURITY DEPOSIT	EXCESS INSURANCE	REPORTS REQUIRED	TAXES, FEES AND ASSESSMENTS
GA	State Board of Workers' Comp Suite 1000 South Tower One CNN Center Atlanta, GA 30303 – 2788 (404) 656-3875	Self-Insurance Association. Form requires manual premium data for each location and financial statements	$500 fee to Georgia Self-Insurers Guaranty Trust Fund	Continuous, until revoked	Automatic	Minimum: $250,000 surety bond, or letter of credit confirmed by a Georgia Bank	Required in most instances	Annual payroll report, to be filed by March 1	Pro-rata share of cost of administration based on percentage of W/C premium (.58% July 1, 1993 to July 1, 1994), plus $300. Also pro-rata share for administration of Subsequent Injury Fund based on previous year's claims paid, usually 1-6% of claims paid 1st year assessment fee of $4,000 paid to Georgia Self-Insurers Guaranty Trust Fund; then 1.5% of previous years indemnity payments after 1st year
HI	State of Hawaii Department of Labor & Industrial Relations Workers' Compensation Division 830 Punchbowl St., Room 209 P.O. Box 3769 Honolulu, HI 968103 (808) 586-9166	WC-21 (Rev. 9/71) Application for Self-Insurance Authorization	None	Perpetual, subject to revocation by the Director	Automatic	Minimum $500,000, surety bond or letter of credit from Hawaiian Financial Institution	Specific or aggregate excess insurance not mandatory, but may be required depending on financial condition & loss history	Annual Report (WC-23) on open claims, benefits paid and reserves for future payments, payroll, and audited financial report	Special compensation fund and administrative expenses assessments, determined yearly
ID	Industrial Commission of Idaho 317 Main street State House Mail Boise, ID 83720 – 6000 (208) 334-6000 Attn: Fiscal Dept.	Form 1C-4006 Application to Self-Insure and latest financial statement Form IC-4050 for each included wholy – owned subsidiary	None	Continuous until revoked or withdrawn	Automatic with annual financial statement Continuation of self-insured status is reviewed with each change of corporate structure, spin-offs, etc.	Minimum: $50,000 plus 5% of employer's annual average 3-year payroll up to $550,000, in form of surety bond or Idaho municipal bonds. Also IC Form 36 "Outstanding Awards Unpaid Balance"	Specific excess or aggregate excess is allowed but not required	File I.C. 36 quarterly (or monthly if requested) regarding outstanding claims; semi-annual premium tax return and annual financial reports	Premium tax of 2.5% of standard premium. 4 to 5% of Permanent Partial Awards and Lump Sum Settlements for Second Injury Fund
IL	Illinois Industrial Commission Office of Self-Insurance 701 S. Second St., Springfield, IL 62704 (217) 785-7084	IC-50 – Application for Self-Insurance Includes: • Certified Financial Statement (12 years) • 3 yrs. loss runs • Copy of Excess Insurance Quote • Current W/C coverage • Rating Experience Modification Factor	$500 per application; each subsidiary requires a separate application and fee	Continuous, until revoked	Automatic if reports filed pass annual review and security requirement has been met	Amount determined upon review of application, initially and annually Minimum: $200,000. Surety bond, cash or government negotiable securities acceptable. Letter of credit permitted	Specific and/or aggregate excess insurance may be required	Annual Financial Statement and loss runs	Annual renewal fee – $500 per self-insured entity

STATE	MAILING ADDRESS	FORMS REQUIRED	FILING FEE	TERM	RENEWAL	SECURITY DEPOSIT	EXCESS INSURANCE	REPORTS REQUIRED	TAXES, FEES AND ASSESSMENTS
IN	Insurance Division Supervisor 402 West Washington Street Rm W196 Indianapolis, IN 46204 – 2753 (317) 232-3808	SI-1 – Application for Permission to Carry Risk Without Insurance SI-2 – Surety Bond SI-3 – Certificate of Excess Insurance SI-4 – Indemnity Agreement One application may include all subsidiaries	$500	One year	August 1, regardless of inception date $250 Renewal Fee $250 Extra for late renewal filing	Surety bond in a minimum amount of $500,000	Specific and aggregate excess insurance may be required as a condition of approval	Annual audited financial report with renewal application due in August for preceding calendar year	Second Injury Fund – 1% of total compensation paid, if fund is below $500,000. No asssessment fee is over Residual Asbestos Injury Fund – ½% of total compensation paid, if fund is below $50,000 (both based on weekly indeminty). OSHA assessment ¾% of total compensation paid the prior year due April 1 (only if fund drops below 600,000)
IA	Insurance Division of Iowa Lucas State Office Building Des Moines, IA 50319 (515) 242-6550	Application of Employer for Relief – requires financial reports, payroll, prior loss experience and safety program	$100 Application Fee and $100 fee when Certificate is issued	Annual. All Certificates expire July 31	Renewal application must be returned by June 1	Amount set by formula; minimum of $200,000. Department Actuary makes final determination	At commissioner's discretion	Financial statement and annual report must be filed annually by June 1 with application for renewal	None, other than Second Injury Fund contributions
KS	State of Kansas Department of Human Resources Division of Workers' Compensation 800 S.W. Jackson, Suite 600 Topeka, KS 66612-1227 (913) 296-3606	105 – Employer's Application to Become Self-Insurer Under the Workers' Compensation Act 120 – Application Information Sheet – financial statement and loss run	None	One year from date of issue	Annual renewal: Form 120 - financial statement from previous fiscal year	Security amount determined upon application. Surety bond or letter of credit are acceptable	Required. Amount depends on financial statement and other relevant factors	Annual financial statement and loss runs 5 years of financial reports	Assessment for administrative costs in 1992 was 2.126% of all claims paid during 1993. Assessment for Second Injury Fund determined each year; most recent assessment – 8.9%
KY	Department of Workers' Claims Perimeter Park West 1270 Louisville Road, Building C Frankfort, KY 40601 (502) 564-5550	Certified Financial report Employer's Application for Permission To Carry His Own Risk Without Insurance. Includes manual payroll data, 5 years of loss run reports, certified financial reports	None	One year	15 days prior to expiration of current authority	If required, minimum of $500,000. Surety bond and letter of credit acceptable or Investment account in Kentucky Bank	Not required, but may be recommended. (Required for a "deep mine.")	Statement of outstanding workers' compensation liabilities due two months prior to recertification date	Special Fund Assessment: for non-coal companies, 12.3% of simulated premium calculated by Workers' Compensation Board; for coal companies, 61.2%

STATE	MAILING ADDRESS	FORMS REQUIRED	FILING FEE	TERM	RENEWAL	SECURITY DEPOSIT	EXCESS INSURANCE	REPORTS REQUIRED	TAXES, FEES AND ASSESSMENTS
LA	Department of Employment & Training Office of Workers' Compensation P.O. Box 94040 Baton Rouge, LA 70804–9040 (504) 342-5658	Application for Individual WC Self-Insurer (Form WDOL – WC 2005) Application for Third Party Administrator (optional) Required form for posting a Surety Bond (Form WDOL – WC 2006)	$100 for self-insurer; $200 for third party administrator (service company)	One year	Yearly renewal fee for self-insured is $100 Third party administrator fee (renewal) $200	Surety bond, U.S. Treasury Bond, or certificate of deposit equal to average of last three years claim experience, or $100,000, whichever is greater	Aggregate or specific excess acceptable to agency	Audited financial statement for last 3 years WC summary loss data for last 3 years	Second Injury Fund – amount approximately 2% of the W/C manual premium. Minimum – $10. This assessment is made annually, with payment due by December 31 **Note:** In addition to the Second Injury Fund assessments, there is an assessment for the Office of Workers' Compensation. Actual assessment is 1% of previous year's paid benefits
ME	Department of Professional and Financial Regulation Bureau of Insurance State House Station 34 Augusta, ME 04333 (207) 582-8707	Application for Self-Insurance, payroll by manual premium classes, loss runs for three years, description of safety program, financial statements	$1,000 new application fee	One year	Employer must request 21 days before expiration $300 renewal fee $100 reporting fee at time of renewal	Amount determined by state formula Surety bond, negotiable securities or letter of credit from Maine Bank are acceptable Minimum: $50,000	Specific and/or aggregate may be required, depending on financial standing **Note:** All Self-Insurers must belong to: Maine Self-Insurers' Guarantee Association P.O. Box 127 Hallowell, ME 04347 Assessment: 1% of standard premium	Survey Questionnaire, Claims Report, Payroll Report with manual premium classes, Audited Financial Statement	Employment Rehabilitation Fund – 1% of actual paid losses Administrative fund – .1% of standard premium
MD	Director of Self-Insurance Workers' Compensation Commission 6 N. Liberty St, 9th Floor Baltimore, MD 21201-3785 (410) 333-1035	A05 – "Employer's Application To Carry His Own Risk," 3 years of audited financial reports and latest 10K report	Application Fee of $250	Continuous until revoked	Automatic on meeting reporting and compliance requirements. Annual renewal fee of $500	Required. Based on claims history and payroll. Minimum $100,000. Surety bonds, or negotiable securities, or state or federal bonds are allowed	Required. Copy of policy must be filed with the Commission	Annual payroll report and 10K or annual audited financial statement, quarterly, and annual claims reports	• Maintenance Fee: Has averaged 40 cents per $1,000 of payroll for last few years • Subsequent Injury Fund assessments (6.5% of all awards from previous yr.) • Uninsured Employer Fund assessment (1% of all awards from previous yr.) 250.00 for adding subsidiary to Self-Insurance Program

STATE	MAILING ADDRESS	FORMS REQUIRED	FILING FEE	TERM	RENEWAL	SECURITY DEPOSIT	EXCESS INSURANCE	REPORTS REQUIRED	TAXES, FEES AND ASSESSMENTS
MA	Director of Self-Insurance Department of Industrial Accidents Office of Insurance, 7th Floor 600 Washington Street Boston, MA 02111 (617) 727-4900	IAB50 Employer's Application for the Privilege of Being a Self-Insurer. (New applications will not be considered from November 1 to January 31 of each year.)	None	One year	Application within 30 days of expiration of current approval. Quarterly reports must also be filed	Amount determined upon application. Minimum $100,000. A surety bond or negotiable securities are acceptable. Generally, the amount is equal to employer's workmen's compensation liabilities	Either aggregate or specific excess insurance is required. Amounts are to be approved by the Department. Minimum is usually $500,000	Annual Application for Renewal (Form IAB50) Quarterly Claims Reports	Maintenance Fund: Annual assessment in varying amounts for expense of regulating self-insurers
MI	Department of Labor Bureau of Workers' Compensation 7150 Harris Drive Box 30016 Lansing, MI 48909 (517) 322-1868 Attn: Self-Insurance Division	MDL-1-402 – Application for Self-Insurance. Includes Financial Information for past five years, and Michigan payroll data by manual class	None	One year	Application for renewal must be submitted 30 days prior to renewal date	Minimum $100,000 Security Determinated after considering application (initial or renewal) and all supportive data. Security is in form of surety bond or letter of credit from Michigan Bank or Federally Chartered Bank with branch in Michigan	Specific and/or aggregate excess is usually required; Director determines which type is necessary, based upon strength of financial statements	Annual application and current Annual Report of corporation. With the initial application, must also file 5-year Profit and Loss Information, yearly Report to Stockholders and 3-year Loss Run Summary	Second Injury Fund – assessment for 1993 is .03013 of paid compensation claims; Dust Disease Fund – .0098 of paid compensation claims; Self-Insured Security Fund – .009; Safety, Education & Training Fund – .005
MN	Department of Commerce Attn: Self-Insurance Division 133 East 7th Street St. Paul, MN 55101 (612) 297-7035	Application for Self-Insurance; Checklist for Application of Self-Insurance; Annual certified financial statements for 5 years 10K Report if filed with the Security and Exchange Commission	$1,000	5 years	10K and Certified audited statements within 4 months of fiscal year end. Status and loss reports due by August 1 annually. In addition, payroll by classification shall be reported to the Workers' Compensation Reinsurance Association on forms available from the Association Financial review occurs annually. Authority renewal every 5 year	Security bond, letter of credit, savings certificates, certificates of deposit, U.S. Treasury notes accepted. Amount of deposit is determined by a certified actuarial opinion that must be prepared by a member of the Casualty Actuarial Society of America, projecting 2 years for individual applicant and 1 year for group applicant. Actuarial determination is then 110% of certified amount. Deposit may not be less than retention limit selected with Workers' Compensation Reinsurance Association. Must be accompanied by sworn affidavit signed by officer of Self-Insurance policy	Specific excess mandatory with W.C.R.A	See renewal	Due biannually is Department of Labor Special Compensation Fund (30% of paid indemnity 1993) Self-Insured Security Trust Fund 3% of paid indemnity for previous year

STATE	MAILING ADDRESS	FORMS REQUIRED	FILING FEE	TERM	RENEWAL	SECURITY DEPOSIT	EXCESS INSURANCE	REPORTS REQUIRED	TAXES, FEES AND ASSESSMENTS
MO	Department of Labor Division of Workers' Compensation P.O. Box 58 Jefferson City, MO 65102 (314) 751-4231	Form 81 – Application for Authority to Self-Insure. Includes 3 years of Financial Reports, 3 years of Loss Runs, Profited Loss 10K's Payroll report	$150	Continuous until revoked	Automatic, if reports duly filed	Required with amount determined upon review of application. Minimum, $180,000. Surety bond, U.S. or State of Missouri obligations are acceptable	Required	Annual financial statements, payroll by manual classification, and loss runs	Administrative Fund: Tax – 2% of standard modified premium. Second Injury Fund up to 3% of manual premimum, Private Ennuity Guaranty Corp. of Missouri Fund ⅛% of premimums for each 1st 3 years
MS	Executive Director Mississippi Workers' Compensation Commission P.O. Box 39296 – 5300 Jackson, MS 39216 (601) 987-4204	A-2 – Employer's Application for the Privilege of Paying Compensation Provided in the Mississippi Workers' Compensation Act as a Self-Insurer	$100	One year	Automatic after 2nd year	Determined upon review of applicaiton; minimum $100,000, plus excess insurance in amount determined by Commission Surety bond only	Required; carrier must be licensed in state and have a rating from Best of AVIII or better	• Annual Financial Statement • Quarterly Safety Report (by competent Safety Examiner) • Semi-Annual Report listing total compensation payments made for 6-month period	Annual assessment for second Injury Fund based on actual amount of compendation paid (current rate is 1.5%)
MT	Department of Labor & Industry Employment Relations Division W/C Regulation Bureau Helena, MT 59604 – 8011 P.O. Box 8011 (406) 444-6530	The completed applicaiton, containing: Audited financial statements for the last two years; loss run and summary from insurance carriers who provided coverage during the preceding four years; and designation of at least one adjuster, maintaining an office in Montana, which shall pay compensation when due and which shall have authority to settle claims	None	One year	A certificate must be renewed Renewals staggered. Application must be submitted 30 days prior to assigned renewal date	If required, the Division determines the amount of the security deposit; minimum required $250,000 security	Specific excess and aggregate excess insurance in an amount determined by the Division	Financial Statement of most recent fiscial year for renewal	A fee must be paid to cover the operating costs of workers' compensation. This fee consists of a self-insurer's pro rata share of the fund costs, with the proration based upon gross annual payroll for the past calendar year. The minimum fee is $200

STATE	MAILING ADDRESS	FORMS REQUIRED	FILING FEE	TERM	RENEWAL	SECURITY DEPOSIT	EXCESS INSURANCE	REPORTS REQUIRED	TAXES, FEES AND ASSESSMENTS
NE	State of Nebraska Workers' Compensation Court Capitol Building P.O. Box 98908 Lincoln, NE 68509–8908 (402) 471-2953 Attn: Self-Insurance Division	Form SIA-86 – Application for Authority to Self–Insure 5 years of audited financial statements, payroll by Nebraska classification, loss run, and medical/hospital payment report	50 – 150.00	One year	Form SIAR-86, used to calculate premium tax and assessment, is sent to self-insureds in mid-December, must be returned by January 31, and payments are due by March 1. Form SIA-86 will be mailed two months before the end of each self-insured's fiscal year and will be due one month later	Required but variable	Required. Both retention and total coverage may be designated by the Court. Nebraska endorsement is required. Policy must be filed	Audited financial statements, loss runs	In lieu of premium tax – 2% of manual premium Second Injury Fund – 2% of manual Benefits Paid Vocational Rehabilitation – 1% of manual premium (Assessments for latter two funds only when they drop below the minimum.)
NV	Nevada Insurance Division Worker's Compensation Self-Insurance Section 1665 Hot Springs Road, #152 Carson City, NV 89710 (702) 687-4270	Employer's Application for Self-Insurance, accompanied by 3 years of audited financial statements	$200 (non-refundable)	Continuous until terminated or withdrawn	Annual report form (provided by Division) must be filed by September 30	The greater of $100,000 or 105% of the employer's expected annual incurred costs, in form of a bond, negotiable securities, cash, or a letter of credit (form a Nevada Bank)	Required. Amount determined upon application, minimum self-insured retention $100,000. Must be countersigned by licensed Nevada resident agent	Annual audited financial statements. Employer's Annual Report (provided by the Division)	Initial Insolvency Fund Assessment .5% of security deposit; thereafter annual Insolvency Fund – .25% of security deposit Annual pro-rata assessment for operation of Department of Industrial Relations and self-insurance program amount levied by Division Industrial Relations Formula based on insurer's claims expenditure (702) 687-3305)
NH	New Hampshire Labor Department State Office Park South, 95 Pleasant Street Concord, NH 03301 (603) 271-3176 Attn: Administration of Self-Insurance	WCSI – Self-Insurance Application. Financial statements and payroll by manual premium classes, 5 years loss history	None	Continuous until revoked	Subject to review and cancellation at any time	Bond is required as additional security over and above financial status. Bond amount is discretionary, but minimum is $250,000 Security Deposit agreement or surety bond	Specific and aggregate excess coverages are required.	• Certified Annual Financial Report or 10K Report • Annual Claims Report: 291A Questionaire overing benefits paid, Future Reserves, Annual actuary report	Second Injury Fund: A special assessment is conducted on indemnity payments made during the prior self-insured year. Approx. 2% of paid benefits

STATE	MAILING ADDRESS	FORMS REQUIRED	FILING FEE	TERM	RENEWAL	SECURITY DEPOSIT	EXCESS INSURANCE	REPORTS REQUIRED	TAXES, FEES AND ASSESSMENTS
NJ	New Jersey Department of Insurance 20 West State Street CN325 Trenton, NJ 08625 (609) 984-2717	$1,500 Fee for credit assessment report (291 Form) 3 years of Financial Statements	$1,000 Application Fee after initial credit financial assessment	1 year	$1,000 Renewal fee due May 1. Possible $1,500 Credit assessment fee with renewal	Surety bond required $500,000 minimum	Required	Audited financial statement	Compensation Court Cash Fund is 1% of manual premium. Also. Sender Inquiring Fund & Guaranty Fund Assessment due annually
NM	(New Mexico has reorganized its workers' compensation, from a judicial to an administrative law system, with some changes through in 1990. As the new system evolves, there may be more changes.)								
	Self-Insurance Bureau Workers' Compensation Administration P.O. Box 27198 Albuquerque, NM 87125-7198 (505) 841-6818	Application for Self-Insurance Audited Financial Statement less than six months old Three Year Loss History	$150	Continuous unless revoked		Minimum $200,000 surety bond; more may be required or letter of credit from New Mexico financial institution	Specific required – retention of $250,000 maximum of statutory upper limit	• Annual Financial Report • Claims Experience Report	Subsequent Injury Fund (½% of previous years losses), and Self-Insured Guarantee Fund (1% of losses for previous year as of 1/1/92)
NY	Self-Insurance Office New York Workers' Compensation Board 180 Livingston Street Brooklyn, NY 11248 (718) 802-6795	SI-1 – Application for Self-Insurance Annual Financial Statement (Form 10-K if public corporation)	None	Continuous until revoked	Automatic if reports filed	In amount necessary to secure liability under the Workers' Compensation Law. Usual minimum is $530,000, but Chair may adjust upward or downward. Surety bond or letter of credit permitted	In amounts acceptable to the Chair	Annual Financial Statement (10-K if public corporation) Payroll, loss data and outstanding claim reports on forms provided by the Board	Second Injury Fund, Special Disability Fund, and Fund for Reopened Cases. Administrative assessment. Special Fund tax
NC	North Carolina Dept. of Insurance Self-Insured Workers' Compensation Dobbs Building 430 N. Salisbury Street P.O. Box 26387 Raleigh, NC 27611 (919) 733-5631	Form 10.Financial statements, payroll by manual codes, three years of loss runs	None	Continuous	Automatic, if proper reports filed. Reports reviewed annually	$500,000 Acceptable negotiable securities, surety bond, or certificate of deposit	Required in amount of $5-million	Form 17 (Payroll Report) submitted by January 31 of each year. Certified financial reports and listings of corporate officers and directors. Statement of Financial Condition	Maintenance Fund Tax: 2.5% of premium (1 time) Annual Regulatory charge 7.25% of maintenance Fund Tax Self Insurance Guaranty Fund: 0.5% of manual premium
ND	North Dakota workers' compensation is under an exclusive state fund. Neither self-insurance nor insurance companies are permitted								

STATE	MAILING ADDRESS	FORMS REQUIRED	FILING FEE	TERM	RENEWAL	SECURITY DEPOSIT	EXCESS INSURANCE	REPORTS REQUIRED	TAXES, FEES AND ASSESSMENTS
OH	Self-Insured Department Bureau of Workers' Compensation 30 West Spring Street Columbus, OH 43266-0581 (614) 466-6737	SI-6 – Application by Employer to Pay Compensation Direct	None	One year	State sends out Form SI-7 (Renewal Application) 120 days prior to expiration of current authority. This form should be returned 90 days prior to expiration of such authority	None	Specific excess is not required, but is permissible on amounts over $50,000 on any one accident. Excess aggregate is not permitted	SI-7 (Renewal Application) with copy of latest financial statement for parent company, as well as for any subsidiary. Must be filed 90 days prior to end of effective date. Financial information may not be more than six (6) months old. Also, SI-8, SI-9 and SI-220	Administrative Fund – fee based on cost of operations Surplus Fund – rate set by cost, thus it varies Disabled Workmen's Relief Fund – effective 8/22/86, companies are billed for any payments made to claimants from this fund. These taxes are two times a year; assessment is a percentage of "paid compensation." Due February 28 and August 31
OK	Workers' Compensation Court 1915 Stiles Oklahoma City, OK 73105 (405) 557-7680 Attn: Insurance Dept.	1-B – Employer's Application for Permission to Carry His Own Risk Without Insurance, Financial Statements and Loss Runs	$500	Annual	Must file application, financial report and corporate annual report 60 days before effective date. State should send forms 90 days before expiration date. $500 renewal fee	Bond or securities. Minimum $100,000	Required. Amount determined by Workers' Compensation Court, usually $500,000 to $1 million	Financial reports, corporate annual report for preceding year	W/C Administration Fund: 3% of award paid to claimant (excluding medical) Special Indemnity Fund: 5% assessment on permanent total disability payments and partial disability payments (5% is paid by us and 5% comes from claimant's award) Occupational Health and Safety Fund Tax: ¾% of 1% assessment paid by us based on W/C awards (medical excluded)

STATE	MAILING ADDRESS	FORMS REQUIRED	FILING FEE	TERM	RENEWAL	SECURITY DEPOSIT	EXCESS INSURANCE	REPORTS REQUIRED	TAXES, FEES AND ASSESSMENTS
OR	Department of Consummer & Business Services Workers' Compensation Division Compliance Section 21 Labor and Industries Building Salem, OR 97310 (503) 945-7716 Attn: Self-Insurance Specialist	Application To Become a Self-insured Employer, payroll by manual classes, loss runs for last two years Recent experience rating modification worksheet and supporting documents	None	Continuous until revoked	No renewal fee	Minimum $300,000 plus amount determined upon review of application. After first year, amount is based on claim reserves. Minimum $100,000. Surety bond or securities acceptable. (Claim reserves, excess insurance, self-insurer retention, and financial soundness determine amount of security deposit.)	Required. Must be in an amount appropriate to cover employer's potential liability	Annual reports of all losses; payroll by manual classes, audited financial statements	Administration expenses: assessment based on manual premium (4.5%) Assessment for Handicapped Workers Reserve and Workers Compensation Reserve Taxes: Quarterly self-insurer's tax. Workday assessment 14¢/day due from employer, 14¢/day due from employee
PA	Bureau of Workers' Compensation Attn: Self-Insurance Division 1171 S. Cameron St., Room 103 Harrisburg, PA 17104-2501 (717) 783-4476	Employer's Application (LIBC-366) – new and renewal applicants	$500 must accompany each application (Each subsidiary has own fee)	One year	Renewal application must be filed 60 days prior to expiration of current insurance exemption $100 renewal fee Listing of Open Disability Cases (Form LIBC-413) Listing of Open Fatal Cases (Form LIBC-414)	Minimum $200,000: surety bond or letter of credit from Pennsylvania Financial Institution. Affiliates may be combined under one surety bond for the total amount of security required	Specific excess is almost always required	Loss records are to be kept on a calendar year basis. Annual Report of Compensation Paid, LIBC-673, must be filed by April 15 each year	Assessments are made in July for Supersedeas Fund and Subsequent Injury Fund; in November for the Administration Fund. Assessments are a percentage of prior year's paid losses. Percentages for all 3 runs 2.5 – 3% of paid losses. One time Guaranty Trust Fund Assessment .5% of modified manual premium
RI	Rhode Island Dept. of Labor Self-Insurance Unit 610 Manton Avenue Providence, RI 02909 (401) 457-1800	SI-2 Self-Insurance Application, financial statements, loss runs. Tax records, owner's data, corporate resolution, parent guarantor, etc.	$300 – $500 depending on company size (# of employee)	A self-insured who wishes to continue as such must file an application and surety annually; 60 days lead time	60 days notice usually sent by state prior ot renewal date	If an application is approved, employer will be notified to file a $500,000 annual minimum surety bond, letter of credit, certificate of deposit, securities, or combinations of securities Amount determined by department	Almost always required, retention fixed by Department	Same as for initial application	Each self-insurer is required to pay assessments annually The Workers' Compensation Administration Fund based on group premimum (for 1993 approx. 4.75%). Also Self-Insurers' Assessment that based on percent of surety bond to whole pool of surety bonds

STATE	MAILING ADDRESS	FORMS REQUIRED	FILING FEE	TERM	RENEWAL	SECURITY DEPOSIT	EXCESS INSURANCE	REPORTS REQUIRED	TAXES, FEES AND ASSESSMENTS
SC	South Carolina Worker's Compensation Commission 1612 Marion Street P.O. Box 1715 Columbia, SC 29202-1715 Attn: Self-Insurance Administrator (803) 737-5706	SCWCC Form #7. 3 years audited financial statements and three year loss history	$100 Application Fee ($25 for each subsidiary)	Continuous until revoked	Automatic, if reports filed	Amount determined upon review. Minimum is $250,000. Surety bond or letter of credit from South Carolina Financial Institution	Amount and type are determined on an individual basis	Audited Financial Report or 10-K	Self-Insurer's Tax: Premium Tax: 2.5% of paid expenses. Second Injury Fund is variable, based on claims
SD	Division of Labor and Management South Dakota Department of Labor 700 Governors Drive Pierre, SD 57501-2291 (605) 773-3681	Workers' Compensation Proof of Solvency Report. Financial statements, loss runs	$600	One year. All expire on August 31	Department sends renewal form to self-insurer in mid-June $600 renewal fee	Required – determined on individual applicant basis. Security bond or letter of credit acceptable. Minimum Security 250,000	Expected	Financial Statement	A Second Injury Fund financed by 4% tax on all payments by carriers and self-insurers, plus $500 in no dependency death cases. In lieu of Premimum Tax $\frac{6}{10}$% of straight premimum
TN	Department of Insurance Self-Insurance Section 500 James Robertson Parkway Nashville, TN 37243-1132 (615) 741-1756	Form IN-0120 Employer's Application. Financial statements, payroll by manual classes, loss runs	None	One year	Annually if reports filed	Surety bond in the amount of $350,000 minimum. Insurance Commissioner may adjust amount	Required	Financial report, loss runs, payroll	4.4% of modified standard premium for Administrative Fund, and a Second Injury Fund assessment made from this 4.4% of modified standard premium
TX	Texas Workers' Compensation Commission Division Self-Insurance MS 60 4000 South IH35 Austin, TX 78704 – 7491 (512) 440-3954	Inital Application Packet 3 years financial statements Loss Runs Third Party Administration requirements Safety Planed Inspection	$1,000	One year	Yearly upon certificate anniversary	$300,000 or 125% of outstanding liability whichever is larger Cash, Texas Securities, letter of credit or surety bond	$5 million of specific excess insurance	Annual claim and safety report	Regulating fee based on indemnity payment. Also Texas Workers' Compensation Fund Research Center Tax. Texas Department of Insurance maintenance tax surcharge
UT	Industrial Commission of Utah Industrial Accidents Division 160 East 300 South, 3rd Floor P.O. Box 146610 Salt Lake City, UT 84114-6610 (801) 530-6800	Form 109 – Application for Self-Insurance with Financial Statements	$900 on initial application; $500 on annual renewal	Continuous until Revoked, but reviewed annually	Annual Renewal Application (to be submitted at least 60 days before self-insurance anniversary date) with financial statements	Minimum $100,000 surety bond or an irrevocable letter of credit	Specific or aggregate excess insurance, as set by the agency, are required	Annual Financial Reports (certified), payroll data, and claims information	Approximately 5.73% premium tax based on premimum of UTAH W/C Fund. (same as for insurance companies) paid to Utah Tax Commission

STATE	MAILING ADDRESS	FORMS REQUIRED	FILING FEE	TERM	RENEWAL	SECURITY DEPOSIT	EXCESS INSURANCE	REPORTS REQUIRED	TAXES, FEES AND ASSESSMENTS
VT	Division of Workers' Compensation Department of Labor and Industry Drawer 20 National Life Drive Montpelier, VT 05602 – 3401 (802) 828-2286	No. 30 – Application for Self-Insurance. Financial statements, payroll by manual class, loss runs for three years	None	One year	Renew each year. Process same as initial filing	Surety bond, letter of credit or a cash escrow account in a Vermont bank equal to Self-Insurance Excess retention level	Required	Annual report of total compensation paid and financial statements	1% annually of total paid losses in workers' compensation for Administration Fund
VA	Virginia Workers' Compensation Commission Controller's Office 1000 DMV Drive Richmond, VA 23220 Attn: Self-Insurance (804) 367-0580	No. 20 – Employer's Application. Financial statements and loss runs	$200	Continuous until revoked	Automatic, if reports filed	Amount determined by the Commission. Only a corporate surety bond is acceptable. Minimum is $750,000	Excess insurance may be required at the discretion of the Commission	Must submit financial, payroll reports with manual classes, and loss runs annually	Annual maintenance tax calculated on the basis of a maximum of up to 2½% of the premium that would have been paid to a private carrier (1989 rate – .625%) Uninsured Employer's Fund – up to ¼ of 1% of manual premium. Second Injury Fund: same. No tax assessed in recent years
WA	Department of Labor and Industries Self-Insurance Section P.O. Box 44891 Olympia, WA 98504 – 4891 (206) 956-6901	SIF #1 – Application for Certification 3 years audited financial statements Written accident prevention program List of locations Number of Employees Safety Contact Person	$250	Continuous until withdrawn by the Director or surrendered by the employer with Director's approval	Automatic, if reports and surety filed	Minimum – $345,000 in form of bond, cash or securities in escrow, or letter of credit. Director determines amount based on the developed liabilities	Not required	Quarterly reports on claim costs and hours worked. Annual reports on summary of liabilities plus audited financial statements	Administrative Assessment – assessed each quarter as a percentage of claims cost. (Is .0453 beginning July, 1993.) Second Injury Fund – rate varies. Supplemental Pension Fund Premium – assessed each quarter at a rate of .0472 per man-hour worked; ½ may be deducted from the employee's wages

STATE	MAILING ADDRESS	FORMS REQUIRED	FILING FEE	TERM	RENEWAL	SECURITY DEPOSIT	EXCESS INSURANCE	REPORTS REQUIRED	TAXES, FEES AND ASSESSMENTS
WV	Workers' Compensation Fund 601 Morris St. Charleston, WV 25301 (304) 558-0380 Attn: Self-Insurance Unit	360 – Election to Carry Own Risk	$2,500.00 non-refundable	One year	Automatic with reports and yearly bond renewal	Amount determined upon review of application. Minimum $1,000,000. Surety bond, letter of credit, or negotiable securities	Not required	Quarterly audited financial reports	Assessments are based on premimum for: 1. Administrative Contribution (2.7%) 2. Disabled Workers' relief Fund (3.5%) 3. Other Losses (.8%) 4. Second Injury Fund (17 – 30%; variable) 5. Catastrophe Fund (optional) (1%)
WI	Self-Insurance Unit Works' Compensation Division 201 E. Washington Avenue P.O. Box 7901 Madison, WI 53707 (608) 266-8961	Self-Insurance Application and financial statements for last 5 years	$300 for initial application; $100 for renewal	One year	Annually – the application must be returned by the deadline date on renewal notice; self-insurance permission begins on July 1	If required, there is a $500,000 minimum surety bond. Excess insurance is considered when establishing bond amount	Specific excess insurance required. OSHA report. Safety data Aggregate excess may be required	Loss runs and financial statements OSHA report and safety data	Annual assessment to maintain state program, based on proportion of all indemnity paid; amount varies, usually between 3% and 5%
WY	For Coverage: Wyoming Workers' Compensation Division Office of the State Treasurer Herschler Building 122 West 25th Street Cheyenne, WY 82002 – 0900 (307) 777-7374	**Note:** Self-insurance candidates are subject to statutory review based on type of business (SIC codes). Wyoming has no process for reviewing and monitoring self-insurers							

INDEX